Laser-Driven Accelerators, Radiations, and Their Applications

Laser-Driven Accelerators, Radiations, and Their Applications

Editors

Hyung Taek Kim
Daniele Margarone

MDPI • Basel • Beijing • Wuhan • Barcelona • Belgrade • Manchester • Tokyo • Cluj • Tianjin

Editors
Hyung Taek Kim
Gwangju Intituts of Science
and Technology
Korea

Daniele Margarone
Queen's University Belfast, UK
ELI Beamlines Centre, Czech Republic

Editorial Office
MDPI
St. Alban-Anlage 66
4052 Basel, Switzerland

This is a reprint of articles from the Special Issue published online in the open access journal *Applied Sciences* (ISSN 2076-3417) (available at: https://www.mdpi.com/journal/applsci/special_issues/LDA2019).

For citation purposes, cite each article independently as indicated on the article page online and as indicated below:

LastName, A.A.; LastName, B.B.; LastName, C.C. Article Title. *Journal Name* **Year**, *Volume Number*, Page Range.

ISBN 978-3-0365-4233-1 (Hbk)
ISBN 978-3-0365-4234-8 (PDF)

Cover image courtesy of Daniele Margarone, ELI Beamlines, FZÚ AVČR

© 2022 by the authors. Articles in this book are Open Access and distributed under the Creative Commons Attribution (CC BY) license, which allows users to download, copy and build upon published articles, as long as the author and publisher are properly credited, which ensures maximum dissemination and a wider impact of our publications.

The book as a whole is distributed by MDPI under the terms and conditions of the Creative Commons license CC BY-NC-ND.

Contents

About the Editors vii

Preface to "Laser-Driven Accelerators, Radiations, and Their Applications" ix

Hyung Taek Kim and Daniele Margarone
Laser-Driven Accelerators, Radiations, and Their Applications
Reprinted from: *Appl. Sci.* **2022**, *12*, 3662, doi:10.3390/app12073662 1

Andreea Groza, Alecsandru Chirosca, Elena Stancu, Bogdan Butoi, Mihai Serbanescu, Dragana B. Dreghici and Mihai Ganciu
Assessment of Angular Spectral Distributions of Laser Accelerated Particles for Simulation of Radiation Dose Map in Target Normal Sheath Acceleration Regime of High Power Laser-Thin Solid Target Interaction—Comparison with Experiments
Reprinted from: *Appl. Sci.* **2020**, *10*, 4390, doi:10.3390/app10124390 3

Junho Won, Jaehyeon Song, Sasi Palaniyappan, Donald Cort Gautier, Wonhee Jeong, Juan Carlos Fernández and Woosuk Bang
Monte Carlo Study of Imaging Plate Response to Laser-Driven Aluminum Ion Beams
Reprinted from: *Appl. Sci.* **2021**, *11*, 820, doi:10.3390/app11020820 19

Timofej Chagovets, Stanislav Stanček, Lorenzo Giuffrida, Andriy Velyhan, Maksym Tryus, Filip Grepl, Valeriia Istokskaia, Vasiliki Kantarelou, Tuomas Wiste, Juan Carlos Hernandez Martin, Francesco Schillaci and Daniele Margarone
Automation of Target Delivery and Diagnostic Systems for High Repetition Rate Laser-Plasma Acceleration
Reprinted from: *Appl. Sci.* **2021**, *11*, 1680, doi:10.3390/app11041680 31

Filip Grepl, Josek Krása, Andriy Velyhan, Massimo De Marco, Jan Dostál, Miroslav Pfeifer and Daniele Margarone
Distortion of Thomson Parabolic-Like Proton Patterns Due to Electromagnetic Interference
Reprinted from: *Appl. Sci.* **2021**, *11*, 4484, doi:10.3390/app11104484 45

Itamar Cohen, Yonatan Gershuni, Michal Elkind, Guy Azouz, Assaf Levanon and Ishay Pomerantz
Optically Switchable MeV Ion/Electron Accelerator
Reprinted from: *Appl. Sci.* **2021**, *11*, 5424, doi:10.3390/app11125424 53

Hyung Taek Kim, Vishwa Bandhu Pathak, Calin Ioan Hojbota, Mohammad Mirzaie, Ki Hong Pae, Chul Min Kim, Jin Woo Yoon, Jae Hee Sung and Seong Ku Lee
Multi-GeV Laser Wakefield Electron Acceleration with PW Lasers
Reprinted from: *Appl. Sci.* **2021**, *11*, 5831, doi:10.3390/app11135831 61

Fernando Brandi, Luca Labate, Daniele Palla, Sanjeev Kumar, Lorenzo Fulgentini, Petra Koester, Federica Baffigi, Massimo Chiari, Daniele Panetta and Leonida Antonio Gizzi
A Few MeV Laser-Plasma Accelerated Proton Beam in Air Collimated Using Compact Permanent Quadrupole Magnets
Reprinted from: *Appl. Sci.* **2021**, *11*, 6358, doi:10.3390/app11146358 73

Majid Masnavi and Martin Richardson
Spectroscopic Studies of Laser-Based Far-Ultraviolet Plasma Light Source
Reprinted from: *Appl. Sci.* **2021**, *11*, 6919, doi:10.3390/app11156919 85

Sergio Mingo Barba, Francesco Schillaci, Roberto Catalano, Giada Petringa, Daniele Margarone and Giuseppe Antonio Pablo Cirrone
Dosimetric Optimization of a Laser-Driven Irradiation Facility Using the
G4-ELIMED Application
Reprinted from: *Appl. Sci.* **2021**, *11*, 9823, doi:10.3390/app11219823 . . . . **97**

Daniele Margarone, Julien Bonvalet, Lorenzo Giuffrida, Alessio Morace, Vasiliki Kantarelou, Marco Tosca, Didier Raffestin, Philippe Nicolai, Antonino Picciotto, Yuki Abe, Yasunobu Arikawa, Shinsuke Fujioka, Yuji Fukuda, Yasuhiro Kuramitsu, Hideaki Habara and Dimitri Batani
In-Target Proton–Boron Nuclear Fusion Using a PW-Class Laser
Reprinted from: *Appl. Sci.* **2022**, *12*, 1444, doi:10.3390/app12031444 . . . . **109**

About the Editors

Hyung Taek Kim

Hyung Taek Kim is the head research scientist of Advanced Photonics Research Institute at Gwangju Institute of Science's. He recently founded and became the director of "Research Center for Plasma Applications with Ultraintense Lasers (PAUL center). He is one of the most active experimental physicists in the field of laser–plasma interactions, particularly electron accelerations and the generation of radiation sources using petawatt lasers. He has published over 60 articles on laser–plasma interactions in SCI-indexed journals. His research interests include laser wakefield acceleration, ultrashort x-ray/gamma-ray generation by laser–plasma interactions, muon generation with laser-accelerated electron beams, femtosecond laser filamentation, and nonlinear quantum electrodynamic processes in laser–electron collisions.

Daniele Margarone

Daniele Margarone is a lecturer in Experimental Plasma Physics at Queen's University Belfast (Centre for Plasma Physics) and head of the Department of Ion Acceleration and Applications of High Energy Particles at the ELI Beamlines Research Centre. His main research interests include laser-driven ion acceleration; innovative target geometries for ion acceleration; real-time diagnostics of particles and radiation generated in laser plasmas; generation of brilliant particle streams from nuclear fusion reactions; and production of laser-based secondary sources for multidisciplinary applications, including new compact approaches to hadrontherapy for cancer treatment and enhancement of cancer cell killing efficacy through the proton boron nuclear fusion reaction. He is the author of around 200 scientific papers (>2300 citations) on these research topics (h-index 25 from WoS).

Preface to "Laser-Driven Accelerators, Radiations, and Their Applications"

This Special Issue aims to provide an overview of the rapidly progressing field of laser-driven particle accelerations, radiation sources, and their applications. The Special Issue covers the latest developments in laser drivers and laser–particle accelerators, radiation sources based on these laser–plasma accelerators, theoretical studies on novel accelerator concepts, diagnostics for laser–particle accelerators, other laser-driven particle sources, applications of laser-driven particle beams and radiations, and exotic physics in laser–particle interactions.

Hyung Taek Kim and Daniele Margarone
Editors

Editorial

Laser-Driven Accelerators, Radiations, and Their Applications

Hyung Taek Kim [1],* and Daniele Margarone [2,3],*

[1] Advanced Photonics Research Institute, Gwangju Institute of Science and Technology (GIST), Gwangju 61005, Korea
[2] Centre for Plasma Physics, School of Mathematics and Physics, Queen's University of Belfast, Belfast BT7 1NN, UK
[3] ELI–Beamlines Center, Institute of Physics, Czech Academy of Sciences, Za Radnicí 835, 252 41 Dolní Břežany, Czech Republic
* Correspondence: htkim@gist.ac.kr (H.T.K.); d.margarone@qub.ac.uk (D.M.)

Citation: Kim, H.T.; Margarone, D. Laser-Driven Accelerators, Radiations, and Their Applications. *Appl. Sci.* **2022**, *12*, 3662. https://doi.org/10.3390/app12073662

Received: 28 March 2022
Accepted: 31 March 2022
Published: 5 April 2022

Publisher's Note: MDPI stays neutral with regard to jurisdictional claims in published maps and institutional affiliations.

Copyright: © 2022 by the authors. Licensee MDPI, Basel, Switzerland. This article is an open access article distributed under the terms and conditions of the Creative Commons Attribution (CC BY) license (https://creativecommons.org/licenses/by/4.0/).

Particle accelerators and radiation based on radio-frequency (RF) cavities have significantly contributed to the advancement of science and technology in the last century. However, the rising costs and scales for building cutting-edge accelerators form barriers to accessing these particle and radiation sources. Since the introduction of chirped pulse amplification technology [1] in the 1990s, short-pulse, high-power lasers have enabled the realization of laser-driven accelerations and radiation sources. Laser-driven accelerators and radiation sources could be a viable alternative to providing compact and cost-effective particle and photon sources. The accelerating field in a plasma, driven by intense laser pulses, is typically several orders of magnitude greater than that of RF accelerators, while controlling the plasma media and intense laser pulses is highly demanding. Therefore, numerous efforts have been directed toward developing compact, high-quality particle beams and radiation sources based on intense laser-plasma interactions, with the goal of paving the way for these novel sources to be used in a variety of applications.

This Special Issue covers the latest developments in laser-based ion and electron accelerators, laser-plasma radiation sources, advanced targetry and diagnostic systems for laser-driven particle accelerators, particle beam transport solutions for multidisciplinary applications, ionizing radiation dose map determination, and new approaches to laser-plasma nuclear fusion using high-intensity, short laser pulses. This collection of research articles is a complementary set of experimental results, achieved using cutting-edge laser technologies with a broad range of parameters (from 10 TW to 1 PW and from 10 fs to 1 ps) and numerical simulation studies, carried out through particle-in-cell, hydrodynamic, and Monte Carlo advanced modelling.

The versatility of laser-plasma accelerators is demonstrated through an optically switchable, multi-MeV ion/electron accelerator using the same target geometry (thin-foil) [2]. A review of the recent developments, limitations, and perspectives of multi-GeV electron accelerators with PW-class lasers using the laser-wakefield acceleration approach is provided [3]. Advanced spectroscopic investigations of laser-based, far-ultraviolet plasma sources are also presented [4]. Recent progress in the design and development of automated systems to refresh solid targets at a high repetition rate during the interaction with high-intensity laser pulses are presented, along with ion diagnostics and corresponding data collection and real-time analysis methods [5]. Experimental studies on the correlation between the frequency spectrum of the large electro-magnetic pulse generated in the high-intensity laser–target interaction and the distortion of Thomson parabola spectrometer proton tracks are also reported [6]. A dedicated Monte Carlo Study of Imaging Plate Response to Laser-Driven Aluminum Ion Beams is presented [7]. The design, implementation, and characterization of a multi-MeV laser-plasma proton beamline using compact and cost-effective particle beam transport solutions is presented [8]. On the other hand, feasibility studies aimed to perform radiobiological experiments using laser-accelerated proton beams with intermediate-energy (few tens of MeV), properly focused and selected through advanced particle beam transport solutions, are reported [9]. The angular spectral distribution of laser-accelerated particles is assessed for the subsequent modelling of radiation dose maps and a comparison with the experimental results [10]. Finally, the first proof-of-principle experiment to demonstrate the efficient generation of α-particle beams through proton–boron fusion reactions using a PW-class laser in the "in-target" geometry is presented [11].

Author Contributions: H.T.K. and D.M. equally contributed to the preparation of this manuscript. All authors have read and agreed to the published version of the manuscript.

Funding: H.T.K. was supported by GIST Research Institute (GRI) grant funded by the GIST in 2022, and the National Research Foundation of Korea (NRF) grant funded by the Korea government (MSIT) Grant No. NRF-2020R1F1A1070538. DM was supported by the Ministry of Education, Youth, and Sports of the Czech Republic through the project "Advanced Research Using High-Intensity Laser-Produced Photons and Particles" (CZ.02.1.010.00.016_0190000789).

Institutional Review Board Statement: Not applicable.

Informed Consent Statement: Not applicable.

Data Availability Statement: Not applicable.

Acknowledgments: This publication was only possible with the invaluable contributions of the authors and reviewers of *Applied Sciences*.

Conflicts of Interest: The authors declare no conflict of interest.

References

1. Strickland, D.; Mourou, G. Compression of amplified chirped optical pulses. *Opt. Commun.* **1985**, *56*, 219–221. [CrossRef]
2. Cohen, I.; Gershuni, Y.; Elkind, M.; Azouz, G.; Levanon, A.; Pomerantz, I. Optically Switchable MeV Ion/Electron Accelerator. *Appl. Sci.* **2021**, *11*, 5424. [CrossRef]
3. Kim, H.T.; Pathak, V.B.; Hojbota, C.I.; Mirzaie, M.; Pae, K.H.; Kim, C.M.; Yoon, J.W.; Sung, J.H.; Lee, S.K. Multi-GeV Laser Wakefield Electron Acceleration with PW Lasers. *Appl. Sci.* **2021**, *11*, 5831. [CrossRef]
4. Masnavi, M.; Richardson, M. Spectroscopic Studies of Laser-Based Far-Ultraviolet Plasma Light Source. *Appl. Sci.* **2021**, *11*, 6919. [CrossRef]
5. Chagovets, T.; Stanček, S.; Giuffrida, L.; Velyhan, A.; Tryus, M.; Grepl, F.; Istokskaia, V.; Kantarelou, V.; Wiste, T.; Hernandez Martin, J.C.; et al. Automation of Target Delivery and Diagnostic Systems for High Repetition Rate Laser-Plasma Acceleration. *Appl. Sci.* **2021**, *11*, 1680. [CrossRef]
6. Grepl, F.; Krása, J.; Velyhan, A.; De Marco, M.; Dostál, J.; Pfeifer, M.; Margarone, D. Distortion of Thomson Parabolic-Like Proton Patterns due to Electromagnetic Interference. *Appl. Sci.* **2021**, *11*, 4484. [CrossRef]
7. Won, J.; Song, J.; Palaniyappan, S.; Gautier, D.C.; Jeong, W.; Fernández, J.C.; Bang, W. Monte Carlo Study of Imaging Plate Response to Laser-Driven Aluminum Ion Beams. *Appl. Sci.* **2021**, *11*, 820. [CrossRef]
8. Brandi, F.; Labate, L.; Palla, D.; Kumar, S.; Fulgentini, L.; Koester, P.; Baffigi, F.; Chiari, M.; Panetta, D.; Gizzi, L.A. A Few MeV Laser-Plasma Accelerated Proton Beam in Air Collimated Using Compact Permanent Quadrupole Magnets. *Appl. Sci.* **2021**, *11*, 6358. [CrossRef]
9. Mingo Barba, S.; Schillaci, F.; Catalano, R.; Petringa, G.; Margarone, D.; Cirrone, G.A.P. Dosimetric Optimization of a Laser-Driven Irradiation Facility Using the G4-ELIMED Application. *Appl. Sci.* **2021**, *11*, 9823. [CrossRef]
10. Groza, A.; Chirosca, A.; Stancu, E.; Butoi, B.; Serbanescu, M.; Dreghici, D.B.; Ganciu, M. Assessment of Angular Spectral Distributions of Laser Accelerated Particles for Simulation of Radiation Dose Map in Target Normal Sheath Acceleration Regime of High Power Laser-Thin Solid Target Interaction—Comparison with Experiments. *Appl. Sci.* **2020**, *10*, 4390. [CrossRef]
11. Margarone, D.; Bonvalet, J.; Giuffrida, L.; Morace, A.; Kantarelou, V.; Tosca, M.; Raffestin, D.; Nicolai, P.; Picciotto, A.; Abe, Y.; et al. In-Target Proton–Boron Nuclear Fusion Using a PW-Class Laser. *Appl. Sci.* **2022**, *12*, 1444. [CrossRef]

Article

Assessment of Angular Spectral Distributions of Laser Accelerated Particles for Simulation of Radiation Dose Map in Target Normal Sheath Acceleration Regime of High Power Laser-Thin Solid Target Interaction—Comparison with Experiments

Andreea Groza [1], Alecsandru Chirosca [2,*], Elena Stancu [3], Bogdan Butoi [1], Mihai Serbanescu [4,5], Dragana B. Dreghici [1,2] and Mihai Ganciu [1]

1. Low Temperature Plasma Department, National Institute for Laser, Plasma and Radiation Physics (INFLPR), Atomistilor Str. No. 409, 077125 Magurele, Ilfov County, Romania; andreea.groza@inflpr.ro (A.G.); ro_medeus@yahoo.com (B.B.); dragana.dreghici@inflpr.ro (D.B.D.); mihai.ganciu@inflpr.ro (M.G.)
2. Nuclear Physics Department, Faculty of Physics, University of Bucharest, 077125 Magurele, Romania
3. STARDOOR Department, National Institute for Laser, Plasma and Radiation Physics, Atomistilor Str. No. 409, 077125 Magurele, Romania; elena.stancu@inflpr.ro
4. Centre for Advanced Laser Technology (CETAL-PW), National Institute for Laser, Plasma and Radiation Physics, Atomistilor Str. No. 409, 077125 Magurele, Ilfov County, Romania; mihai.serbanescu@inflpr.ro
5. Faculty of Electronics, Telecommunications and Information Technology, Politehnica University of Bucharest (UPB), Splaiul Independentei 313, 060042 Bucharest, Romania
* Correspondence: alecsandru.chirosca@ccpr.ro

Received: 27 April 2020; Accepted: 23 June 2020; Published: 26 June 2020

Abstract: An adequate simulation model has been used for the calculation of angular and energy distributions of electrons, protons, and photons emitted during a high-power laser, 5-μm thick Ag target interaction. Their energy spectra and fluencies have been calculated between 0 and 360 degrees around the interaction point with a step angle of five degrees. Thus, the contribution of each ionizing species to the total fluency value has been established. Considering the geometry of the experimental set-up, a map of the radiation dose inside the target vacuum chamber has been simulated, using the Geant4 General Particle Source code, and further compared with the experimental one. Maximum values of the measured dose of the order of tens of mGy per laser shot have been obtained in the direction normal to the target at about 30 cm from the interaction point.

Keywords: spectra of laser accelerated particle beams; mapping of radiation dose; GEANT4 simulations

1. Introduction

High-intensity lasers have progressively been used in contemporary research for the study of matter under extreme conditions and to generate beams of accelerated particles [1–6].

As result of the interaction of high-power laser pulses (I > 10^{19} W/cm^2, fs to ps pulse duration) with solid micrometer flat [1,2] or structured thin targets [2,6], by the target normal sheath acceleration (TNSA) mechanism, electron and proton beams with high directionality, small divergence, and energies up to tens of MeV [1–6] are generated.

The TNSA regime involves complex physical phenomena and is usually considered to be the main rear surface ion acceleration mechanism. When the laser pre-pulse interacts with the target's front side, it produces a pre-plasma. The subsequent arrival of the main laser pulse leads to the generation of hot electrons, as the pre-plasma electrons absorb a percentage of laser pulse energy. The mean free path of such hot electrons in the target is larger than its thickness, and thus part of them pass through the target and form a dense sheath of negative charge in the proximity of the target rear surface up to its rear surface, where it generates a dense sheath. The further expansion of the electrons sheath into the vacuum determine a TV/m electric field, normal to the target surface. The impurities (water and organic molecules) adsorbed on the rear side of the target can be ionized in this strong electric field. Thus, the generated protons are accelerated in the normal direction to the target.

Besides electron and proton beams, bremsstrahlung radiation is also produced due to electron interaction with target nuclei [2]. At the same time, X-ray bremsstrahlung photons can be provided by the "hot" electrons and laser accelerated electrons which reach the vacuum chamber walls [7,8].

The mixed field of photons and electrons might create a hazardous radiation environment, as dose levels of tens of mGy/per laser shot, depending on the target thickness and material characteristics, can be obtained [7,8].

In order to distinguish between different kinds of laser accelerated particle beams, complex detection systems needed to be envisaged. For such goals, magnetic or Thomson parabola spectrometers coupled with Lanex foils, image plates, radiochromic films (RCF), microchannel plates, or CR-39 detectors have been used [2,9–11]. These spectrometers, placed at different distances and angles with respect to the laser–target interaction point, can reveal the energy spectral distribution of the electron and proton beams. The spectra of photons emitted in TNSA regime can be measured using X-ray spectrometers and estimated from the energy distribution of electron beams [12]. The charts of electron-photon distribution in the mixed field of radiation were calculated and experimentally determined [7,8].

It was shown [5] that the spectral distribution of laser accelerated particle beams in high power laser–solid target experiments can reproduce the space radiation environment. The values of radiation dose per laser shot measured during such experiments, inside the target vacuum chambers [7,8], are similar to those measured onboard space vessels [13–18]. On the NASA website [13], daily values of hundreds of µGy were reported for the cumulative radiation dose inside spacecrafts. Similar conditions can be obtained using laser plasma accelerator facilities available worldwide [19–23].

Inside the spacecrafts and space stations there are lots of electronic systems that need to be tested in dedicated facilities on Earth, before being used in extreme conditions. In addition, the assessment of detectors' response in ground-based facilities is essential for overcoming the problems intrinsic to space dosimetry. As shown in Hidding's et al. paper [5], to test electronics, a proper knowledge of the fluxes of ionizing radiation is an important issue.

In this context, the measurement and estimation of the spatial and angular spectral distribution of the ionizing radiation generated in high power laser-thin solid target experiments can be extremely useful.

In this paper, we propose a simulation model to be used for the assessment of the radiation dose map in a TNSA regime for a high power laser-thin solid target interaction experiment. First, the energy spectral distribution of electron, proton and photon beams, have been calculated within 0–360° for a 5 µm thick Ag target irradiated with a high-power laser pulse of about 5×10^{19} W/cm^2 intensity. To this goal, the TNSA plasma expansion model has been considered in conjunction with the Geant4 Monte-Carlo radiation transport code. Then, the angular and energy spectral distributions of ionizing particles were used as input data for the calculation of electron, proton, and photon fluencies around the high power laser-thin solid target interaction point.

The values of input parameters are characteristics to a high power laser-thin solid target experiment performed at the CETAL laser facility [24].

In the Groza's et al. paper [24], we reported a method for the assessment of the energy of the accelerated proton beams produced in high power laser-thin solid target experiments using a stack of CR-39 detectors. It was also stated that a compact experimental set-up which connect the target holder with the detector holder, and the laser spot optical analysis system can be useful for practical applications. For example, by using such a system, the misalignments between targets and detectors can be avoided [24].

In this paper, we introduced an updated version of the above-mentioned experimental set-up which is also suitable for estimation of laser-accelerated electron beam energies. It includes a magnetic spectrometer and a cylindrical holder for positioning the EBT3 RCF passive detectors. The calibration of the RCF was performed for both X-ray photon beams and monoenergetic electrons.

The radiation dose map measured inside the interaction chamber during the high power laser-Ag thin target interaction experiments using EBT3 RCF detectors, will be presented. It will be compared with the simulated one, generated by implementing the data characteristic to angular and energy spectral distribution of electrons, protons, and photons in the geometry mesh of the experimental set-up designed using the GEANT4 standard geometry components.

2. Description of the Simulation Models and Experimental Set up

2.1. Description of the Model for Generation of Angular Spectra of Electrons, Protons and Photons; GEANT4 Model for Compute the Dose Map inside the Interaction Chamber

(a) Description of TNSA Model

The simulation model is based upon the Geant4 [25] framework. The mathematical models for sources description and data processing pipelines have been implemented in the Python language [26]. The integration between the sources description and the custom GEANT4 based application developed in C++, was performed using the Geant4 General Particle source. We used the command line scoring system for the region of interest and the output data were analyzed using another Python pipeline. The particle sources were implemented considering the target normal sheath acceleration (TNSA) mechanism and the plasma expansion model [1].

In TNSA regime, the interaction of a high power laser beam with a thin target generates on its front surface energetic electrons, which are accelerated in forward direction through the target. During their interaction with the target material, these hot electrons can generate bremsstrahlung radiation [7,8]. The electrons, which attain the back of the target and enter in vacuum, create an electrostatic space charge sheath and thus an electric field with an intensity of about 10^{12} V/m. Due to this field, the protons from the rear target surface can be accelerated up to MeV energies [1–6]. The temperature of hot electrons, is related to the laser intensity, [1]:

$$T_{hot} = [(1 + I\,[\text{W/cm}^2]\lambda^2\,[\mu\text{m}]/(1.37 \times 10^{18}))^{1/2} - 1]m_0 c^2, \tag{1}$$

where I represent the laser intensity in beam focus, λ is laser wavelength, m_0 electron mass, and c light velocity [1]. The number of electrons accelerated into the target, N_e, depends on the energy fraction absorbed by hot electrons $f = 1.2 \times 10^{-15} \, I^{0.74}$ (W/cm^2), through the formula [1,27]:

$$N_e = f\,E_L/T_{hot} \tag{2}$$

where E_L is the laser energy.

The electron density at the rear side of the target is $n_{e,0} = N_e/(c\,\tau_L S_{sheath})$, where $S_{sheath} = \pi(r_0 + d \times \tan\theta)^2$ [1], τ_L is laser pulse duration, d is the target thickness, r_0 is the radius of laser beam in focus and θ is the half angular broadening of the hot electrons inside the target. Roth calculated this formula as a function of target thickness and laser intensity [27]:

$$n_{e,0} = [\eta E_L]/[c\tau_L \pi(r_0 + (d\tan\theta/2))^2 k_B T_{hot}] \sim 1.5 \times 10^{19}\,[r_0^2/(r_0 + (d\tan\theta/2)^2][I_{18}^{7/4}/[(1 + 0.73 I_{18}\lambda)^{1/2} - 1]\,[\text{cm}^{-3}] \tag{3}$$

where I_{18} is the laser intensity in terms of 10^{18} W/cm^2 [27].

The energy spectrum of electrons leaving the rear side of the target is given by different formulas, depending on how large the laser intensity is:

$$dN/dE \sim E^2 e^{-E/T_{hot}} \quad (4)$$

(relativistic Maxwelian distribution) for $I > 10^{19}$ W/cm^2 [7,12] and

$$dN/dE \sim E^{1/2} e^{-E/T_{hot}} \quad (5)$$

(Maxwelian distribution) for $I < 10^{19}$ W/cm^2 [7,12].

The energy spectrum of accelerated protons within the plasma expansion model is [1]:

$$dN/dE = [n_{e,0} c_s t_{acc} S_{sheat}/(2ET_{hot})^{1/2}] \exp(-(2E/T_{hot})^{1/2}), \text{ where } c_s = (Z_i \times T_{hot}/m_i)^{1/2} \quad (6)$$

where $t_{acc} = 1.3 \times \tau_L$ while m_i and Z_i ($Z_i = 1$) are referred to as protons.

The energy spectrum of bremsstrahlung photons is derived from the energy spectrum of the electrons which interact with the Ag target ($Z = 49$) and was calculated considering the temperature of hot electrons. The bremsstrahlung radiation is due to energy deposited by the hot electrons while passing through the target.

(b) Description of Electron and Proton Sources Used for Calculation of Electron, Proton and Photon Spectra and Fluencies, around the High Power Laser—Thin Solid Target Interaction Point

The simulation model used for calculation of angular distribution of laser driven accelerated particles was developed considering mainly the above formulas (Equations (1)–(6)). A 2 MeV temperature for the hot electrons was calculated using Formula (1) and the following experimental parameters [24]: 5×10^{19} W/cm^2 laser intensity, 40 fs laser pulse duration, 207 µm^2 laser spot area.

Two volume sources of radiation were considered in order to compute the spectra of electrons, protons and photons emitted in the 0–360° range (with a 5-degree angular step) at 3 cm distance, around the interaction point.

The first source represents the source of electrons (a disk of 9 µm radius) generated in the pre-plasma obtained after the interaction of the PW laser with the target surface. It provides the electrons for the simulation of radiation transport. The electrons were considered to have a Maxwellian energy distribution in accordance with Equations (4) and (5). This source is position in front of the target [28–31]. The energy distribution of electrons was calculated, based on mathematical equations from (1) to (5). The angular distribution of electron source was assumed isotropic. The electrons generated in the pre-plasma which emit in 4π are the main source for radiation in the vacuum chamber [7,8].

The energy distribution of photons has been calculated considering the hot electrons interaction with the target nuclei.

The second source (a disk of 9-µm radius) of radiation included in the simulation was placed behind the target and provides the accelerated protons. There are considered the TNSA mechanism (Equations (1)–(3) and (6)) and the plasma expansion model [1,28,29]. The divergence of this source is an independent parameter and is defined through its half angle which was 25° in accordance with [1].

The incidence angle of the laser beam on the target was not considered in these simulations. Previously, in the paper of Morita's et al. [32] by Particle in Cell simulations it was shown that an oblique incidence angle of laser on the target increases the energy of accelerated protons without changing the distribution of electrons. At laser intensities of ~10^{19} W/cm^2, the incidence angle of the laser beam on the target influences only the efficiency of the energy transfer from photons to electrons into the pre-plasma.

The characteristics of source terms are summarized in Table 1.

Table 1. Characteristics of source terms.

Source of Radiation	Electrons (Source 1)	Protons (Source 2)
Laser intensity (W/cm^2)	5×10^{19}	5×10^{19}
Laser pulse duration (fs)	40	40
Laser spot area (μm^2)	207	207
Source radius (μm)	9	9
Source position	ahead	behind
Angular distribution	4π	25° half angle
Number of events	1.97×10^{12}	1.29×10^{9}

The two volume sources described above were used to compute the angular and energy spectral distributions of electrons, protons and photons around the high power laser-thin solid target interaction point using the GEANT4 simulation toolkit [25,33,34]. Particle fluencies were also determined.

The general particle sources (GPS) defined in GEANT4 provide a complex environment which allows the inclusion into the simulation of both proton and electron sources, with a specific ratio of particle numbers. It was considered a 1.97×10^{12} total events number, (1.97×10^{12} electron events number and 1.29×10^{9} proton events number) and a proton to electron number ratio of 1.53×10^{3}. The total events number and the ratio between electron and proton events number were generated by analytical calculations using the TNSA model (Equations (1)–(6)) for the experimental parameters mentioned above.

Geant4 simulations were performed using the G4EmLivermore interaction library for electromagnetic radiation and QGSP_BIC_HP for proton interaction. Binary cascade models were activated for Ion interactions [33,34].

Monte Carlo algorithms provide a statistical approach for radiation transport within environments and detectors, the uncertainties being lower than 1% for simulations that runs for 10^{12} events number. The main source of inconsistencies in Monte Carlo simulations are represented by the variance reduction techniques [35] usually employed for decreasing the simulation run time. Such method was not applied here.

Scoring was performed using the Geant4 command line-based scoring system and a cylindrical mesh. The scoring mesh was binned in polar coordinates and had 5 degree angular and 0.2 cm radial steps, respectively. Proton, electron, and photon spectra, as well as their corresponding fluencies were assessed.

The simulations were performed using a 32 core XENON E5-2650 with 20 GB RAM. The run time was approximately of 70 ± 4 h per simulation and the statistical fluctuations were less than 1%.

The data were made available in a familiar web interface using Jupyter Notebooks [36]. This approach allowed for interactive data processing techniques to be applied to validate the simulation results. Thus, the output data files were easily integrated into other software packages for data analysis and further processing.

(c) Description of the Geometry Mesh of the Experimental Set-Up Used for Calculation of Radiation Dose Map Inside the Vacuum Chamber

The simulation of radiation dose map was also performed with the Geant4 v.10.5 framework tools described above [25,33,34].

Firstly, the electron and proton sources were implemented into a mesh (see Figure 1) adapted to the specific parameters of the experimental set-up presented in Figure 2. The electron source (the first source of radiation) is illustrated as a yellow disk, the red disk represent the 5 μm thick target behind which is positioned the proton source (the second source of radiation) designed as a green disk. The two sources were integrated into the simulation model using the GPS that allows the positioning of more than one source within an experimental set-up. Also, it was considered, that, the electrons that propagate in vacuum can generate nuclear reactions when interact with experimental set-up components (see Figure 2), producing secondary radiation such photons. For the considered particles energy range, in the simulation model, all available nuclear processes (in GEANT4 General Particle Source tools) were considered. The mesh of the experimental set-up was implemented using GEANT4 standard geometry components without any Boolean operations, and the overlapping regions were tested at the beginning of each run.

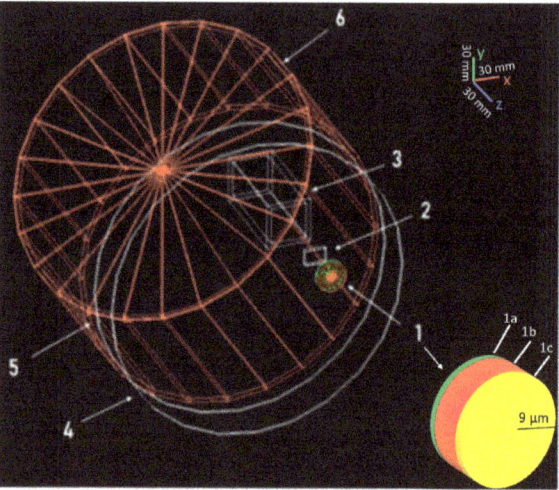

Figure 1. Geometry mesh of the GEANT4 simulation model: 1a—source of electrons; 1b—target; 1c—source of protons; 2—hole; 3—magnetic spectrometer; 4—target holder; 5—detector holder; 6—aluminum cylinder. The structure of the electron, proton sources and target are presented in the right corner of the image.

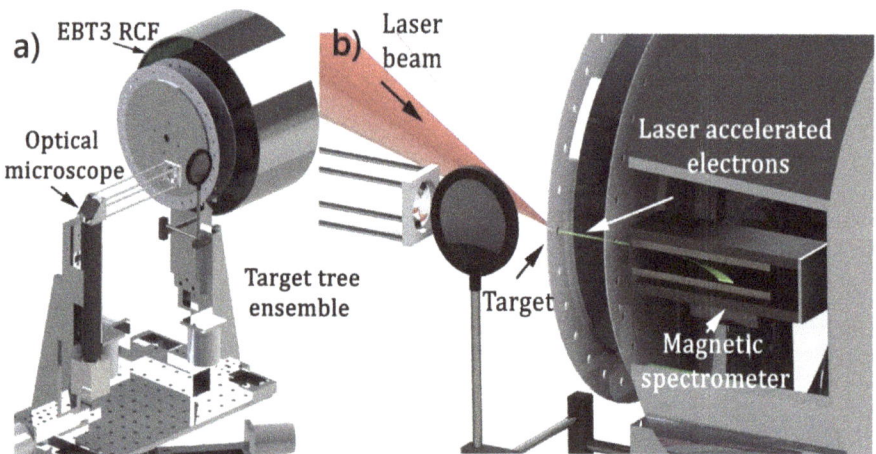

Figure 2. (**a**) Experimental set-up; (**b**) Detailed of the experimental set-up.

The angular and energy spectral distributions of electrons, protons and photons obtained as result of the interaction of laser spot with the Ag target, as well as the geometry mesh from Figure 1, were used to simulate the radiation dose map inside the vacuum chamber.

2.2. Experimental Setup Used to Measure Electron and Proton Spectra at 3 cm Distance from Target n

The mapping of the radiation dose inside the target chamber has been performed during experiments [24] of high power-thin solid target interaction for a laser intensity in focus of about 5×10^{19} W/cm^2 (40 fs pulse duration [24,37]). The target was tilted at 45° with respect to the laser beam focus position. The laser spot surface area was (9×23) 207 µm^2 and the fraction of energy in the laser spot (at full width half maximum) was ~30%. The elliptical shape of the focal spot was previously attributed to the slightly ellipticity of the incoming beam [8,38].

The experimental set-up from Figure 2, was designed to allow a straightforward analysis of laser accelerated electron and proton beams.

It is composed of the targets and passive detectors holder ensemble, a magnetic spectrometer (B ~ 0.6 T), and an optical analysis ensemble. The target and detector holder system consist in two parallel metallic plates centered using a horizontal metallic ax. The targets were positioned on the first plate while the passive detectors used for proton beams analysis were placed on the second plate. The spectral analysis of the proton beams achieved using CR-39 detectors was reported in [24]. Behind the second plate a centered (to the drilled holes) magnetic spectrometer, for the estimation of the energy of the laser accelerated electrons, was placed in a fix position, while the target and detector holder ensemble can be rotated. Around the magnetic spectrometer can be observed a metallic cylinder that can be simultaneous rotated with the target and detector holder plates. On the inner surface of the cylinder (see Figure 2) EBT3 radiochromic films were positioned. A maximum electron energy of about 13 MeV was estimated from the coloring of the EBT3 radiochromic films. Such values of the electron energies were also reported in similar experimental conditions [5].

The target and detector holder ensemble are placed on mechanical translation and rotation stages for precise alignment of each target in the focus of the laser beam. The optical analysis system is described in detail in [24].

2.3. Calibration of EBT3 Radiochromic Films used for Mapping of the Radiation Field

The dosimetry assessment during high power laser-thin solid target interaction performed using the EBT3 radiochromic films (RCF) proved to be useful [39] and offers two-dimensional information on the radiation dose. The EBT3 films have a symmetrical layer's structure as the active layer (28 µm thick) is sandwiched between two 125 µm matte-polyester substrates (Ashland Advanced Materials). These polyester layers prevent the formation of Newton ring interference patterns when the irradiated EBT3 films are scanned with flatbed scanners [39].

The EBT3 films were calibrated using both high energy photons generated by a 40 kV X-ray source [40] and electrons with an energy of about 5 MeV using a classical medical accelerator. In the paper of Sorriaux et al. [41], it was shown that EBT3 RCF can be used for dosimetry measurements of photon, electron and proton beams as their calibration curves (in the same dose range), are similar. The uncertainties of the EBT3 calibration curves presented there were within 1.5% for photons and protons and 2% for electrons [41].

A high precision measurement of the optical density of each EBT3 film is essential for the evaluation of the ionizing particles radiation dose values inside the target chamber.

The EBT3 films exposed during the high-power laser thin solid target experiments, as well as those used for the determination of the calibration curve (see Figure 3b) were scanned using an EPSON Expression 11000XL professional scanner with a resolution of 4800 dpi in transmission mode. The scanned area was about 0.5×0.5 cm^2 for each film.

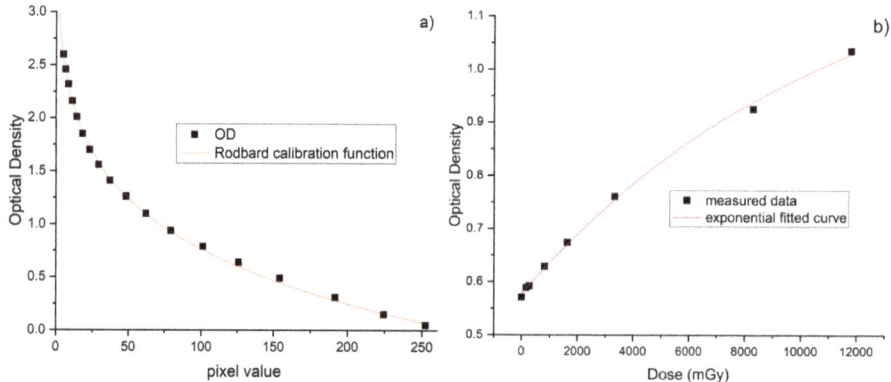

Figure 3. (a) Pixel values to optical density Rodbard calibration curve. (b) The dependence of optical density on radiation dose.

The scanned images of the EBT3 films were processed with ImageJ software in order to convert the pixel values into standard optical density (OD) [42]. For this purpose, a Kodak calibrated optical density step tablet [42] has been used and the images were converted into 8 bits grey scale. The pixel values range from 0–255 gray units. A so-called Rodbard calibration function [43,44] was used for pixel values to obtain an optical density transformation: $y = d + (a - d)/(1 + (x/c)^b)$ where $a = 80.147399$, $b = 0.102551$, $c = 1.109687 \times 10^{12}$, $d = 8.304216$. The R^2 was 0.997. This function was identified to be suitable for pixel values to OD calibration in medical applications and for the establishment of dose response curves [43,44]. The graph of the Rodbard function is presented in Figure 3a.

The calibration graph presented in Figure 3b was obtained for a 40 keV photons beam. The calibration curve obtained for 5 MeV electrons is similar (within ±7%) with that one from Figure 3b. Both curves were used for calculation of the radiation dose inside the target chamber as well as for the electron maximum energy (of about 13 MeV) estimation. The black squares represent the measured data values and in red is the curve used for fitting. As fitted function, we used an exponential one. The fitting parameters was: $R^2 = 0.997$, and standard error was about 0.069.

3. Results and Discussions

(a) Simulation Results on the Angular Spectral Distribution of Electron, Proton and Photon Beams Generated in TNSA Regime

Laser accelerated electron and proton beams in vacuum are the primary sources of radiation in a high power laser-thin solid target interaction experiment in the TNSA regime. The secondary radiation source consists mainly of bremsstrahlung X-ray photons or gamma rays both produced by the interaction of hot electrons with target nuclei. The interaction of primary radiation, (mainly of electrons) with the vacuum chamber walls and detectors placed at different distances and inclination angles with respect to the laser–target interaction point, also generate bremsstrahlung radiation on a nanosecond time scale.

The opening angle of proton and electron accelerated beams depend on few parameters such as: target thickness, laser intensity, laser focal spot size, emittance, and source dimensions [1–6]. Many authors [1–6,27,45–47] reported that electron and proton beams generated in TNSA regime have the highest number and energy in forward direction, normal to the target. The decrease of protons energy with the increase of opening angle was reported both by calculations and experimental measurements [9,45].

The spectra of proton and electron accelerated beams as well as of the emitted photons calculated using the simulation model described above (without considering the mesh of the experimental set-up presented in Figure 1) allowed us to find angular and energy distributions of primary and secondary radiation (see Figures 4 and 5).

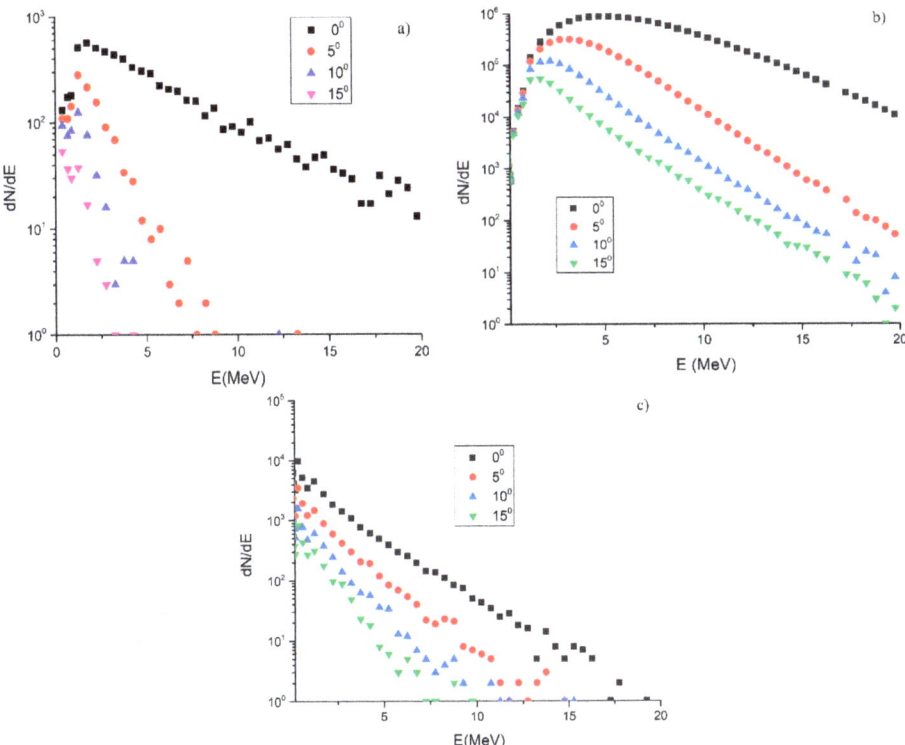

Figure 4. Simulated spectra of laser accelerated: (**a**) protons; (**b**) electrons beams and (**c**) emitted photons at different angles within 0–15 degrees range. 0° is considered in forward direction normal to target.

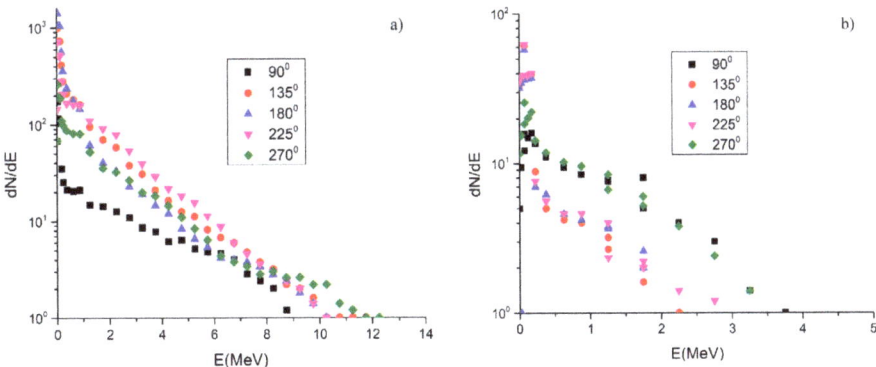

Figure 5. Simulated spectra of laser accelerated: (**a**) electron and (**b**) photon beams at different angles.

Within 0–15 degrees of angle, the spectra of electrons, protons, and photons are shown in Figure 4 (0° is considered in forward direction normal to the target position). These spectra are calculated for the pulse duration time, 5×10^{19} W/cm^2 laser intensity, and at 3 cm distance from the laser–target interaction point. In Figure 4a can be observed, that the most energetic protons are emitted in normal direction to the target position. Within 5 degrees angle the energy of protons drastically decreases. However, the electron spectra presented in Figure 4b indicate only the decrease of electron numbers as the angle increases (see Figure 4b). The spectra of photons also display an angular dependence (see Figure 4c). The spectra obtained for angles between 345° and 0° degrees are similar.

The interaction between the laser focused spot and target was considered to produce ionizing radiation within 0–360°. The spectra of electrons and photons at different angles between 90° and 270° are presented in Figure 5. The number of emitted electrons and photons as well as their energy are lower than those emitted in the 0–15° range (see Figure 4). Proton spectra were not generated in this angular range.

The spectra of electrons, protons, and photons (see Figures 4 and 5) display some fluctuations in the distribution of particles as function of energy. It appears mainly at the highest energies and at angles different from 0°. This is probably due to the statistical approach characteristic to the Monte Carlo simulations [33,34] and to the fact that the number of generated particles at high energies, is low. Anyway, these fluctuations are relatively small and do not affect the estimations of the electron, proton, and photon spectral distributions. Similar distributions, but without any fluctuations, can be obtained when the spectra are analytically calculated. However, such calculations are possible only at 0°.

The main advantage of the constructed simulation model is that the simultaneous calculations of electron, proton and photon spectra and it angular dependence within 0–360° can offer an overall image on the ionizing radiation distribution around the high power laser-thin solid target interaction point. Thus, we can evaluate the evolution of the number of produced electrons, protons, and photons both with energy and angle as a function of experimental parameters such as: laser intensity, laser pulse duration, and the target thickness.

(b) Simulation results on Electron, proton, and Photon Fluencies

High-power laser–thin solid target interaction generates mixed radiation fields of electrons and photons. The radiation dose measured inside the vacuum chamber by passive detectors, is mainly attributed to photons and laser accelerated electrons. The interaction of electrons with the metallic components of the chamber also generates bremsstrahlung radiation [7,8]. The protons are emitted in the target normal direction, forwards, and backwards [27], being stopped in materials in accordance to their stopping powers [48].

For near target radiation field assessment, the simulation model described above, allowed us the estimation of total fluencies of radiation generated by the interaction of the high power laser beam with the thin solid target. The fluencies of electrons, protons, and photons were also calculated (see Figure 6), using as input data the spectra presented in Figures 4 and 5. It turns out that electrons contribute ~98.9%, photons ~1%, and protons ~0.1%, respectively, to the total fluencies. The electrons, and photons are produced almost uniformly around the interaction point, having a maximum in the normal direction to the target position. The protons are emitted mainly in the forward direction.

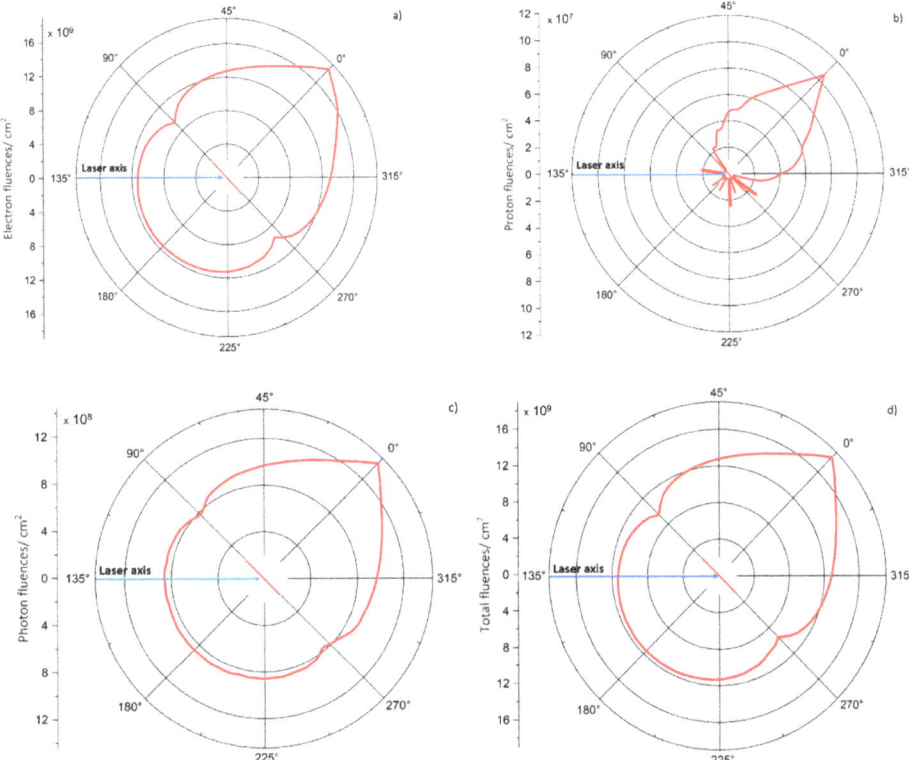

Figure 6. Angular dependence of particle fluencies/cm² at 3 cm from the interaction point on logarithmic scale: (**a**) electrons (**b**) protons (**c**) photons and (**d**) total fluencies.

(c) Simulated and Experimental Dose Maps

By implementing the angular and energy spectral distributions in the mesh associated with the experimental set-up displayed in Figure 2, the simulated dose map was generated.

In the experiments performed using the experimental set-up from Figure 2, the radiation dose inside the target chamber was charted, using EBT3 RCF placed at different distances and inclination angles with respect to the high power laser-thin solid target interaction point. The calibration curve from Figure 3b was used for calculation of the radiation dose inside the vacuum chamber.

In Figure 7a, the radiation dose measured around the interaction point is shown, in comparison with the simulated one. The dose values are per laser shot and were normalized to 30 cm distance. As can be observed the maximum values of the radiation dose were reached in the forward target normal direction.

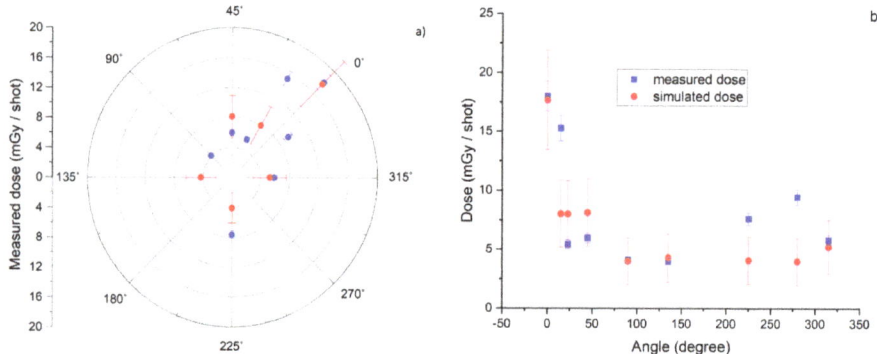

Figure 7. (**a**) Map of the measured dose (blue dots) inside the target chamber and of the simulated radiation dose (red dots); (**b**) The fluctuations in the angular distribution of measured and simulated dose.

There are certain inadequacies between experimental data and simulations (see Figure 7b). We suppose that these discrepancies appear as the scattering of the radiation on the walls of the vacuum chamber and from metallic cylinders placed around the magnetic spectrometer (see Figure 2), which was not considered in the simulation model. Otherwise, it would determine a percentage of uncertainties higher than 1% for 10^{12} events number, and the simulation run time would have increased accordingly. Therefore, a simplified geometry was considered.

Moreover, the vacuum chamber has a rectangular parallelepiped geometrical shape [20] and the maximum measured dose values away from the forward direction are in the proximity of the chamber corners. Measured dose values of tens of mGy/per laser shot were obtained in similar experimental conditions [8].

Considering the electron and photon fluency data presented in Figure 6, we suppose that the electrons have the largest contribution to the radiation dose (98.9%) while photons contribute only 1%. Protons do not influence the dose value by more than 0.1%. Anyway, the protons with the highest energy are emitted in the forward direction (see Figure 6 and Ref. [27]), even if in the backward direction to the target position, they were also observed (see Figure 6 and Ref. [27]). The protons emitted forward are stopped in the detectors placed at 3 cm distance from the target position (see Figure 2).

Thus, based on the calculation of the angular dependence of particle fluencies, the radiation dose map reconstruction was performed in any point within the area of interest. The presented simulation model can be further developed for the calculation of dose in any material, by considering the energy and type of incident radiation as well as possible reactions.

4. Conclusions

The results presented in this paper link the angular and energy distributions of electrons, protons, and photons calculated within 0–360°, with an angular step of five degrees, to the radiation dose map. This is achieved through integration into the simulation model and the use of an experimental set up mesh. The geometry of the experimental set-up was designed in the Geant4 General Particle Source code and was considered for the calculation of the radiation dose around the high-power laser-solid thin foil interaction point. When comparing the calculated dose map with the experimental one, certain discrepancies between the values of dose obtained at different angles were observed. This is most probably because the scattering of radiation into the vacuum chamber was not considered in the simulation model.

Integrated dose per laser shot of about 15 mGy (due to electrons and photons) in the normal direction to the target, at 30 cm distance from the laser–target interaction point was experimentally measured.

Excepting the geometry of our experimental set-up, the presented simulation model allows for the calculation of the fluencies of electrons, protons, and photons based on their energy and angular spectral distributions. Our results show that electrons contribute almost ~99% to the value of total fluencies generated around the interaction point, while photons have a 1% share.

The numerical and experimental investigations presented in this paper suggest that high power laser–thin solid target experiments can be used as a test environment for electronic devices placed onboard spacecraft and space stations, the main advantage being the simultaneous generation of electrons, protons, and photons.

Author Contributions: Conceptualization, A.G., A.C., B.B., and M.S.; methodology, A.G, B.B., M.S., E.S., and D.B.D.; investigation, B.B., M.S., E.S., and D.B.D.; software, A.C. and D.B.D.; validation, A.G., A.C., M.G., B.B., M.S., and E.S., D.B.D.; formal analysis, A.G. and A.C.; writing—original draft preparation A.G., A.C., E.S., B.B., E.S., M.S., D.B.D., and M.G.; writing—review and editing A.G., A.C., E.S., and D.B.D. All authors have read and agreed to the published version of the manuscript.

Funding: Work has been funded by European Space Agency within the ESA contract No. 4000121912/17/NL/CBi/2017.

Acknowledgments: We acknowledge support from the CETAL-PW facility at the National Institute for Laser, Plasma and Radiation Physics, Magurele, Romania. We also thank to Șerban Udrea from GSI-Darmstadt for fruitful discussions.

Conflicts of Interest: The authors declare no conflict of interest. The funders had no role in the design of the study; in the collection, analyses, or interpretation of data; in the writing of the manuscript, or in the decision to publish the results.

References

1. Fuchs, J.; Antici, P.; d'Humieres, E.; Lefebvre, E.; Borghesi, M.; Brambrink, E.; Cecchetti, C.A.; Kaluza, M.; Malka, V.; Manclossi, M.; et al. Laser-driven proton scaling laws and new paths towards energy increase. *Nat. Phys.* **2006**, *2*, 48–56. [CrossRef]
2. Macchi, A.; Borghesi, M.; Passoni, M. Ion acceleration by superintense laser-plasma interaction. *Rev. Mod. Phys.* **2013**, *85*, 751–793. [CrossRef]
3. Bolton, P.R.; Borghesi, M.; Brenner, C.; Carroll, D.C.; Martinis De, C.; Flacco, A.; Floquet, V.; Fuchs, J.; Gallegos, P.; Giove, D.; et al. Instrumentation for diagnostics and control of laser-accelerated proton (ion) beams. *Phys. Med.* **2014**, *30*, 255–270. [CrossRef] [PubMed]
4. Ledingham, K.W.D.; Galster, W. Laser-driven particle and photon beams and some applications. *New J. Phys.* **2010**, *12*, 045005. [CrossRef]
5. Hidding, B.; Karger, O.; Konigstein, T.; Pretzler, G.; Manahan, G.G.; McKenna, P.; Gray, R.; Wilson, R.; Wiggins, S.M.; Welsh, G.H.; et al. Laser-plasma-based Space Radiation Reproduction in the Laboratory. *Sci. Rep.* **2017**, *7*, 42354. [CrossRef]
6. Zigler, A.; Eisenman, S.; Botton, M.; Nahum, E.; Schleifer, E.; Baspaly, A.; Pomerantz, I.; Abicht, F.; Branzel, J.; Priebe, G.; et al. Enhanced Proton Acceleration by an Ultrashort Laser Interaction with Structured Dynamic Plasma Targets. *Phys. Rev. Lett.* **2013**, *110*, 215004. [CrossRef]
7. Liang, T.T.; Bauer, J.M.; Liu, J.C.; Rokni, S.H. Radiation protection around high-intensity laser interactions with solid targets. *Health Phys.* **2018**, *115*, 6. [CrossRef]
8. Liang, T.; Bauer, J.; Cimeno, M.; Ferrari, A.; Galtier, E.; Granados, E.; Lee, H.J.; Liu, J.; Nagler, B.; Prinz, A.; et al. Radiation dose measurements for high-intensity laser interactions with solid targets at SLAC, Rad. *Prot. Dosim.* **2016**, *172*, 346–355. [CrossRef]
9. Nurnberg, F.; Schollmeier, M.; Brambrink, E.; Blazevic, A.; Carroll, D.C.; Flippo, K.; Gautier, D.C.; Geißel, M.; Harres, K.; Hegelich, B.M.; et al. Radiochromic film imaging spectroscopy of laser accelerated proton beams. *Rev. Sci. Instrum.* **2009**, *80*, 033301. [CrossRef]

10. Jeong, T.W.; Singh, P.K.; Scullion, C.; Ahmed, H.; Hadjisolomou, P.; Jeon, C.; Yun, H.; Kakolee, K.F.; Borghesi, M.; Ter-Avetisyan, S. CR-39 track detector for multi-MeV ion spectroscopy. *Sci. Rep.* **2017**, *7*, 2152. [CrossRef]
11. Jeong, T.W.; Singh, P.K.; Scullion, C.; Ahmed, H.; Kakolee, K.F.; Hadjisolomou, P.; Alejo, A.; Kar, S.; Borghesi, M.; Ter-Avetisyan, S. Experimental evaluation of the response of micro-channel plate detector to ions with 10s of MeV energies. *Rev. Sci. Instrum.* **2016**, *87*, 083301. [CrossRef] [PubMed]
12. Fiorini, F.; Neely, D.; Clarke, R.J.; Green, S. Characterization of laser-driven electron and photon beams using the Monte Carlo code FLUKA. *Laser Part. Beams* **2014**, *32*, 233–241. [CrossRef]
13. Zell, H. Space Weather. Text. NASA. Available online: http://www.nasa.gov/mission_pages/rbsp/science/rbsp-spaceweather.html (accessed on 1 March 2020).
14. Tokumaru, M. Three-dimensional exploration of the solar wind using observations of interplanetary Scintillation. *Proc. Jpn. Acad. Ser. B* **2013**, *89*, 67–79. [CrossRef] [PubMed]
15. Cannon, P. Extreme Space Weather: Impacts on Engineered Systems and Infrastructures, in Royal Academy of Engineering. Available online: https://www.raeng.org.uk/publications/reports/space-weather-full-report (accessed on 5 March 2020).
16. Delzanno, G.L.; Borovsky, J.E.; Thomsen, M.F.; Moulton, J.D.; Macdonald, E.A. Future beam experiments in the magnetosphere with plasma contactors: How do we get the charge off the spacecraft? *J. Geophys. Res. Space Phys.* **2015**, *120*, 3647–3664. [CrossRef]
17. Holly, Z. National Aeronautics and Space Administration. Available online: https://www.nasa.gov/mission_pages/rbsp/science/rbsp-spaceweather-human.html (accessed on 4 August 2017).
18. Konigstein, T.; Karger, O.; Pretzler, G.; Rosenzweig, J.B.; Hidding, B. Design considerations for the use of laser-plasma accelerators for advanced space radiation studies. *J. Plasma Phys.* **2012**, *78*, 383–391. [CrossRef]
19. Danson, C.; Hillier, D.; Hopps, N.; Neely, D. Petawatt class lasers worldwide. *High Power Laser Sci. Eng.* **2015**, *3*, e3. [CrossRef]
20. Center for Advanced Laser Technologies (CETAL), Ultra-intense Lasers Laboratory. Available online: http://cetal.inflpr.ro/newsite/cetal-pw (accessed on 20 February 2020).
21. Asavei, T.; Tomut, M.; Bobeica, M.; Aogaki, S.; Cernaianu, M.O.; Ganciu, M.; Kar, S.; Manda, G.; Mocanu, N.; Neagu, L.; et al. Materials in extreme environments for energy, accelerators and space applications at ELI-NP. *Rom. Rep. Phys.* **2016**, *68*, S275–S347.
22. Ganciu, M.; Groza, A.; Cramariuc, O.; Mihalcea, B.; Serbanescu, M.; Stancu, E.; Surmeian, A.; Butoi, B.; Dreghici, D.; Chirosca, A.; et al. Hardware and software methods for radiation resistance rising of the critical infrastructures. *Rom. Cyber Secur. J.* **2019**, *1*, 3–13.
23. Narici, L.; Casolino, M.; Fino, L.; Di Larosa, M.; Picozza, P.; Rizzo, A.; Zaconte, V. Performances of Kevlar and Polyethylene as radiation shielding on-board the International Space Station in high latitude radiation environment. *Sci. Rep.* **2017**, *7*, 1–11. [CrossRef]
24. Groza, A.; Serbanescu, M.; Butoi, B.; Stancu, E.; Straticiuc, M.; Burducea, I.; Balan, A.; Chirosca, A.; Mihalcea, B.; Ganciu, M. Advances in Spectral Distribution Assessment of Laser Accelerated Protons using Multilayer CR-39 Detectors. *Appl. Sci.* **2019**, *9*, 2052. [CrossRef]
25. Allison, J.; Amako, K.; Apostolakis, J.; Arce, P.; Asai, M.; Aso, T.; Bagli, E.; Bagulya, A.; Banerjee, S.; Barrand, G.J.N.I.; et al. Recent developments in Geant4. *Nucl. Instrum. Methods Phys. Res. A* **2016**, *835*, 186–225. [CrossRef]
26. Python Core Team. *Python: A Dynamic, Open Source Programming Language*; Python Software Foundation, 2015. Available online: https://www.python.org/ (accessed on 20 May 2020).
27. Roth, M.; Schollmeier, M. Ion Acceleration—Target Normal Sheath Acceleration. In Proceedings of the CAS-CERN Accelerator School: Plasma Wake Acceleration Geneva, Geneva, Switzerland, 23–29 November 2014.
28. Mora, P. Plasma expansion in vacuum. *Phys. Rev. Lett.* **2003**, *90*, 185002. [CrossRef] [PubMed]
29. Tampo, M.; Awano, S.; Bolton, P.R.; Kondo, K.; Mima, K.; Mori, Y.; Kodama, R. Correlation between laser accelerated MeV proton and electron beams using simple fluid model for target normal sheath acceleration. *Phys. Plasmas* **2010**, *17*, 7. [CrossRef]
30. Xiao, K.D.; Zhou, C.T.; Jiang, K.; Yang, Y.C.; Li, R.; Zhang, H.; He, X.T. Multidimensional effects on proton acceleration using high-power intense laser pulses. *Phys. Plasmas* **2018**, *25*, 2. [CrossRef]

31. Volpe, L.; Fedosejevs, R.; Gatti, G.; Pérez-Hernández, J.A.; Méndez, C.; Apiñaniz, J.; Roso, L. Generation of high energy laser-driven electron and proton sources with the 200 TW system VEGA 2 at the Centro de Laseres Pulsados. *High Power Laser Sci. Eng.* **2019**, *7*, 6–11. [CrossRef]
32. Morita, T.; Esirkepov, T.Z.; Bulanov, S.V.; Koga, J.; Yamagiwa, M. Tunable High-Energy Ion Source via Oblique Laser Pulse Incident on a Double-Layer Target. *Phys. Rev. Lett.* **2008**, *100*, 145001. [CrossRef]
33. Agostinelli, S.; Allison, J.; Amako, K.A.; Apostolakis, J.; Araujo, H.; Arce, P.; Asai, M.; Axen, D.; Banerjee, S.; Barrand, G.; et al. Geant4—a simulation toolkit. *Nucl. Instrum. Methods Phys. Res. A* **2003**, *506*, 250–303. [CrossRef]
34. Allison, J. Geant4 developments and applications. *IEEE Trans. Nucl. Sci.* **2006**, *53*, 270–278. [CrossRef]
35. Kong, R.; Ambrose, M.; Spanier, J. Efficient, Automated Monte Carlo Methods for Radiation Transport. *J. Comput. Phys.* **2008**, *227*, 9463–9476. [CrossRef]
36. The Jupyter Notebook. Available online: https://jupyter.org/ (accessed on 21 May 2020).
37. Giubega, G. Proton Acceleration in Ultra-Intense Laser Interaction with Solid Targets at CETAL-PW Laser, WORKSHOP CETAL 2018. Available online: http://cetal.inflpr.ro/newsite/workshop_abstracts.php (accessed on 15 December 2019).
38. Zeil, K.; Kraft, S.D.; Bock, S.; Bussmann, M.; Cowan, T.E.; Kluge, T.; Metzkes, J.; Richter, T.; Sauerbrey, R.; Schramm, U. The scaling of proton energies in ultrashort pulse laser plasma acceleration. *New J. Phys.* **2010**, *12*, 045015. [CrossRef]
39. Najafi, M.; Geraily, G.; Shirazi, A.; Esfahani, M.; Teimouri, J. Analysis of Gafchromic EBT3 film calibration irradiated with gamma rays from different systems: Gamma Knife and Cobalt-60 unit. *Med. Dosim.* **2017**, *3*, 159–168. [CrossRef] [PubMed]
40. Available online: http://tomography.inflpr.ro/ (accessed on 15 March 2020).
41. Sorriaux, J.; Kacperek, A.; Rossomme, S.; Lee, J.A.; Bertrand, D.; Vynckier, S.; Sterpin, E. Evaluation of Gafchromic EBT3 films characteristics in therapy photon, electron and proton beams. *Phys. Med.* **2013**, *6*, 599–606. [CrossRef] [PubMed]
42. Available online: https://imagej.nih.gov/ij/docs/examples/calibration/ (accessed on 30 January 2020).
43. Available online: https://imagej.nih.gov/ij/docs/guide/146-30.html#sub:Curve-Fitting (accessed on 30 January 2020).
44. DeLean, A.; Munson, P.J.; Rodbard, D. Simultaneous analysis of families of sigmoidal curves: Application to bioassay, radioligand assay, and physiological dose-response curves. *Am. J. Physiol.* **1978**, *235*, E97–E102. [CrossRef] [PubMed]
45. Hatchett, S.P.; Brown, C.G.; Cowan, T.E.; Henry, E.A.; Johnson, J.S.; Key, M.H.; Koch, J.A.; Langdon, A.B.; Lasinski, B.F.; Lee, R.W.; et al. Electron, photon, and ion beams from the relativistic interaction of Petawatt laser pulses with solid targets. *Phys. Plasmas* **2000**, *7*, 5. [CrossRef]
46. Cowan, T.E.; Fuchs, J.; Ruhl, H.; Kemp, A.; Audebert, P.; Roth, M.; Stephens, R.; Barton, I.; Blazevic, A.; Brambrink, E.; et al. Renard-Le Galloudec, N.; Ultralow Emittance, Multi-MeV Proton Beams from a Laser Virtual-Cathode Plasma Accelerator. *Phys. Rev. Lett.* **2004**, *92*, 20. [CrossRef]
47. Carroll, D.C.; McKenna, P.; Lundh, O.; Lindau, F.; Wahlström, C.G.; Bandyopadhyay, S.; Pepler, D.; Neely, D.; Kar, S.; Simpson, P.T.; et al. Active manipulation of the spatial energy distribution of laser-accelerated proton beams. *Phys. Rev. E* **2007**, *76*, 065401R. [CrossRef]
48. Ziegler, J.F.; Biersack, J.P. *The Stopping and Range of Ions in Matter*; Bromley, D., Ed.; Treatise on Heavy-Ion Science, Volume 6: Astrophysics, Chemistry, and Condensed Matter; Springer: Boston, MA, USA, 1985; pp. 93–129.

© 2020 by the authors. Licensee MDPI, Basel, Switzerland. This article is an open access article distributed under the terms and conditions of the Creative Commons Attribution (CC BY) license (http://creativecommons.org/licenses/by/4.0/).

Article

Monte Carlo Study of Imaging Plate Response to Laser-Driven Aluminum Ion Beams

Junho Won [1,2], Jaehyeon Song [1,2], Sasi Palaniyappan [3], Donald Cort Gautier [3], Wonhee Jeong [1], Juan Carlos Fernández [3] and Woosuk Bang [1,2,*]

1 Department of Physics and Photon Science, Gwangju Institute of Science and Technology (GIST), Gwangju 61005, Korea; wonder112@gist.ac.kr (J.W.); songjh8975@gist.ac.kr (J.S.); wonhee1990@gist.ac.kr (W.J.)
2 Center for Relativistic Laser Science, Institute for Basic Science, Gwangju 61005, Korea
3 Los Alamos National Laboratory, Los Alamos, NM 87545, USA; sasi@lanl.gov (S.P.); gautier@lanl.gov (D.C.G.); juanc@lanl.gov (J.C.F.)
* Correspondence: wbang@gist.ac.kr

Abstract: We measured the response of BAS-TR imaging plate (IP) to energetic aluminum ions up to 222 MeV, and compared it with predictions from a Monte Carlo simulation code using two different IP response models. Energetic aluminum ions were produced with an intense laser pulse, and the response was evaluated from cross-calibration between CR-39 track detector and IP energy spectrometer. For the first time, we obtained the response function of the BAS-TR IP for aluminum ions with a kinetic energy as high as 222 MeV. On close examination of the two IP response models, we confirm that the exponential model fits our experimental data better. Moreover, we find that the IP sensitivity in the exponential model is nearly constant in this energy range, suggesting that the response function can be determined even with little experimental data.

Keywords: Monte Carlo simulation; laser-driven ion acceleration; imaging plate

1. Introduction

An imaging plate (IP) is a film-like image sensor that records the incident radiation flux on a thin sheet called a phosphor layer. It is known to be sensitive to energetic charged particles, X-rays, and gamma rays [1–4]. Since IPs were developed by Fuji film Co. in the early 1980s, they have been widely used in nuclear science and in medicine. While an IP is a passive detector and cannot be used in high repetition rate experiments, IPs have several advantages over other particle detectors: (1) immunity to electromagnetic pulse (EMP), (2) high dynamic range (4–5 orders of magnitude), (3) high spatial resolution (resolving to as low as 10 µm), and (4) reusability (signals of IPs can be erased with white light) [1,5–7]. For radiation detection, Biological Analysis System (BAS) IP types are commonly used [8]. Specifically, BAS-MS, SR, and TR IPs were primarily designed for high sensitivity, high resolution, and detection of beta particles from tritium, respectively [9,10].

BAS IPs typically consist of three or four layers with various thicknesses: a protective layer, a phosphor layer, a support layer, and a magnetic layer. The BAS-TR IP has no protective layer [11], and the lack of a protective layer makes BAS-TR IP particularly well suited to measure heavy ions with short ranges within matter. Incoming ions deposit kinetic energy in the 50 µm thick phosphor layer [11]. Beneath the 250 µm thick support layer, there is a 160 µm thick magnetic layer which allows for magnetic attachment of the IP to the scanner [12].

When an IP is exposed to radiation, the electrons of Eu^{2+} in the phosphor layer are ionized and trapped in FBr or FI sites forming metastable states. The lifetimes of the metastable states range from 10 min to several days. When a scanner irradiates the phosphor layer with 2 eV photons from a laser diode, the electrons in the metastable state are re-excited and recombine with Eu^{3+} and emit 3 eV photons. That emission is known as the photostimulated luminescence (PSL). To use an IP as a quantitative radiation detector, it is necessary to calibrate the PSL relative to the spectral intensity of radiation. For ions, the spectral response function of an IP is measured in units of PSL per incident ion of a given energy. This must be done for each type of radiation and IP and scanner combination, because each combination has in general different responses [5,7,13–16].

Researchers have measured the response of IPs to various radiation types such as electrons [5,7,13,17–21], protons [12,14,22–24], and X-ray [16,25] for a wide energy range. The measurement of IP responses to energetic heavy ion beams, however, is more challenging because it is difficult to produce heavy ion beams with sufficient particle fluence for IP calibration at a range of energies in a reasonably short time. For this reason, the published studies of IP response to ions are limited to a few types of heavier elements such as deuterium [23,26], helium [16,23], carbon [6], and titanium [27].

Since Hidding et al. [28] proposed a linear model predicting the response of IP, some researchers have calculated the IP response by calculating stopping powers using Monte Carlo simulation codes. Bonnet et al. designed an exponential model and calibrated the IP response to protons, electrons, photons, and ^{4}He ions, using Geant4 [14,16,29]. Recently, Rabhi et al. reported on the responses of BAS-MS, SR, and TR for 1–200 MeV protons [12] and for 40–180 MeV electrons [21] using Geant4. Singh et al. used FLUKA to calibrate the responses of BAS-MS and SR to 150 keV–1.75 MeV electrons [5].

In this paper, we report on the IP response to aluminum (Al) ions for the first time, with an incident kinetic energy as high as 222 MeV. We have used an Al ion beam driven by an intense laser pulse as the ion source, and detected these ions using BAS-TR IPs for the measurements. We compare both the linear model and the exponential model with our experimental results for Al ions. In our study, we have used the Monte Carlo simulation code SRIM [30] to calculate the stopping powers of a BAS-TR IP for Al ions because SRIM is known to represent the available experimental data well [31,32]. We show that the response function calculations using stopping power from SRIM code agree very well with our experimental data for Al ions up to 222 MeV. We find that the IP sensitivity remains nearly constant for all the incident Al ion energy in the exponential model, which suggests that the IP response function can be calculated for the entire energy range of the ion beams using just a few experimental data points.

2. Experimental Setup

The experiments were performed on the Trident laser facility at Los Alamos National Laboratory (LANL) [33,34]. Figure 1 shows the schematic layout of the experimental setup. 80 J, 650 fs, 1054 nm laser pulses were focused using an f/3 off-axis parabola, and irradiated 110 nm thick aluminum foils with a peak laser intensity of about 2×10^{20} W/cm^2 [33]. The laser-driven Al ion beams diverged with a 20° cone half-angle [35,36]. The ions fly into a high resolution and high dispersion Thomson Parabola Spectrometer (TPS) [33,37], which measures an energy spectrum of the ions separately depending on their charge to mass (Z/A) ratio. The TPS symmetry axis is aligned with the ion propagation direction, and the ion flux into the TPS is limited by a pinhole aperture along that axis. Over a portion of the ion flight within the TPS, strong electric (E) and magnetic (B) fields parallel to each other and normal to the symmetry axis deflects ions depending on their Z/A and kinetic energy (E_{ion}). After a drift distance within the TPS, they arrive at the detector plane laid normal to the axis. The Z/A and E_{ion} are given by their location on this plane [33,37]. Specifically, the TPS disperses a given Z/A on the detector plane along a narrow (as defined by the pinhole) parabolic curve in the $\hat{x}$ (horizontal, B-field deflection) and $\hat{y}$ (vertical, E-field deflection) directions originating at the intersection with the symmetry axis according to E_{ion}. The origin (= zero point in Figure 2) corresponds to an infinite E_{ion}, and X-rays or neutral particles are recorded as well. The TPS uses 10 cm long magnets producing 0.82 T and 50 cm long electrodes that can be charged up to 15 kV potential., enabling high energy resolutions of $\Delta E/E < 5\%$ at 100 MeV/nucleon [33,37]. The IP used in the

TPS was covered with an 18 µm thick Al filter in order to eliminate background noise originating from scattered laser lights, low energy protons (<1 MeV), low energy electrons (<50 keV), and soft X-rays [33]. Incident Al ions with kinetic energy greater than 50 MeV penetrated through the filter and reached the IP surface. For counting the absolute number of aluminum ions, strip-shaped CR-39 track detectors with a width of a few mm were placed on the IP surface [33].

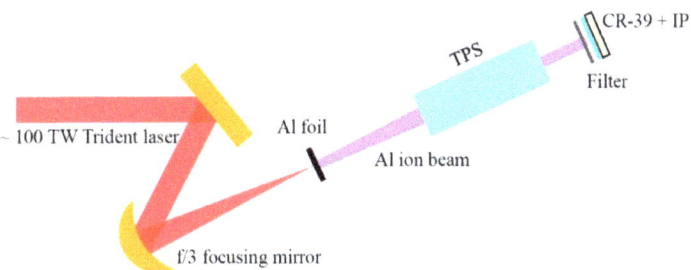

Figure 1. Schematic layout of the experimental setup. An intense laser pulse produces energetic Al ions, which are detected using CR-39 and IP.

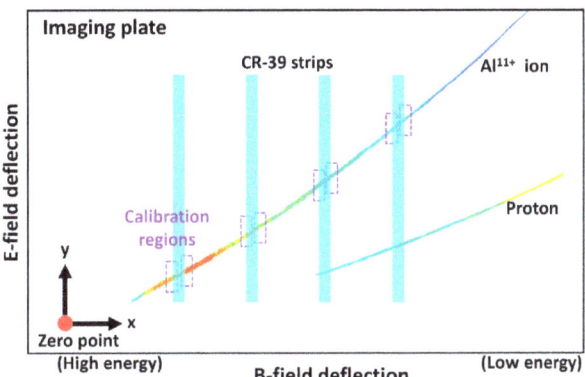

Figure 2. Schematic layout of the CR-39 strips on the IP. The laser-driven Al ions that are deflected inside the TPS leave traces on the CR-39 strips and BAS-TR IP. Calibration regions are marked as purple rectangles in the figure. At each boundary of the calibration region, PSL/ion values are measured by comparing the number of tracks on the CR-39 and the amount of PSL from the IP.

It is known that the IP response does not depend on the charge state of the incident ions [6,23,38,39]. This is because the incident ions quickly arrive at an equilibrium charge state as soon as they enter the target surface. This characteristic is assumed by Freeman et al. [23], and is confirmed by Doria et al. [6] and J. Strehlow et al. [27] in experiments using multiply charged carbon ions and titanium ions, respectively. Therefore, we do not need to specify the charge state of Al ions incident on the BAS-TR IP in our SRIM simulations.

3. Measurement of PSL/Ion

After exposing the calibration region of an IP to energetic aluminum ions, PSL is measured experimentally using a scanner. In this experiment, we scanned each IP 5 min after exposing it to an ion beam. The BAS-TR IP was scanned by a commercial scanner (Fujifilm Typhoon FLA-7000). The input light in the scanner is converted to electronic signals, which are stored in a PC as quantum level (QL) pixel-resolved image data. Since

QL encodes a logarithmic response, a conversion is required to extract the linear PSL data. The conversion formula from a QL value to a PSL value is [6]

$$\text{PSL} = \left(\frac{R}{100}\right)^2 \times \frac{4000}{S} \times 10^{L \times \left(\frac{QL}{2^G - 1} - \frac{1}{2}\right)}, \quad (1)$$

where $R = 25$ µm is the resolution of the scanner, S is the scanner sensitivity setting selected from 1000 to 10,000, $L = 5$ is the latitude parameter which relates to the dynamic range of the scanner, and $G = 16$ is the gradation parameter for 16-bit image data.

The PSL/ion value was obtained from cross-calibration between the amount of PSL scanned in the Al^{11+} trajectory adjacent to a CR-39 strip and the number of ions counted in the pits of the strip. This calibration method assumes that there is no sharp discontinuity in the areal density of Al^{11+} ions on the track nearby the edges of the CR-39 bars. These calibration regions are illustrated in Figure 2, which shows the schematic layout of the CR-39 strips on the BAS-TR IP. E_{ion} is readily obtained from the TPS data based on the analytic expressions for the ion deflection at the detector plane. The x-direction deflection (due to the known E) is used to obtain E_{ion}/q, where q is the ion charge. That value is plugged into the equation for the y-direction deflection (due to the known B) to obtain Z/A. Since we know A (Al), we obtain q and E_{ion}. Thus, PSL/ion value for Al^{11+} ions can be obtained for the E_{ion} of Al^{+11} ions corresponding to each edge of the CR-39 strip along the track.

4. Fading Effect

As time elapses after activation, some of the electrons in the metastable states spontaneously decay to the Eu^{3+} state and emit PSL. This phenomenon is called the fading effect, and the resulting PSL loss when the IP is scanned subsequently should be taken into account in the analysis. Several studies have measured fading curves for electrons [13,17], protons [14], X-rays [5,7,15,26], and γ-rays [14]. Although the radiation sources used in fading measurements are different in each experiment, fading curves are not very sensitive to the type and energy of radiation. Bonnet et al. find that fading signals are nearly independent of the radiation type with less than 10% differences between photons and protons [14]. Ohuchi et al. also report that the fading effect is similar for electrons and for protons regardless of their kinetic energies [40]. The known parameters contributing to fading effect are ambient temperature and scanner type [7]. Although the fading effect becomes bigger as the ambient temperature increases, its change can be considered negligible for a small temperature fluctuation [7].

Zeil et al. [13] report different fading behaviors between their data measured by BAS-1800II and the data of Tanaka et al. [17] measured by BAS-5000. Their findings suggest that PSL signals measured using different scanners can be quite different [13]. Ohuchi et al. also compared BAS-1000 and BAS-5000 and observed that fading of BAS-5000 is larger than that of BAS-1000 [40]. Therefore, we need to apply a fading model benchmarked using the same IP with the same scanner. Bonnet et al. [14] and Boutoux et al. [7] have used the same FLA-7000 scanner as in our measurements, and their fading functions are quite comparable each other. They have both used two exponential functions to fit their data, and we have adopted the fading function of Boutoux et al. as shown below [7].

$$f(t) = 0.535\, e^{\frac{-t}{\tau_1}} + 0.465\, e^{\frac{-t}{\tau_2}}, \quad (2)$$

where $\tau_1 = 23.812$ (min), $\tau_2 = 3837.2$ (min). In our experiment, fading loss is expected to be about 10% at $t = 5$ (min), and thus the experimentally measured PSL values have been scaled upwards to the values that would have been measured at time zero.

5. Calculation of PSL/Ion from SRIM Data

There are two models commonly used to predict the amount of PSL from a given radiation. Hidding et al. [28] propose a linear model assuming that the yield of PSL is proportional to the total deposited energy in the sensitive layer of an IP.

$$R(E_{ion}) = \alpha E_{dep}(E_{ion}), \tag{3}$$

where $R(E_{ion})$ is the IP response for ions with incident kinetic energy of E_{ion} and α is the IP sensitivity. The IP sensitivity varies depending on the type of radiation and IPs. It also depends on the waiting time before scanning because of the fading loss. The total deposited energy, $E_{dep}(E_{ion})$, is obtained from the integral of the ion-stopping power $S(z)$ at depth z. In the phosphoric layer of the IP,

$$E_{dep} = \int_0^W S(z) dz, \tag{4}$$

where $S(z) = -dE_{ion}/dz$ and W is the thickness of the layer.

The incident ion loses its kinetic energy to electrons in the target by ion-electron collisions resulting from Coulomb interaction and to target nuclei by ion-nucleon collisions (called recoil process). In our SRIM simulations, the predominant process is Coulomb interaction, and the recoil energy contributes only $\sim 10^{-4}$ to the entire collision process. The cross-section for ion-electron interaction is inversely proportional to the square of the approaching speed of the ion.

Bonnet et al. [14] proposed a model for the deposited energy that accounts for the optical thickness of the IP to the PSL radiation by weighting the stopping power by an exponential decay term, i.e.,

$$E_{dep} = \int_0^W S(z) e^{-\frac{z}{L}} dz, \tag{5}$$

where L is the absorption length of PSL photons within the phosphor layer of the IP [14], which is 44 ± 4 μm for BAS-TR IPs [16]. A large L implies that the PSL photons pass through the phosphor layer easily without being absorbed within it [16], and thus a negligible correction. However, $L = 44$ μm indicates that a significant amount of PSL is absorbed since the thickness phosphor layer of BAS-TR IP is 50 μm. Equation (4) can also be interpreted as a special case when the absorption length is infinity and there is no absorption [14]. We refer IP models proposed by Hidding et al. and Bonnet et al. as the linear model and the exponential model, respectively, in the following analysis.

To obtain the stopping power for Al beams, we use the Monte Carlo simulation code SRIM which calculates the stopping and range of ions in matter using a quantum mechanical treatment of ion-atom collision [30]. Each simulation is performed with 10,000 incidences and calculated stopping power and other values are averaged over the 10,000 incidences. We calculate E_{dep} using two different methods (1) by using the averaged $S(z)$ obtained directly from SRIM, and (2) by calculating the absorbed energy and $e^{-\frac{z}{L}}$ at each step from individual incidence then averaging E_{dep} over 10,000 incidences. SRIM divides the target depth into 100 steps in the first method, and about 700 uniform steps in the second method, which determines the simulation resolution. Although the second method has seven times higher target depth resolution in computing the total deposited energy in the phosphor layer, the discrepancy in the deposited energy calculations by each method is found to be only 0.01–0.1%.

In the linear model, we have calculated $S(z)$ using the first method for simplicity. In the exponential model, we have used the second method to calculate $S(z)$ since more steps can potentially reduce errors involved in calculating the weighting factor $e^{-\frac{z}{L}}$. For each IP model, the total deposited energy is calculated as follows

$$E_{dep} = \sum_{i=1}^{I} \left[\frac{S(z_i) + S(z_{i+1})}{2}\right](z_{i+1} - z_i), \quad \text{(Linear model)} \tag{6}$$

$$E_{dep} = \sum_{i=1}^{l}\left(-\frac{dE}{dz}\right)e^{-\frac{1}{L}\left(\frac{z_{i+1}+z_i}{2}\right)}dz = \sum_{i=1}^{l} -(E_{i+1} - E_i)e^{-\frac{1}{L}\left(\frac{z_{i+1}+z_i}{2}\right)}, \quad (7)$$
(Exponential model)

where z_i is the target depth (the distance that an Al ion passes through the target), $S(z_i)$ is the stopping power of target at depth z_i, E_i is the kinetic energy of the Al ion at z_i, and l is the total number of steps ($l = 100$ or $l = 700$). In the linear model, the area under the curve of stopping power as a function of target depth represents the deposited energy. We use the average of two stopping power values in each interval, and estimate the target depth of each thin layer as $\frac{z_{i+1}+z_i}{2}$ in the exponential model.

The average stopping powers of phosphor layer for mono-energetic Al ions are shown as functions of the target depth in Figure 3 for 130 MeV Al ions (dashed green line) and for 200 MeV Al ions (dot dashed blue line). The 50 µm thick phosphor layer of BAS-TR IP is thick enough to stop all Al ions with $E_{ion} \leq 130$ MeV, so the entire E_{ion} is absorbed within the phosphor layer. For 200 MeV Al ions, on the other hand, the stopping power gradually increases as the ions lose their kinetic energy, but the ions penetrate through the phosphor layer with significant energy remaining.

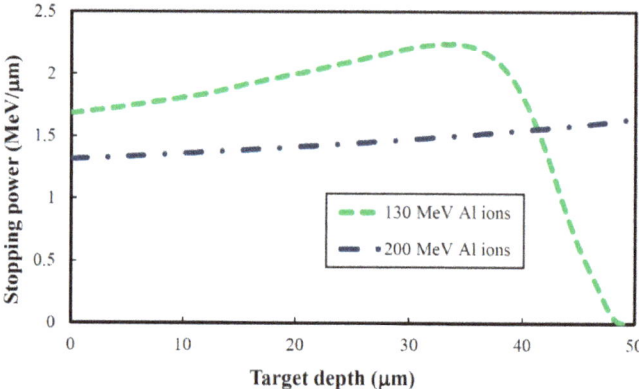

Figure 3. Stopping power of the 50 µm thick phosphor layer of a BAS-TR IP for 130 MeV and 200 MeV Al ions as functions of the target depth. The area under the curve represents the deposited energy in the phosphor layer.

Figure 4a shows the IP response, $R(E_{ion})$, as a function of Al ion energy for our setup. Solid black circles indicate the experimental measurements of PSL/ion data. Error bars are estimated to be ±15%, which account for the decay uncertainty from the fading effect during the time gap (5 min), PSL stimulated by diode laser during scanning, inaccurate calibration of the PMT, and IP surface quality (roughness) [6]. The dashed black line represents the IP response calculated using the linear model, and the solid red line shows the IP response calculated using the exponential model with L = 44 µm. The calculated IP responses with ± one standard deviation (±4 µm) of L are shown when L = 48 µm (dashed red line) and L = 40 µm (dot dashed red line). In both models, the total deposited energy increases as the kinetic energy of Al ion increases from 50 MeV to 140 MeV, but it decreases beyond 140 MeV. The IP response from the exponential model increases more gradually and it fits the experimental data better.

As is described in the experimental setup section, there was an 18 µm thick filter in front of our BAS-TR IP, and only ions with sufficient kinetic energy (larger than 50 MeV) arrived at the IP front surface. Since filter arrangements can differ for each experiment, beyond the computation of our specific filter conditions, we aim to produce a response model applicable to arbitrary filter arrangements. We start with the computed incident ion energy on the front phosphor layer surface obtained by subtracting the energy loss in the 18 µm thick filter from the incoming E_{ion} measured with the TPS. We computed

Al ion energy loss in the filter with SRIM. Figure 4b shows energy loss from an 18 μm thick Al filter as a function of the incident Al ion energy. The dashed green line indicates the kinetic energy loss of energetic Al ions. The solid blue line shows the incident kinetic energy of Al ions on the phosphor layer after penetrating through the filter as a function of the initial Al ion energy before the filter. Figure 4c shows the IP response as a function of the incident Al ion energy on the phosphor layer. The horizontal axis corresponds to the kinetic energy of the incident Al ion after penetrating through the filter, which is calculated in Figure 4b. Solid black circles represent the experimentally measured IP responses, and the dashed black line indicates the IP response calculated using the linear model. The solid red line represents the IP response calculated using the exponential model with an absorption length of $L = 44$ μm. For both the linear and the exponential model, we have used the method of least squares and determined the IP sensitivity, α, from Figure 4c. The IP responses with ± one standard deviation of the absorption length are also plotted in the same figure for $L = 48$ μm (dashed red line) and for $L = 40$ μm (dot dashed red line).

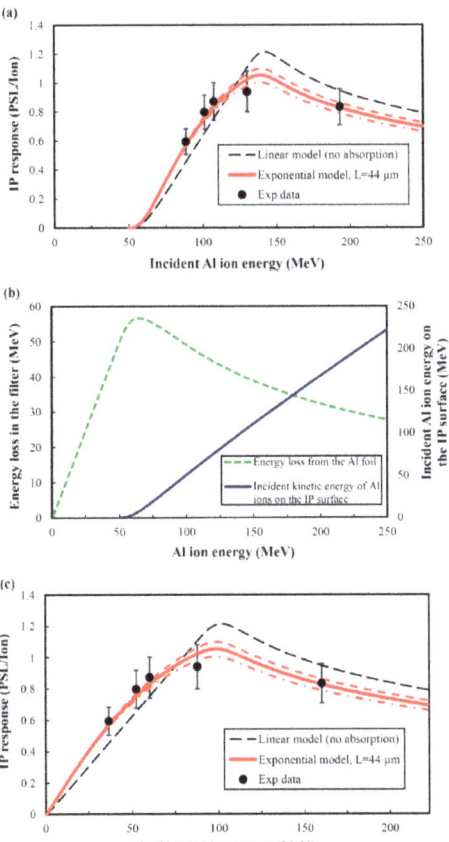

Figure 4. (**a**) IP response of BAS-TR IP is shown as a function of incoming Al ion energy before the filter. (**b**) Energy loss in the filter is shown as a function of Al ion energy (dashed green line). The incident kinetic energy of Al ions on the phosphor layer after penetrating through the filter is also shown as a function of Al ion energy (solid blue line). (**c**) IP response of BAS-TR IP is shown as a function of the incident Al ion energy on the phosphor layer.

6. IP Sensitivity

We examined how IP sensitivities at different incident Al ion energy deviate from the IP sensitivity obtained by least squares method in each model. Figure 5 shows the IP sensitivities as functions of the incident Al ion energy for both the linear model and the exponential model. The IP sensitivities calculated using the exponential model are shown as hollow red circles, and those calculated using the linear model are plotted as hollow black circles. These values are derived from experimentally measured IP responses and the calculated deposited energy from the incident Al ions using each model. In Figure 5, the IP sensitivity fluctuation in the exponential model is less than that in the linear model. The IP sensitivity is nearly constant at $\alpha_{exp} = 0.019$ in the exponential model with a standard deviation of 5% of α_{exp}. In the linear model, the IP sensitivity is $\alpha_{lin} = 0.013$ with a standard deviation of 21% of α_{lin}. This suggests that the exponential model describes the IP response better.

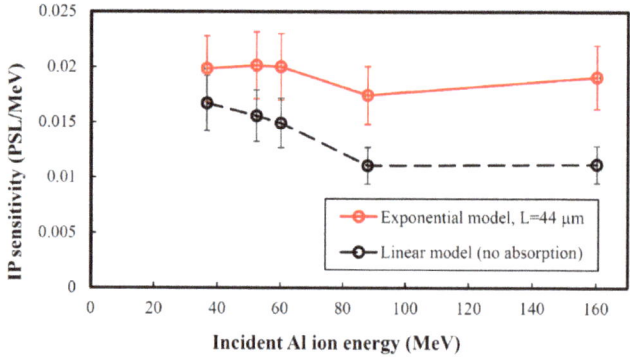

Figure 5. Sensitivity of BAS-TR IP is shown as a function of the incident Al ion energy on the IP surface.

Since the IP sensitivity in the exponential model remains nearly unchanged regardless of the incident kinetic energy of Al ions in Figure 5, we can treat α_{exp} as a constant value in Equation (3) and determine the IP response function by multiplying the deposited energy function calculated from the Monte Carlo simulations. This implies that the IP response function can be calculated even with little experimental data.

The overall sensitivity of BAS-TR IP to Al ions is found to be much smaller than the known sensitivity of IPs to electrons, protons, and alpha particles. This is consistent with the findings reported by Freeman et al. [23] and Bonnet et al. [16] for alpha particles. Bonnet et al. report that the IP sensitivity to ^{4}He ions is about 10 times smaller than the IP sensitivity to protons with BAS-MS and BAS-SR IPs and around five times smaller than the IP sensitivity to protons with BAS-TR IP [16]. Bonnet et al. explain this using a quenching effect. According to their study, the IP sensitivity depends on both the type of incident ions and the stopping power of IPs for those ions [16,23].

In our experiment, a similar quenching effect is also observed. The measured sensitivity of BAS-TR IP to Al ions is about 13 times less than the known IP sensitivity to protons, and it is about half of the known IP sensitivity to ^{4}He [16]. As shown in Figure 5, IP sensitivities decrease with increasing incident Al ion energy. This decrease is larger in the linear model than in the exponential model. The large variations of the IP sensitivities in the linear model seem to be caused by the quenching effect, which results in large discrepancy with the experimental IP response data. In comparison, the exponential model has smaller variations of the IP sensitivity and agrees well with the experimental data. The exponential factor in Equation (5) offsets the IP sensitivity decline coming from the stopping power increase of Al ions.

7. Conclusions

For the first time, we measured the response of BAS-TR IP to Al ions up to 222 MeV. The PSL/ion values were measured experimentally using CR-39 track detectors and an ion energy spectrometer, and the measurements were compared with calculated deposited energy. We propose a technique to calculate deposited energy in the phosphor layer using stopping power calculations from SRIM code. The response function taking the absorption length into account is in very good agreement with the experimental data. We find that the exponential model predicting the response of an IP fits the experimental data better. The IP sensitivity is nearly constant regardless of the incident energies of aluminum ion beams, suggesting that the IP response function can be calculated even with little experimental data. Our simulations and analysis provide a straightforward method using stopping power calculations to find the response function of an imaging plate to other energetic heavy ion beams.

Author Contributions: Conceptualization, W.B.; methodology, S.P., D.C.G., and J.C.F.; formal analysis, J.W., J.S., and W.J.; writing—original draft preparation, J.W., W.B.; writing—review and editing, J.W., W.B.; visualization, J.W.; supervision, W.B.; project administration, W.B.; funding acquisition, J.C.F. and W.B. All authors have read and agreed to the published version of the manuscript.

Funding: This research was funded by NRF, grant number NRF-2018R1C1B6001580, by the U.S. DOE under Contract No. DE-AC52-06NA25396, and by the Institute for Basic Science under IBS-R012-D1. The APC was funded by NRF-2018R1C1B6001580.

Data Availability Statement: The data that support the findings of this study are available from the corresponding author upon reasonable request.

Acknowledgments: This work was supported by NRF-2018R1C1B6001580. The experimental work was performed at LANL, operated by Los Alamos National Security, LLC, for the U.S. DOE under Contract No. DE-AC52-06NA25396, and was supported in part by the LANL LDRD program. J.W., J.S., and W.B. were supported by the Institute for Basic Science under IBS-R012-D1. W.B. was partly supported by the GIST Research Institute (GRI) grant funded by the GIST in 2020. The authors would like to thank M. Cordoba and C.E. Hamilton for target fabrication, and thank the Trident laser team for operation of the laser and assistance with the imple-mentation of TPS diagnostics.

Conflicts of Interest: The authors declare no conflict of interest.

References

1. Amemiya, Y.; Miyahara, J. Imaging plate illuminates many fields. *Nature* **1988**, *336*, 89. [CrossRef] [PubMed]
2. Amemiya, Y.; Wakabayashi, K.; Tanaka, H.; Ueno, Y.; Miyahara, J. Laser-stimulated luminescence used to measure X-ray diffraction of a contracting striated muscle. *Science* **1987**, *237*, 164. [CrossRef] [PubMed]
3. Cipiccia, S.; Islam, M.R.; Ersfeld, B.; Shanks, R.P.; Brunetti, E.; Vieux, G.; Yang, X.; Issac, R.C.; Wiggins, S.M.; Welsh, G.H.; et al. Gamma-rays from harmonically resonant betatron oscillations in a plasma wake. *Nat. Phys.* **2011**, *7*, 867. [CrossRef]
4. Ta Phuoc, K.; Corde, S.; Thaury, C.; Malka, V.; Tafzi, A.; Goddet, J.P.; Shah, R.C.; Sebban, S.; Rousse, A. All-optical Compton gamma-ray source. *Nat. Photonics* **2012**, *6*, 308. [CrossRef]
5. Singh, S.; Slavicek, T.; Hodak, R.; Versaci, R.; Pridal, P.; Kumar, D. Absolute calibration of imaging plate detectors for electron kinetic energies between 150 keV and 1.75 MeV. *Rev. Sci. Instrum.* **2017**, *88*, 075105. [CrossRef] [PubMed]
6. Doria, D.; Kar, S.; Ahmed, H.; Alejo, A.; Fernandez, J.; Cerchez, M.; Gray, R.J.; Hanton, F.; MacLellan, D.A.; McKenna, P.; et al. Calibration of BAS-TR image plate response to high energy (3-300 MeV) carbon ions. *Rev. Sci. Instrum.* **2015**, *86*, 123302. [CrossRef]
7. Boutoux, G.; Rabhi, N.; Batani, D.; Binet, A.; Ducret, J.E.; Jakubowska, K.; Nègre, J.P.; Reverdin, C.; Thfoin, I. Study of imaging plate detector sensitivity to 5-18 MeV electrons. *Rev. Sci. Instrum.* **2015**, *86*, 113304. [CrossRef]
8. Boutoux, G.; Batani, D.; Burgy, F.; Ducret, J.E.; Forestier-Colleoni, P.; Hulin, S.; Rabhi, N.; Duval, A.; Lecherbourg, L.; Reverdin, C.; et al. Validation of modelled imaging plates sensitivity to 1-100 keV X-rays and spatial resolution characterisation for diagnostics for the "PETawatt Aquitaine Laser". *Rev. Sci. Instrum.* **2016**, *87*, 043108. [CrossRef]
9. Schlenvoigt, H.P.; Haupt, K.; Debus, A.; Budde, F.; Jäckel, O.; Pfotenhauer, S.; Schwoerer, H.; Rohwer, E.; Gallacher, J.G.; Brunetti, E.; et al. A compact synchrotron radiation source driven by a laser-plasma wakefield accelerator. *Nat. Phys.* **2007**, *4*, 130. [CrossRef]
10. Yu, C.; Qi, R.; Wang, W.; Liu, J.; Li, W.; Wang, C.; Zhang, Z.; Liu, J.; Qin, Z.; Fang, M.; et al. Ultrahigh brilliance quasi-monochromatic MeV γ-rays based on self-synchronized all-optical Compton scattering. *Sci. Rep.* **2016**, *6*, 29518. [CrossRef]

11. Ingenito, F.; Andreoli, P.; Batani, D.; Boutoux, G.; Cipriani, M.; Consoli, F.; Cristofari, G.; Curcio, A.; Angelis, R.D.; Giorgio, G.D.; et al. Comparative calibration of IP scanning equipment. *Comp. Calibration Ip Scanning Equip. J. Instrum.* **2016**, *11*, C05012. [CrossRef]
12. Rabhi, N.; Batani, D.; Boutoux, G.; Ducret, J.-E.; Jakubowska, K.; Lantuejoul-Thfoin, I.; Nauraye, C.; Patriarca, A.; Saïd, A.; Semsoum, A.; et al. Calibration of imaging plate detectors to mono-energetic protons in the range 1-200 MeV. *Rev. Sci. Instrum.* **2017**, *88*, 113301. [CrossRef] [PubMed]
13. Zeil, K.; Kraft, S.D.; Jochmann, A.; Kroll, F.; Jahr, W.; Schramm, U.; Karsch, L.; Pawelke, J.; Hidding, B.; Pretzler, G. Absolute response of Fuji imaging plate detectors to picosecond-electron bunches. *Rev. Sci. Instrum.* **2010**, *81*, 013307. [CrossRef] [PubMed]
14. Bonnet, T.; Comet, M.; Denis-Petit, D.; Gobet, F.; Hannachi, F.; Tarisien, M.; Versteegen, M.; Aleonard, M.M. Response functions of Fuji imaging plates to monoenergetic protons in the energy range 0.6–3.2 MeV. *Rev. Sci. Instrum.* **2013**, *84*, 013508. [CrossRef]
15. Maddox, B.R.; Park, H.S.; Remington, B.A.; Izumi, N.; Chen, S.; Chen, C.; Kimminau, G.; Ali, Z.; Haugh, M.J.; Ma, Q. High-energy X-ray backlighter spectrum measurements using calibrated image plates. *Rev. Sci. Instrum.* **2011**, *82*, 023111. [CrossRef]
16. Bonnet, T.; Comet, M.; Denis-Petit, D.; Gobet, F.; Hannachi, F.; Tarisien, M.; Versteegen, M.; Aléonard, M.M. Response functions of imaging plates to photons, electrons and 4He particles. *Rev. Sci. Instrum.* **2013**, *84*, 103510. [CrossRef]
17. Tanaka, K.A.; Yabuuchi, T.; Sato, T.; Kodama, R.; Kitagawa, Y.; Takahashi, T.; Ikeda, T.; Honda, Y.; Okuda, S. Calibration of imaging plate for high energy electron spectrometer. *Rev. Sci. Instrum.* **2005**, *76*, 013507. [CrossRef]
18. Chen, H.; Back, N.L.; Bartal, T.; Beg, F.N.; Eder, D.C.; Link, A.J.; MacPhee, A.G.; Ping, Y.; Song, P.M.; Throop, A.; et al. Absolute calibration of image plates for electrons at energy between 100keV and 4MeV. *Rev. Sci. Instrum.* **2008**, *79*, 033301. [CrossRef]
19. Nakanii, N.; Kondo, K.; Yabuuchi, T.; Tsuji, K.; Tanaka, K.A.; Suzuki, S.; Asaka, T.; Yanagida, K.; Hanaki, H.; Kobayashi, T.; et al. Absolute calibration of imaging plate for GeV electrons. *Rev. Sci. Instrum.* **2008**, *79*, 066102. [CrossRef]
20. Taniyama, A.; Shindo, D.; Oikawa, T. Sensitivity and Fading Characteristics of the 25 μm Pixel Size Imaging Plate for Transmission Electron Microscopes. *J. Electron Microsc.* **1996**, *45*, 232–235. [CrossRef]
21. Rabhi, N.; Bohacek, K.; Batani, D.; Boutoux, G.; Ducret, J.E.; Guillaume, E.; Jakubowska, K.; Thaury, C.; Thfoin, I. Calibration of imaging plates to electrons between 40 and 180 MeV. *Rev. Sci. Instrum.* **2016**, *87*, 053306. [CrossRef] [PubMed]
22. Choi, I.W.; Kim, C.M.; Sung, J.H.; Kim, I.J.; Yu, T.J.; Lee, S.K.; Jin, Y.Y.; Pae, K.H.; Hafz, N.; Lee, J. Absolute calibration of a time-of-flight spectrometer and imaging plate for the characterization of laser-accelerated protons. *Meas. Sci. Technol.* **2009**, *20*, 115112. [CrossRef]
23. Freeman, C.G.; Fiksel, G.; Stoeckl, C.; Sinenian, N.; Canfield, M.J.; Graeper, G.B.; Lombardo, A.T.; Stillman, C.R.; Padalino, S.J.; Mileham, C.; et al. Calibration of a Thomson parabola ion spectrometer and Fujifilm imaging plate detectors for protons, deuterons, and alpha particles. *Rev. Sci. Instrum.* **2011**, *82*, 073301. [CrossRef] [PubMed]
24. Mančić, A.; Fuchs, J.; Antici, P.; Gaillard, S.A.; Audebert, P. Absolute calibration of photostimulable image plate detectors used as (0.5–20MeV) high-energy proton detectors. *Rev. Sci. Instrum.* **2008**, *79*, 073301. [CrossRef]
25. Dong, Y.; Zhang, Z.; Xu, M.; Du, Y.; Zhang, C.; Dong, X.; He, Y.; Tan, J.; Zhang, Y.; Zhu, C.; et al. Absolute X-ray calibration of an Amersham imaging plate scanner. *Rev. Sci. Instrum.* **2020**, *91*, 033105. [CrossRef]
26. Alejo, A.; Kar, S.; Ahmed, H.; Krygier, A.G.; Doria, D.; Clarke, R.; Fernandez, J.; Freeman, R.R.; Fuchs, J.; Green, A.; et al. Characterisation of deuterium spectra from laser driven multi-species sources by employing differentially filtered image plate detectors in Thomson spectrometers. *Rev. Sci. Instrum.* **2014**, *85*, 093303. [CrossRef]
27. Strehlow, J.; Forestier-Colleoni, P.; McGuffey, C.; Bailly-Grandvaux, M.; Daykin, T.S.; McCary, E.; Peebles, J.; Revet, G.; Zhang, S.; Ditmire, T.; et al. The response function of Fujifilm BAS-TR imaging plates to laser-accelerated titanium ions. *Rev. Sci. Instrum.* **2019**, *90*, 083302. [CrossRef]
28. Hidding, B.; Pretzler, G.; Clever, M.; Brandl, F.; Zamponi, F.; Lübcke, A.; Kämpfer, T.; Uschmann, I.; Förster, E.; Schramm, U.; et al. Novel method for characterizing relativistic electron beams in a harsh laser-plasma environment. *Rev. Sci. Instrum.* **2007**, *78*, 083301. [CrossRef]
29. Bonnet, T.; Comet, M.; Denis-Petit, D.; Gobet, F.; Hannachi, F.; Tarisien, M.; Versteegen, M. Two parameter model of Fuji imaging plate response function to protons. In Proceedings of the SPIE Optics + Optoelectronics, Prague, Czech Republic, 9 May 2013; p. 7. [CrossRef]
30. Ziegler, J.F.; Ziegler, M.D.; Biersack, J.P. SRIM—The stopping and range of ions in matter. *Nucl. Instrum. Methods Phys. Res. Sect. B Beam Interact. Mater. At.* **2010**, *268*, 1818–1823. [CrossRef]
31. Paul, H.; Sánchez-Parcerisa, D. A critical overview of recent stopping power programs for positive ions in solid elements. *Nucl. Instrum. Methods Phys. Res. Sect. B Beam Interact. Mater. At.* **2013**, *312*, 110–117. [CrossRef]
32. Evseev, I.G.; Schelin, H.R.; Paschuk, S.A.; Milhoretto, E.; Setti, J.A.P.; Yevseyeva, O.; de Assis, J.T.; Hormaza, J.M.; Díaz, K.S.; Lopes, R.T. Comparison of SRIM, MCNPX and GEANT simulations with experimental data for thick Al absorbers. *Appl. Radiat. Isot.* **2010**, *68*, 948–950. [CrossRef] [PubMed]
33. Palaniyappan, S.; Huang, C.; Gautier, D.C.; Hamilton, C.E.; Santiago, M.A.; Kreuzer, C.; Sefkow, A.B.; Shah, R.C.; Fernández, J.C. Efficient quasi-monoenergetic ion beams from laser-driven relativistic plasmas. *Nat. Commun.* **2015**, *6*, 10170. [CrossRef] [PubMed]
34. Fernández, J.C.; Cort Gautier, D.; Huang, C.; Palaniyappan, S.; Albright, B.J.; Bang, W.; Dyer, G.; Favalli, A.; Hunter, J.F.; Mendez, J.; et al. Laser-plasmas in the relativistic-transparency regime: Science and applications. *Phys. Plasmas* **2017**, *24*, 056702. [CrossRef] [PubMed]

35. Bang, W.; Albright, B.J.; Bradley, P.A.; Gautier, D.C.; Palaniyappan, S.; Vold, E.L.; Cordoba, M.A.S.; Hamilton, C.E.; Fernández, J.C. Visualization of expanding warm dense gold and diamond heated rapidly by laser-generated ion beams. *Sci. Rep.* **2015**, *5*, 14318. [CrossRef] [PubMed]
36. Bang, W.; Albright, B.J.; Bradley, P.A.; Vold, E.L.; Boettger, J.C.; Fernández, J.C. Linear dependence of surface expansion speed on initial plasma temperature in warm dense matter. *Sci. Rep.* **2016**, *6*, 29441. [CrossRef]
37. Jung, D.; Hörlein, R.; Kiefer, D.; Letzring, S.; Gautier, D.C.; Schramm, U.; Hübsch, C.; Öhm, R.; Albright, B.J.; Fernandez, J.C.; et al. Development of a high resolution and high dispersion Thomson parabola. *Rev. Sci. Instrum.* **2011**, *82*, 013306. [CrossRef]
38. Schiwietz, G.; Grande, P.L. Improved charge-state formulas. *Nucl. Instrum. Methods Phys. Res. Sect. B Beam Interact. Mater. At.* **2001**, *175–177*, 125–131. [CrossRef]
39. Betz, H.-D. Charge States and Charge-Changing Cross Sections of Fast Heavy Ions Penetrating Through Gaseous and Solid Media. *Rev. Mod. Phys.* **1972**, *44*, 465–539. [CrossRef]
40. Ohuchi, H.; Yamadera, A. Dependence of fading patterns of photo-stimulated luminescence from imaging plates on radiation, energy, and image reader. *Nucl. Instrum. Methods Phys. Res. Sect. A Accel. Spectrometers Detect. Assoc. Equip.* **2002**, *490*, 573–582. [CrossRef]

Article

Automation of Target Delivery and Diagnostic Systems for High Repetition Rate Laser-Plasma Acceleration

Timofej Chagovets [1,*], Stanislav Stanček [1], Lorenzo Giuffrida [1], Andriy Velyhan [1], Maksym Tryus [1], Filip Grepl [1,2], Valeriia Istokskaia [1,2], Vasiliki Kantarelou [1], Tuomas Wiste [1], Juan Carlos Hernandez Martin [1], Francesco Schillaci [1] and Daniele Margarone [1,3]

1. ELI Beamlines, FZU—Institute of Physics of the Czech Academy of Sciences, Za Radnicí 835, 25241 Dolní Břežany, Czech Republic; stanislav.stancek@eli-beams.eu (S.S.); lorenzo.giuffrida@eli-beams.eu (L.G.); Andriy.velyhan@eli-beams.eu (A.V.); maksym.tryus@eli-beams.eu (M.T.); filip.grepl@eli-beams.eu (F.G.); valeriia.istokskaia@eli-beams.eu (V.I.); vasiliki.kantarelou@eli-beams.eu (V.K.); tuomas.wiste@eli-beams.eu (T.W.); juancarlos.hernandezmartin@eli-beams.eu (J.C.H.M.); francescoschillaci@eli-beams.eu (F.S.); Daniele.margarone@eli-beams.eu (D.M.)
2. Faculty of Nuclear Sciences and Physical Engineering, Czech Technical University in Prague, Brehova 7, 11519 Praha, Czech Republic
3. Centre for Plasma Physics, School of Mathematics and Physics, Queen's University of Belfast, Belfast BT7 1NN, UK
* Correspondence: timofej.chagovets@eli-beams.eu

Abstract: Fast solid target delivery and plasma-ion detection systems have been designed and developed to be used in high intensity laser-matter interaction experiments. We report on recent progress in the development and testing of automated systems to refresh solid targets at a high repetition rate during high peak power laser operation (>1 Hz), along with ion diagnostics and corresponding data collection and real-time analysis methods implemented for future use in a plasma-based ion acceleration beamline for multidisciplinary user applications.

Keywords: high repetition rate target; ion acceleration; laser–plasma interaction

1. Introduction

The rapid development of high peak, high average power lasers led to the implementation of relatively compact experimental systems, capable of delivering laser energy on target with several tens of Joules at a high repetition rate (1–10 Hz) [1–5]. While the availability of ultrahigh intensity laser pulses has enabled investigation of new physical mechanisms in the field of laser plasma acceleration physics by means of proof-of-principle experiments in single-shot mode [6,7], societal applications (including medical ones) [8,9] require high repetition rate operation, which is very challenging in terms of target delivery systems and real-time detection of plasma radiation. In fact, the current bottleneck in such experiments is not represented by the laser operation mode, but rather by the development of suitable target and diagnostic systems capable of sustaining harsh laser-plasma experimental conditions, such as giant electromagnetic noise, ultrahigh dose rate ionizing radiation, and particle debris generated from the irradiated target [10–16]. Thus, new solutions for fast target delivery, detection, and data acquisition systems have to be developed in order to satisfy recent requirements for potential applications of laser plasma physics.

Recently, the TERESA (TEstbed for high REpetition-rate Sources of Accelerated particles) has been successfully used at ELI-Beamlines [17]. The mission of the project was to provide a developing and testing environment for novel solutions in target delivery and laser–plasma diagnostics at high repetition rates (up to 10 Hz). In this paper, we report on our progress in the development of target delivery and alignment solutions for high repetition rate laser operation, along with ion diagnostics, data acquisition, real-time analysis methods, accurate control of vacuum, and alignment systems. The technologies described in this paper will be further tested at the ELIMAIA (ELI Multidisciplinary Applications of laser-Ion Acceleration) beamline to supply laser-accelerated ion beams to users carrying out research in various disciplines (physics, biology, chemistry, medicine, and material sciences) [18]. In Section 2, we discuss related experimental setups and operation modes. Target supply systems for thin solid films with fast target refreshing capability for operation up to 10 Hz, along with various diagnostics and related data acquisition systems, are presented in Sections 3 and 4. Conclusions and perspectives are outlined in Section 5.

2. Experimental Setup and Control

In general, good experimental conditions in laser-plasma interaction experiments require an optimal energy transfer between the incoming laser beam and the used target. Such a laser-plasma coupling efficiency is a key parameter to enhance the performance of a laser-plasma accelerator. This can be satisfied if both the laser beam focusing element, typically an Off-Axis Parabola (OAP), and the target positioner are handled carefully in order to place the target precisely into the position of the previously optimized focal spot (high encircled energy). The full procedure usually consists of three consecutive steps: (i) Definition and referencing of the interaction point position; (ii) OAP focal spot optimization and its positioning at the interaction point; (iii) Target alignment in 3D and its positioning at the interaction point.

Alignment procedures are typically available and well described in technical manuals at high power laser facilities. Low repetition rate laser beams, with a time interval between shots of several minutes, are typically focused and aligned on targets before each shot using a low power mode (unamplified version) of the laser beam. On the other hand, high repetition rate facilities require overall alignment of the target frames prior to the experimental run, due to the fact that the focus position must be optimized. Subsequently, all the targets must be pre-aligned before each irradiation sequence (at least few hundreds of shots) with high accuracy. Therefore, standard focal spot alignment procedure needs to be combined with a reliable target positioning system, which is capable of precise and repeatable operation, as described below. Naturally, overall pointing stability and vibration-free transport of the beam up to the focusing optics was ensured by careful engineering of both the mirror mounts and the vacuum systems, typically using decoupling between vacuum vessels and optical breadboard. Furthermore, additional potential unwanted effects, such as thermal lensing of optical components and slow laser beam drift, must be compensated.

The interaction point in the experimental chamber must be precisely defined since ion/plasma diagnostics and other experimental equipment (e.g., magnetic systems) are pointed at it, and it is considered a reference point for ideal observation of the laser-target interaction and further utilization of the accelerated particles.

The interaction point definition relies on the mechanical precision of the used components and is usually realized by placing a reference tip in the desired position. The tip is usually a conically sharpened (stainless steel) wire reaching a diameter of a few tens of micrometers. The alignment of different detectors with the interaction point itself is usually carried out using a small alignment laser beam (laser pointer perpendicularly attached to the detectors case front surface) propagating from the detectors towards the expected interaction point. This simple check ensures that the detector is oriented to the interaction point, and it has a clear view of the interaction. The intersection of the different detector alignment beams marks the interaction point where a reference tip is placed. Since the laser beam path in the experimental chamber was typically aligned horizontally (the beam axis is at the same height above the breadboard), the interaction point also remained at this defined height. Subsequently, the laser focal spot must be positioned in this point.

As soon as the interaction point is precisely defined and marked with a reference object, the monitoring system, consisting of a microscope objective with a given magnification, can be pre-aligned with the laser optical axis (the direction is given by the off-axis angle of the OAP) and pointed at the reference object placed at the objective's working distance. The microscopic objective is then fixed, and the OAP focal spot is optimized and positioned onto the reference tip. The laser beam is centered onto the OAP reflective surface and the mirror is tilted vertically until the focal spot lies in the same horizontal plane as the axis of the beam inside the interaction chamber. Subsequently, the OAP is tilted in the horizontal plane to bring the focus close to the reference tip. As soon as the magnified focus becomes visible through the objective, the OAP optimization can start.

The monitoring system is moved towards and outwards of the incoming beam to evaluate the size and shape of the beam close to the focal point. One can achieve a small focal spot size with a large value of encircled energy (i.e., minimal wave front distortion and high laser intensity) on target only when the focusing OAP is properly optimized, which is evident from the circular shape of the converging and diverging beam in the proximity of the laser focus.

If the focal spot is not circular, the OAP alignment shall be optimized. The tip and tilt of the OAP are used while scanning the focal spot in the longitudinal direction. During this optimization, the focal spot moves away from the tip. This must be simultaneously compensated using the movement of the OAP holder since the focal spot follows the X, Y, Z movement of the OAP. This procedure is normally done manually step by step until the desired result is reached. As soon as a circular focal spot is achieved in front of and behind the focal plane, the transversal optimization ends. The monitoring system is then pointed back on the reference tip and the OAP is finally moved to place the focus (now a very small circle) onto the top of the reference tip. This ensures that the optimized focal spot sits in the interaction point. As the last step, the target is moved into the same position.

3. Target Delivery System

Modern systems, which are capable of delivering laser energy on target with several tens of Joules at high repetition rates (1–10 Hz) require at least several thousands of targets per hour since the target is destroyed after each laser shot. Moreover, there are strict technical requirements for the target system, such as fast target refreshing, positioning, and alignment. Currently, a wide range of targets has been developed for laser-plasma acceleration, such as thin solid foils, tapes [19], gas [20] or liquid jets [21,22], clusters [23], cryogenic targets [24,25], and liquid crystals [10,26]. Hereafter, we aim to address the need for high repetition rate planar thin target delivery as a continuous sheet of material (thin foil) that is refreshed by a motorized stage.

A picture of the planar target delivery systems (PTDS) used in our experimental tests is presented in Figure 1a. The main part of the device is modular to allow holding of various types of target frames. The system can accommodate 900 foil targets, with an average distance of 5 mm between neighboring positions. The foils are secured using a special frame system made of two metallic plates that hold the foils in between them. Both plates contain a matrix of conical holes of about 1 mm in diameter. The conical shape helps to avoid the shock wave propagation from one target to the neighbors, permitting use of all the available targets during the laser irradiation. Moreover, this design provides good protection of individual targets from excessive evaporation or overheating effects occurring during laser-target interaction, or contaminations from neighboring targets after the shot. The current modification of the system uses nine of these frame holders and is able to hold any kind of foil (metallic, semiconductor, or plastic targets) with a very broad range of possible thicknesses (from foils of few tens of nanometers to few hundreds of micrometers thick).

 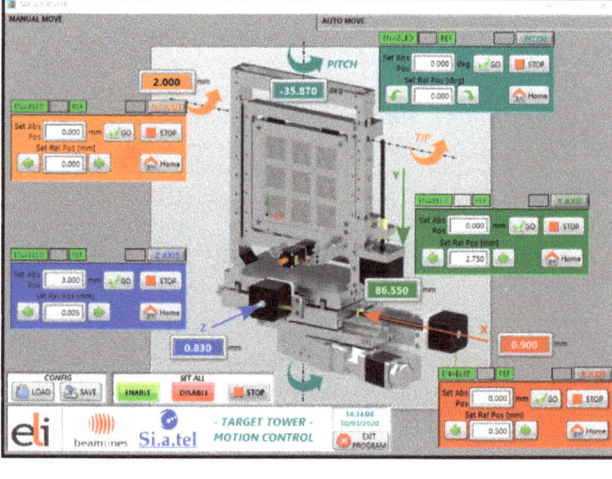

(a) (b)

Figure 1. A picture of (**a**) the planar target delivery system and (**b**) the graphical user interface for control of the target system.

A motorized system of PTDS has five degrees of freedom (x, y, z, pitch, and tip) and allows the device to align and to hit each individual target at 1 Hz with an accuracy better than 10 µm on each axis. To control the position of the device to avoid unwanted clashing with neighboring devices, each actuator is supplied with two linear limit switches to define the range of motion of the corresponding axis. The used motors are suitable for operation in a harsh environment where very strong electro-magnetic pulses (EMP), associated with high intensity laser-matter interaction, may affect the operation of electronics and high precision motorized systems. To reduce electrical discharge effects induced by laser-target interaction, the target holder is decoupled from the other metallic parts of the device with a polytetrafluoroethylene plate. The target holder itself is directly grounded to the vacuum chamber, thus the electrical conductor runs directly from the target plate to the ground.

The use of sophisticated optical systems imposes additional stringent requirements in terms of cleanliness levels of the vacuum systems. All PTDS parts, such as frames, motors, actuators, and limit switches, are made of high vacuum compatible materials. The connection cables are encased in copper braid with Kapton insulation to reduce the outgassing of particles detrimental to the vacuum system cleanliness.

A custom-made software is used for manual positioning of individual targets during the alignment phase and allows automatic refreshing of targets during a laser shot sequence. The graphical user interface shown in Figure 1b allows setting of either absolute or relative target positions, using five degrees of freedom with an accuracy of 5 µm and recording an individual position of the target for the high repetition-rate laser shot sequence.

Accurate alignment of each individual target before the laser shot sequence is one of the most important parts of the experimental run preparation since the accurate positioning of the target into the laser focal plane heavily affects the laser-target interaction conditions and, consequently, the laser-plasma acceleration process.

The alignment procedure consists of several key steps to be followed: (i) defining the interaction point by placing a reference object (sharp pin) in the desired position; (ii) aligning a monitoring system that monitors the interaction point; (iii) fixing the monitoring system to use it as a reference for the next steps of target alignment; and (iv) removing the tip and placing the PTDS to allow its large metallic frame to be at the same position of the tip.

Once the frame is set according to the imaging system focal plane (typically with an accuracy of 10–20 µm), the alignment of each individual target includes recording of its unique coordinates (x, y, and z, when the target is in focus). The other two coordinates (pitch and tip) are usually common for the whole target frame. Damaged or broken targets can be marked and automatically bypassed during the high repetition-rate laser shot sequence. Alignment of one frame with 100 targets generally takes about 10 min and usually can be done in advance.

Ultimately, the software provides a recorded table of target coordinates that is used for automatic target switch to the subsequent position by means of an external trigger sent by the laser system during the experimental run. It is crucial to prevent any hit of the target holder frame by the laser beam during the shot sequence. For this purpose, the control unit of the PTDS was equipped with a trigger input. The target swapping starts right after the incoming trigger is delivered with the laser shot. An output feedback signal indicates the completion of the target tower motion necessary to set the fresh target at the interaction point. A stable performance of the system at the repetition rate of 1 Hz is demonstrated in Figure 2. The PTDS starts motion right after the trigger (blue signal) associated with the laser shot. The finalization of alignment for the new target is indicated by the falling edge of the output feedback (orange signal) before the next laser pulse arrives.

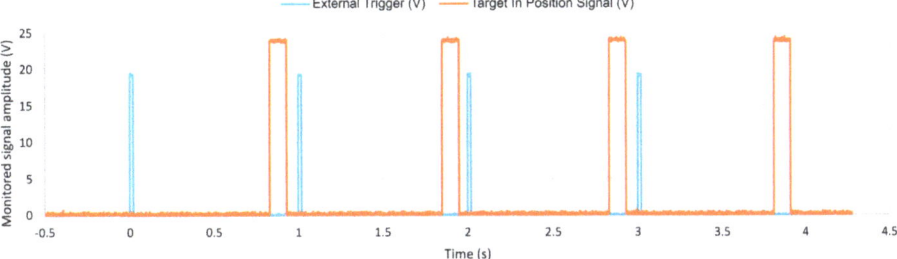

Figure 2. The sequence of four trigger signals (blue) at 1 Hz repetition rate initiating the motion of the following targets. The orange signal corresponds to a reference output confirming that the new target is in the aligned position.

The feedback output provides an estimated value of the potentially reachable target repetition rate during a laser shot sequence operation of about 1.25 Hz. Optical snapshots of the target positions were taken by means of the monitoring system during target renewal (see Figure 3). Monitoring system is supplied with LED placed on monitoring system to improve image quality. In this case, the target frame moves vertically from the upper to the lower target. The image becomes sharp after 800 ms since the target starts its motion, hence clearly indicating that a new target is set to the pre-aligned position and ready for the following shot. This observation is consistent with the feedback signal from the target tower. In fact, the monitoring system can hardly be used for the detection of a new target in the preset position, since image transfer from the camera and online analysis are demanding, with respect to data transfer infrastructure and computing power. Instead, analog feedback can be a reference for the data acquisition system. As a part of the control system, such a signal prevents potential damage of equipment by the laser beam during the target frame motion.

Another important property of the PTDS to be verified is the target position reproducibility when the targets are switching automatically. An accuracy test, with the aim of evaluating potential misalignment of different targets during a shot sequence, was performed using the target tower coupled with the imaging system.

Firstly, a set of targets was aligned, resulting in a table of target coordinates and a corresponding set of target snapshots taken by the imaging system. Then, the target renewal was simulated by a sequence of triggers with repetition rate of 1 Hz. Target snapshots were recorded once the target was in position. Comparing the respective images corresponding to the individual targets, the estimated misalignment was evaluated as less than 10 µm.

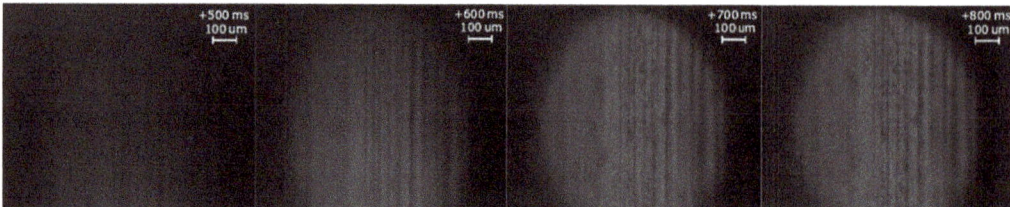

Figure 3. Imaging of the target switching process between two laser shots acquired with monitoring system.

The present configuration of the planar target delivery system demonstrates good ability of target refreshing at 1 Hz repetition rate in a real experimental run at TERESA target area [17]. The OAP with focal length of 330 mm ($\approx$f/3.7) allows to obtain a laser focal spot diameter of about 3.8 µm of full width at half maximum. All targets rastered before the laser firing can keep their position with a repeatability better than 10 µm over the whole laser shot sequence. During the operation of a 30-fs laser with 1 J energy on target (intensity around 5×10^{19} W/cm^2), no substantial damage on individual target frames, nor EMP-related issues, nor nuclear activation were observed after a complete run of about 1000 shots.

Additionally, we have developed and tested a second type of fast target delivery system. The spiral tower is a concept of a target handling system, which allows work at high repetition rates (see Figure 4a). The device consists of a 1-cm-thick Al disk (10 cm diameter) where targets are fixed, a translation and a rotation stage for a motorized roto-translation movement, and two linear stages, one for tilt and one for z micrometer level adjustment. In addition, a linear stage allows adjustment of the height of the device according to the laser interaction point. Similar to the target tower described above, all parts of the device are made of vacuum compatible materials to avoid contamination inside the vacuum chamber.

(a) (b)

Figure 4. Picture presents (**a**) the spiral tower, used at high repetition rate; and (**b**) examples of irradiated Fe, Cu, and Sn target plates with dimensions 50 by 50 mm. Left figure represents a zoomed picture of the irradiated area of Fe target showing a typical spiral shape.

Since the supporting disk is very thick, the device is used in experiments where only the backward plasma emission is of interest for the given experiment. Typically, the employed targets are mm-thick slabs. In contrast to the PTDS system, the number of interaction points is not fixed by the target holder. This device has been tested in single shot and at 1 and 10 Hz repetition rate, delivering thousands of shots continuously using the Bivoj laser (10 J max laser energy delivered in 5–10 ns pulse duration, working at the fundamental wavelength of 1032 nm) at the HiLASE laser center [5].

Dedicated software has been developed for motion control of the tower. It is possible to manually move every single motor or setting for a more complicated series of movements for multi-shot irradiation. A combination of translation and rotation allows the system to move in a spiral trajectory. Few irradiated targets are illustrated in Figure 4b, where the typical spiral shape is demonstrated. The distance between the subsequent interaction points on the target and the number of shots in the same position (if required by the user) can be preset according to the necessity of the experiment. The spiral tower demonstrated stable operation at repetition rates up to 10 Hz during the laser irradiation with stable ion shot-to-shot signal. It can be concluded that any displacement of the target in the direction of the laser propagation caused by the mechanics of the device, or non-ideal form of the target plate, was less than the Rayleigh length (typically 100 μm in this experiment at HiLASE) of the used optical system.

4. Data Acquisition System for High Repetition Rate Performance

Routine operation of PW-class laser-plasma experiments at high repetition rates would represent a new paradigm in terms of statistically relevant discoveries of new plasma acceleration regimes, investigation of complex effects, along with mitigation of laser-plasma instabilities to improve the stability of secondary sources (particles and radiation). This new scenario will require not only fast target delivery devices, but also fast diagnostics and data acquisition systems, along with real-time analysis tools allowing online characterization of laser-plasma generated secondary source parameters.

Online diagnostic systems for laser-generated ion beams at the TERESA and ELIMAIA beamlines are described in detail in [13,17,18], therefore, the following will mainly focus on recently developed and tested data acquisition systems and data analysis tools for high repetition rate operation (up to 10 Hz). Nevertheless, in terms of laser-plasma ion diagnostics, it is worth mentioning that one of the main challenges in the detection of laser-accelerated ions is the high-peak flux (10^{10}–10^{12} ions/pulse) and the short bunch duration (0.1–1 ns), hence the very high dose-rates in a single pulse (around 10^9 Gy/s). Thus, innovative techniques and devices for beam characterization have been developed for the ELIMAIA beamline, since robust online diagnostics represents one of the crucial steps towards multidisciplinary applications of such non-conventional beams [18]. The main online ion diagnostic system is based on the time-of-flight (TOF) technique using diamond and silicon carbide detectors, as reported in the literature [12,13,27], which offers the possibility to monitor shot-by-shot the main ion beam features up to a repetition rate of 10 Hz. Another key ion diagnostic system is the widely used Thomson Parabola Spectrometer (TPS), which allows the detection of energy-resolved ion spectra while discriminating ions with different charge-to-mass ratios by means of combined use of electric and magnetic fields [28,29]. In high repetition rate TPS configuration, deflected ions are typically observed and amplified by means of a microchannel plate (MCP), and are sent to a phosphor screen, thus producing an image of the energy-resolved ion spectra subsequently recorded by a CCD camera. The acquisition of the raw CCD image is controlled by a trigger signal from the laser.

The use of a repetition rate of 1–10 Hz requires a data acquisition system (DAS) with the ability to measure and store a large amount of data. For this purpose, we have developed a data acquisition system based on commercially available oscilloscopes (Agilent Technologies, Santa Clara, CA, USA, DSO9064A; LECROY, Chestnut Ridge, NY, USA, WAVERUNNER 8404M and WAVERUNNER 8254), but with the capability of real-time data transfer to the computer using standard TCP-IP communication over a local area network (LAN).

The DAS system was tested using all three oscilloscopes (with four active channels per device) operated simultaneously in one LAN. After successful triggering, data are acquired into the oscilloscope's memory. The dedicated NI Labview routine that follows the trigger status initiates the transfer of acquired data to the PC. During a test, the code allowed to count the data loss within a series of 200 subsequent triggers at different laser repetition frequencies, 1, 3.3, and 10 Hz (i.e., 1 s, 0.3 s, and 0.1 s), and various sampling rates per channel. Figure 5 depicts the data acquisition time for two extreme configurations: (a) delay between triggers of 1 s/1000 samples per channel; and (b) delay between triggers of 0.1 s/25,000 samples per channel. In the first case, a successful read of data happens in between two triggers without affecting the next measurement, while for the second configuration (where data loss is 29%), after few long data reads (longer than 10 Hz limit, as depicted by the orange line) a subsequent loss of data occurs. A summary of measured data losses for individual oscilloscopes is reported in Table 1.

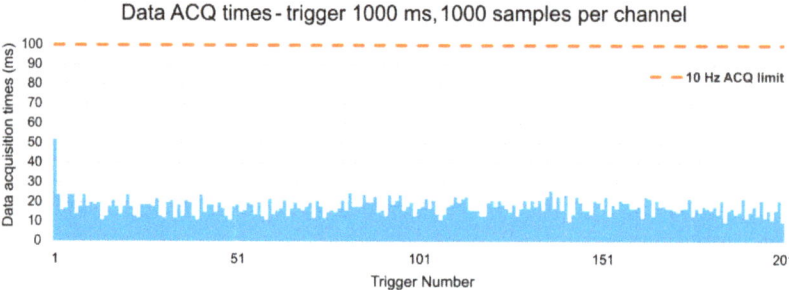

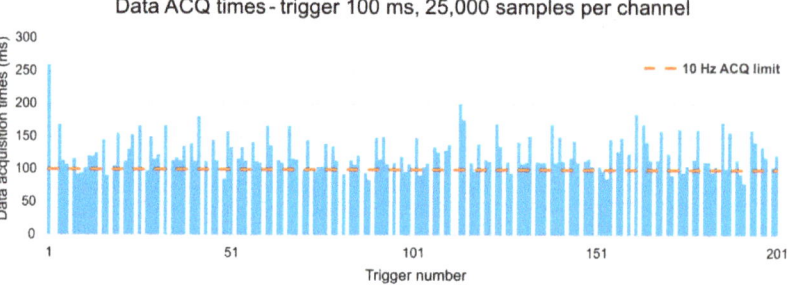

Figure 5. Example of data acquisition times for LeCroy Waverunner 8254: trigger delays of 1 s, 1000 samples per channel (top); trigger delays of 0.1 s, 25,000 samples per channel (bottom). The orange line shows the critical 10 Hz limit for data acquisition time.

Table 1. Measured data loss for a given trigger repetition rate and sampling rate. "X" corresponds to a non-tested configuration; "*" shows data acquisition (ACQ) read for four channels of equal length.

		Agilent Technologies; DSO9064A Delays between Triggers (ms)				LECROY—WAVERUNNER 8404M Delays between Triggers (ms)				LECROY—WAVERUNNER 8254 Delays between Triggers (ms)		
		1000	300	100		1000	300	100		1000	300	100
Samples per channel *	1000	0.0%	0.0%	0.8%	Samples per channel *	0.0%	0.0%	0.3%	Samples per channel *	0.0%	0.0%	0.0%
	5000	0.0%	0.0%	19.3%		0.0%	0.0%	0.8%		0.0%	0.0%	1.0%
	10,000	0.0%	0.0%	55.8%		0.0%	0.0%	6.5%		0.0%	0.0%	1.3%
	25,000	0.0%	1.5%	56.8%		0.0%	0.3%	17.8%		0.0%	0.0%	29.0%
	50,000	0.0%	12.8%	X		0.0%	1.8%	X		0.0%	1.8%	X
	100,000	1.0%	X	X		0.0%	X	X		0.0%	X	X

Data transfer rate from the oscilloscope to the PC depends mainly on the acquisition rate and the number of samples per channel. The oscilloscopes' transfer buffer and internal memory are independent. In case of overlapping between data transfer time and triggering time, there is still a possibility to transfer newly acquired data. However, inability to transfer data between neighboring triggers causes delay accumulation and after few repetitions leads to the loss of data acquired by the oscilloscope. A stable operation of the DAS with three parallel oscilloscopes (four channels per oscilloscope) can be easily achieved for 1 Hz laser repetition rates up to 50,000 samples per channel. On the other hand, operation at 10 Hz shows data loss, even acquiring 1000 samples per channel. However, a still reasonable performance of the DAS with the used oscilloscopes can be achieved even for 10,000 samples per channel and 10 Hz repetition rate (the observed data loss is about 6.5%).

To conclude, the chosen oscilloscopes demonstrate reasonable performance for data collection up to 3 Hz repetition rate. TOF diagnostics typically requires about 1000 samples to record all details of the ion beam spectrum. In case of high requirements to time-resolution (ultrafast ion signal), a relatively low repetition rate (around 1 Hz) is still acceptable in terms of overall data loss. Nevertheless, for application-based experiments, typically requiring a large number of shots, a compromise could be found by recording the ion spectra at a reduced repetition rate (e.g., an average signal acquired during 10 shots), even if the laser is operated at 10 Hz.

PW-class laser systems available at the ELI-Beamlines facility are characterized by high-repetition operating capability (1–10 Hz) that, in combination with suitable target delivery systems and laser-plasma diagnostic devices, provide unique possibilities for investigating new experimental regimes with high statistics. However, such a new scenario makes manual processing of raw data practically impossible. This also applies to typical laser-accelerated ion signals from various diagnostics, e.g., TOF detectors or TPS. In fact, any online analysis of a signal sequence would permit control of, inter alia, the uniformity and stability of TOF spectra that can be a crucial parameter for several applications of the measured particle beams [18]. Therefore, a special routine was developed using Python to perform TOF spectral analyses in real-time during an experiment. The script allows obtaining an average TOF signal based on the last N shots and, at the same time, calculates the standard deviation of the set, plotting the corresponding results (see Figure 6). The spectral changes over a certain time can be seen with high accuracy, and the overall stability can be tracked. This enables monitoring of the progress of the experiment and control of the process for possible errors or system breakdowns.

Real-time analysis of the obtained TPS images during an experiment was performed with specifically developed MATLAB-based graphical user interface (see Figure 7). At the initialization stage, it allows setting up the basic parameter of the used TPS geometry, such as the diameter of the pinhole, length of the electric and magnetic electrodes, distances between electrodes and camera, as well as particularly applied electrode fields strength, orientation, and scaling factor of the camera for the current experimental cycle. The routine can determine the appearance of the new experimental data continuously stored by TPS camera in the predefined folder, automatically start the procedure of their analysis, and save the calculated results.

At the first stage, the code performs a simulated trajectory of the particles inside the TPS device from the collimator down to the detector plane, according to the specified parameters. Furthermore, it controls the precision of the overlap between ion traces, detected with the TPS imaging system, and simulated traces of the ion species that are most commonly present in experiments with solid targets (e.g., protons and carbon ions with charge states from C^{+1} to C^{+6}). If necessary, the developed optimization toolkit corrects the preset parameters responsible for the position and orientation of ion traces in the image and removes possible artificial image noise caused by light scattered from the interior of the diagnostic device. The bulk of the code transforms the image in such a way that parabolic traces with different charge-to-mass ratios are converted into straight stripes, which in turn greatly simplifies the following data analysis.

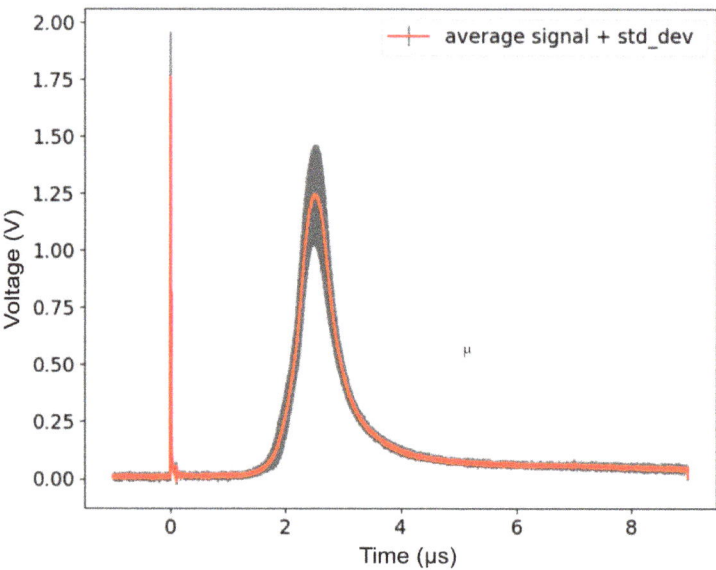

Figure 6. Average time-of-flight (TOF) spectrum and standard deviation calculated from 10 consequent signals recorded by a TOF diagnostic device when an Al target is irradiated with ns-class laser (4 J laser energy) at 10 Hz.

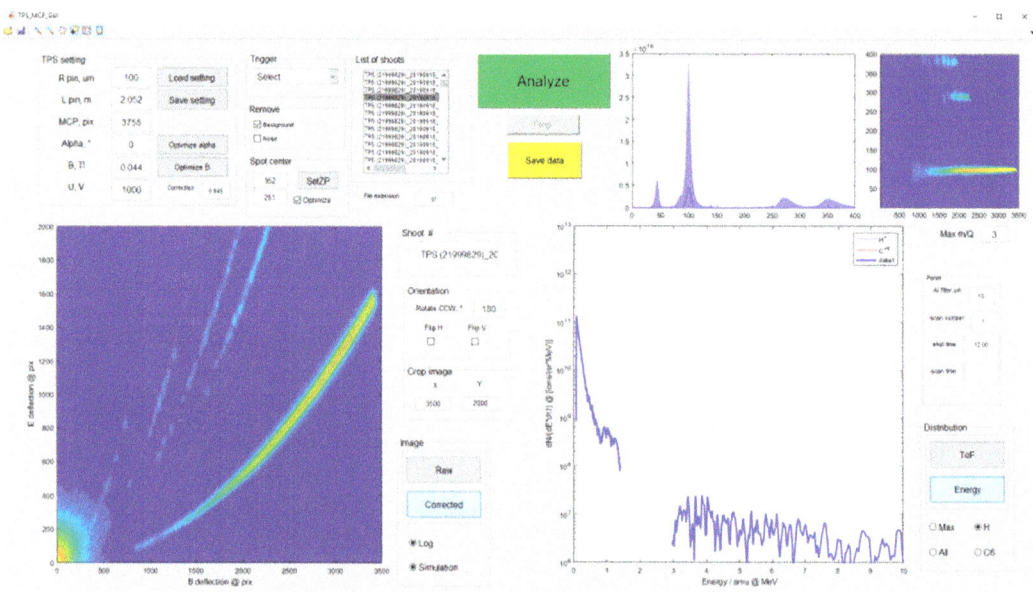

Figure 7. MATLAB-based graphical user interface used for analysis of the Thomson Parabola Spectrometer (TPS) images: (left GUI subfigure) example of the RAW image obtained by the TPS imaging system together with simulated ion traces; (right bottom GUI subfigure) corresponding ion energy distribution of the hydrogen ions as calculated by routine.

Ultimately, the automatically separated stripes representing individual ion species with defined charge-to-mass ratios are converted into corresponding ion energy distributions, and subsequently raw data together with calculated energy spectra are plotted in a user interface windows for visual control. Storing of the calculated results enables provision of simple online statistics (maximum ion energies and their cumulative charge per shot) and control of the shot-to-shot stability in real-time. As a result, this routine can provide complete and quick information on the ion species and the underlying physical processes in the plasma for a shot sequence acquired at a repetition rate of 1 Hz.

5. Conclusions and Perspectives

Operation of high repetition rate, high peak power laser systems focused down to ultrahigh intensity onto solid targets is very beneficial for user experiments, and especially for multidisciplinary applications that require a large number of overall laser shots. In fact, large laser-plasma facilities, such as the ELI pillars, are entering user operations and promising to deliver experiments with high statistical accuracy. In fact, shot-to-shot instabilities are intrinsic features of laser-plasma interaction, thus obviously introducing large experimental uncertainties that can be reduced if experiments with a large number of shots are carried out using the high repetition rate capabilities of the newly available laser technologies at PW-level. This will allow investigation of novel and complex regimes of laser-plasma interaction of interest for fundamental science, as well as optimization of the production of laser-driven secondary sources, along with high average fluxes delivered onto the user sample.

The above-described target and diagnostic technological solutions, along with real-time data acquisition and analysis tools, were developed ad-hoc to be provided to future users of the recently installed ELIMAIA ion beamline at ELI Beamlines, which aims to operate at high repetition rate (1–10 Hz) [18]. These solutions were already successfully tested at 100TW-level [17] and will be further tested and optimized in upcoming commissioning experiments at 1PW-level. Further development is considered based on future beamline performance optimization and user requirements that will certainly aim at an even higher degree of automation.

Author Contributions: Methodology, all co-authors; software, T.C., S.S., A.V., V.I., and F.S.; validation, T.C., S.S., L.G., A.V., M.T., F.G., and V.I.; investigation, all co-authors; writing—original draft preparation, T.C., S.S., L.G., A.V., M.T., F.G., and D.M.; writing—review and editing, T.C. and D.M.; project administration, D.M. All authors have read and agreed to the published version of the manuscript.

Funding: This research was funded by the Ministry of Education, Youth and Sports of the Czech Republic by the project No. LQ1606, and by the project "Advanced Research Using High Intensity Laser Produced Photons and Particles" (CZ.02.1.01/0.0/0.0/16_019/0000789).

Institutional Review Board Statement: Not applicable.

Informed Consent Statement: Not applicable.

Data Availability Statement: Raw data were generated at the ELI Beamlines facility. Derived data supporting the findings of this study are available from the corresponding author upon reasonable request.

Conflicts of Interest: The authors declare no conflict of interest.

References

1. Toth, C.; Evans, D.; Gonsalves, A.J.; Kirkpatrick, M.; Magana, A.; Mannino, G.; Mao, H.-S.; Nakamura, K.; Riley, J.R.; Steinke, S.; et al. Transition of the BELLA PW Laser System Towards a Collaborative Research Facility in Laser Plasma Science. In Proceedings of the Advanced Accelerator Concepts: 17th Advanced Accelerator Concepts Workshop, Harbor, MD, USA, 31 July–5 August 2016; AIP Publishing: Melville, NY, USA, 2017; Volume 1812, p. 110005.
2. Nakamura, K.; Mao, H.-S.; Gonsalves, A.J.; Vincenti, H.; Mittelberger, D.E.; Daniels, J.; Magana, A.; Toth, C.; Leemans, W.P. Diagnostics, Control and Performance Parameters for the BELLA High Repetition Rate Petawatt Class Laser. *IEEE J. Quantum Electron.* **2017**, *53*, 1–21. [CrossRef]
3. Roso, L. High Repetition Rate Petawatt Lasers. *EPJ Web Conf.* **2018**, *167*, 01001. [CrossRef]

4. Sistrunk, E.F.; Spinka, T.; Bayramian, A.; Armstrong, P.; Baxamusa, S.; Betts, S.; Bopp, D.; Buck, S.; Charron, K.; Cupal, J.; et al. All Diode-Pumped, High-Repetition-Rate Advanced Petawatt Laser System (HAPLS). In Proceedings of the Conference on Lasers and Electro-Optics, San Jose, CA, USA, 14–19 May 2017; The Optical Society: Washington, DC, USA, 2017; p. 12.
5. Navratil, P.; Slezák, O.; Pilar, J.; Ertel, K.G.; Hanuš, M.; Banerjee, S.; Phillips, P.J.; Smith, J.; De Vido, M.; Lucianetti, A.; et al. Characterization of Bivoj/DiPOLE 100: HiLASE 100-J/10-Hz Diode Pumped Solid State Laser. In *Solid State Lasers XXVII: Technology and Devices*; SPIE-Intl. Soc. Opt. Eng.: Bellingham, WA, USA, 2018; Volume 10511, p. 105110X.
6. Kar, S.; Kakolee, K.F.; Qiao, B.; Macchi, A.; Cerchez, M.; Doria, D.; Geissler, M.; McKenna, P.; Neely, D.; Osterholz, J.; et al. Ion Acceleration in Multispecies Targets Driven by Intense Laser Radiation Pressure. *Phys. Rev. Lett.* **2012**, *109*, 185006. [CrossRef] [PubMed]
7. Macchi, A.; Borghesi, M.; Passoni, M. Ion Acceleration by Superintense Laser-Plasma Interaction. *Rev. Mod. Phys.* **2013**, *85*, 751–793. [CrossRef]
8. Amaldi, U.; Kraft, G. Radiotherapy with Beams of Carbon Ions. *Rep. Prog. Phys.* **2005**, *68*, 1861–1882. [CrossRef]
9. Cirrone, G.A.P.; Margarone, D.; Maggiore, M.; Anzalone, A.; Borghesi, M.; Jia, S.B.; Bulanov, S.S.; Bulanov, S.; Carpinelli, M.; Cavallaro, S.; et al. ELIMED: A New Hadron Therapy Concept Based on Laser Driven Ion Beams. In Proceedings of the SPIE Optics + Optoelectronics, Prague, Czech Republic, 15–18 April 2013; SPIE-Intl. Soc. Opt. Eng.: Bellingham, WA, USA, 2013; Volume 2, p. 87791I.
10. Prencipe, I.; Fuchs, J.; Pascarelli, S.; Schumacher, D.W.; Stephens, R.B.; Alexander, N.B.; Briggs, R.; Büscher, M.; Cernaianu, M.O.; Choukourov, A.; et al. Targets for High Repetition Rate Laser Facilities: Needs, Challenges and Perspectives. *High Power Laser Sci. Eng.* **2017**, *5*. [CrossRef]
11. Margarone, D.; Torrisi, L.; Cavallaro, S.; Milani, E.; Rinati, G.V.; Marinelli, M.; Tuve', C.; Laska, L.; Krasa, J.; Pfeifer, M.; et al. Diamond Detectors for Characterization of Laser-Generated Plasma. *Radiat. Eff. Defects Solids* **2008**, *163*, 463–470. [CrossRef]
12. Margarone, D.; Krása, J.; Giuffrida, O.L.; Picciotto, A.; Torrisi, L.; Nowak, T.S.; Musumeci, P.; Velyhan, A.; Prokůpek, J.; Láska, L.; et al. Full Characterization of Laser-Accelerated Ion Beams Using Faraday Cup, Silicon Carbide, and Single-Crystal Diamond Detectors. *J. Appl. Phys.* **2011**, *109*, 103302. [CrossRef]
13. Scuderi, V.; Milluzzo, D.; Alejo, A.; Amico, A.; Booth, N.; Cirrone, G.; Doria, D.; Green, J.; Kar, S.; LaRosa, G.; et al. Time of Flight Based Diagnostics for High Energy Laser Driven Ion Beams. *J. Instrum.* **2017**, *12*, C03086. [CrossRef]
14. Prasad, R.; Doria, D.; Ter-Avetisyan, S.; Foster, P.; Quinn, K.; Romagnani, L.; Brenner, C.; Green, J.; Gallegos, P.; Streeter, M.; et al. Calibration of Thomson Parabola—MCP Assembly for Multi-MeV Ion Spectroscopy. *Nucl. Instrum. Methods Phys. Res. Sect. A Accel. Spectrometers Detect. Assoc. Equip.* **2010**, *623*, 712–715. [CrossRef]
15. Mead, M.J.; Neely, D.; Gauoin, J.; Heathcote, R.; Patel, P. Electromagnetic Pulse Generation within a Petawatt Laser Target Chamber. *Rev. Sci. Instrum.* **2004**, *75*, 4225–4227. [CrossRef]
16. Consoli, F.; Tikhonchuk, V.T.; Bardon, M.; Bradford, P.; Carroll, D.C.; Cikhardt, J.; Cipriani, M.; Clarke, R.J.; Cowan, T.E.; Danson, C.N.; et al. Laser Produced Electromagnetic Pulses: Generation, Detection and Mitigation. *High Power Laser Sci. Eng.* **2020**, *8*. [CrossRef]
17. Tryus, M.; Grepl, F.; Chagovets, T.; Velyhan, A.; Giuffrida, L.; Stancek, S.; Kantarelou, V.; Istokskaia, V.; Schillaci, F.; Zakova, M.; et al. TERESA Target Area at ELI Beamlines. *Quantum Beam Sci.* **2020**, *4*, 37. [CrossRef]
18. Margarone, D.; Cirrone, G.A.P.; Cuttone, G.; Amico, A.; Andò, L.; Borghesi, M.; Bulanov, S.S.; Bulanov, S.V.; Chatain, D.; Fajstavr, A.; et al. ELIMAIA: A Laser-Driven Ion Accelerator for Multidisciplinary Applications. *Quantum Beam Sci.* **2018**, *2*, 8. [CrossRef]
19. Nayuki, T.; Oishi, Y.; Fujii, T.; Nemoto, K.; Kayoiji, T.; Okano, Y.; Hironaka, Y.; Nakamura, K.G.; Kondo, K.-I.; Ueda, K.-I. Thin Tape Target Driver for Laser Ion Accelerator. *Rev. Sci. Instrum.* **2003**, *74*, 3293–3296. [CrossRef]
20. Gonsalves, A.J.; Liu, F.; Bobrova, N.A.; Sasorov, P.V.; Pieronek, C.; Daniels, J.; Antipov, S.; Butler, J.E.; Bulanov, S.S.; Waldron, W.L.; et al. Demonstration of a High Repetition Rate Capillary Discharge Waveguide. *J. Appl. Phys.* **2016**, *119*, 033302. [CrossRef]
21. Morrison, J.T.; Feister, S.; Frische, K.D.; Austin, D.R.; Ngirmang, G.K.; Murphy, N.R.; Orban, C.; A Chowdhury, E.; Roquemore, W.M. MeV Proton Acceleration at kHz Repetition Rate from Ultra-intense Laser Liquid Interaction. *New J. Phys.* **2018**, *20*, 022001. [CrossRef]
22. George, K.M.; Morrison, J.T.; Feister, S.; Ngirmang, G.K.; Smith, J.R.; Klim, A.J.; Snyder, J.; Austin, D.; Erbsen, W.; Frische, K.D.; et al. High-Repetition-Rate (kHz) Targets and Optics from Liquid Microjets for High-Intensity Laser–Plasma Interactions. *High Power Laser Sci. Eng.* **2019**, *7*. [CrossRef]
23. Ditmire, T.; Zweiback, J.; Yanovsky, V.P.; Cowan, T.E.; Hays, G.; Wharton, K.B. Nuclear Fusion in Gases of Deuterium Clusters Heated with a Femtosecond Laser. *Phys. Plasmas* **2000**, *7*, 1993–1998. [CrossRef]
24. Margarone, D.; Velyhan, A.; Dostal, J.; Ullschmied, J.; Perin, J.P.; Chatain, D.; Garcia, S.; Bonnay, P.; Pisarczyk, T.; Dudzak, R.; et al. Proton Acceleration Driven by a Nanosecond Laser from a Cryogenic Thin Solid-Hydrogen Ribbon. *Phys. Rev. X* **2016**, *6*, 041030. [CrossRef]
25. Kim, J.B.; Göde, S.; Glenzer, S.H. Development of a Cryogenic Hydrogen Microjet for High-Intensity, High-Repetition Rate Experiments. *Rev. Sci. Instrum.* **2016**, *87*, 11E328. [CrossRef] [PubMed]
26. Poole, P.L.; Willis, C.; Cochran, G.E.; Hanna, R.T.; Andereck, C.D.; Schumacher, D.W. Moderate Repetition Rate Ultra-Intense Laser Targets and Optics Using Variable Thickness Liquid Crystal Films. *Appl. Phys. Lett.* **2016**, *109*, 151109. [CrossRef]

27. Milluzzo, G.; Scuderi, V.; Alejo, A.; Amico, A.G.; Booth, N.; Borghesi, M.; Cirrone, G.A.P.; Cuttone, G.; Doria, D.; Green, J.; et al. A New Energy Spectrum Reconstruction Method for Time-of-Flight Diagnostics of High-Energy Laser-Driven Protons. *Rev. Sci. Instrum.* **2019**, *90*, 083303. [CrossRef]
28. Schillaci, F.; Cirrone, G.; Cuttone, G.; Maggiore, M.; Andó, L.; Amato, A.; Costa, M.; Gallo, G.; Korn, G.; LaRosa, G.; et al. Design of the ELIMAIA Ion Collection System. *J. Instrum.* **2015**, *10*, T12001. [CrossRef]
29. Scuderi, V.; Amato, A.; Amico, A.G.; Borghesi, M.; Cirrone, G.A.P.; Cuttone, G.; Fajstavr, A.; Giuffrida, L.; Grepl, F.; Korn, G.; et al. Diagnostics and Dosimetry Solutions for Multidisciplinary Applications at the ELIMAIA Beamline. *Appl. Sci.* **2018**, *8*, 1415. [CrossRef]

Article

Distortion of Thomson Parabolic-Like Proton Patterns Due to Electromagnetic Interference

Filip Grepl [1,2,*], Josef Krása [3], Andriy Velyhan [2], Massimo De Marco [2,†], Jan Dostál [3], Miroslav Pfeifer [3] and Daniele Margarone [2,4]

[1] Faculty of Nuclear Sciences and Physical Engineering, Czech Technical University in Prague, Břehová 7, 115 19 Prague, Czech Republic
[2] ELI–Beamlines Center, Institute of Physics, Czech Academy of Sciences, Za Radnicí 835, 252 41 Dolní Břežany, Czech Republic; Andriy.Velyhan@eli-beams.eu (A.V.); mdemarco@clpu.es (M.D.M.); Daniele.Margarone@eli-beams.eu (D.M.)
[3] Institute of Physics of the Czech Academy of Sciences, Na Slovance 2, 182 21 Prague, Czech Republic; krasa@fzu.cz (J.K.); dostal@fzu.cz (J.D.); pfeifer@fzu.cz (M.P.)
[4] Centre for Plasma Physics, School of Mathematics and Physics, Queen's University Belfast, Belfast BT7 1NN, UK
* Correspondence: Filip.Grepl@eli-beams.eu
† Current address: Centro de Láseres Pulsados, Calle del Adaja, 8, 37185 Villamayor, Salamanca, Spain.

Abstract: Intense electromagnetic pulses (EMPs) accompany the production of plasma when a high-intensity laser irradiates a solid target. The EMP occurs both during and long after the end of the laser pulse (up to hundreds of nanoseconds) within and outside the interaction chamber, and interferes with nearby electronics, which may lead to the disruption or malfunction of plasma diagnostic devices. This contribution reports a correlation between the frequency spectrum of the EMP and the distortion of Thomson parabola tracks of protons observed at the kJ-class PALS laser facility in Prague. EMP emission was recorded using a simple flat antenna. Ions accelerated from the front side of the target were simultaneously detected by a Thomson parabola ion spectrometer. The comparison of the two signals suggests that the EMP may be considered to be the source of parabolic track distortion.

Keywords: Thomson parabola; laser–plasma interaction; electromagnetic pulse

Citation: Grepl, F.; Krása, J.; Velyhan, A.; De Marco, M.; Dostál, J.; Pfeifer, M.; Margarone, D. Distortion of Thomson Parabolic-Like Proton Patterns Due to Electromagnetic Interference. *Appl. Sci.* **2021**, *11*, 4484. https://doi.org/10.3390/app11104484

Academic Editor: Anming Hu

Received: 19 February 2021
Accepted: 11 May 2021
Published: 14 May 2021

Publisher's Note: MDPI stays neutral with regard to jurisdictional claims in published maps and institutional affiliations.

Copyright: © 2021 by the authors. Licensee MDPI, Basel, Switzerland. This article is an open access article distributed under the terms and conditions of the Creative Commons Attribution (CC BY) license (https://creativecommons.org/licenses/by/4.0/).

1. Introduction

A traditional Thomson parabola ion spectrometer (TP) is a device that can distinguish ions propagating through it according to their charge-to-mass ratio and their kinetic energy [1]. The spectrometer employs parallel magnetic and electric fields that are perpendicularly arranged with respect to the ion propagation direction. Particles entering a pinhole in the front are deflected and they then interact with an image plane where a recording system is installed (e.g., plastic nuclear track detector, photostimulable image plate, or microchannel plate coupled to a phosphor screen and a charge-coupled device camera). Typically, the magnetic field is provided by two parallel magnets, and the electric field is created by applying a voltage to electrical plates through high-voltage cables. Theoretically, perfect parabolic tracks of ions are drawn in the spectrometer detector plane. Nevertheless, the tracks can be perturbed by a high-energy laser pulse under real experimental conditions.

A major source of ion-track distortions is EMP, which is generated during laser–target interaction [2–4]. High-voltage cables connected to the TP can pick up EMP noise during a laser shot, which results in the distortion of the spectrometer electric field. Ions with different energies thus experience varying electric-field strength, and their tracks on the detector plane are distorted. The high-pass filter on high-voltage cables can be incorporated in order to reduce this effect [5]. Alternatively, Faraday cage shielding around cables and the spectrometer can be used to mitigate this effect.

Another source of deviation from perfect tracks is attributed to the emission direction of the laser-accelerated proton beam itself at the the target surface (which is usually called "pointing"). A high-spatial-resolution Thomson spectrometer was employed to measure the pointing of proton beams generated from the rear side of plane target foils. Small bumps and deviations from the perfect parabolic tracks of ions were observed and identified as a feature of the emitted proton beam that occurred due to small fluctuations in the acceleration sheath [6].

Track oscillations and distortions complicate the analysis and interpretation of ion numbers, especially when many different kinds of ion species are detected by the spectrometer. The overlapping of proton tracks and fast ion tracks can appear (as demonstrated in Figure 1) and lead to an incorrect number of detected particles. In addition, fitting and extracting the parabolic trajectories becomes difficult, as they do not follow smooth analytically derived curves. Here, we report the observation of distorted parabolic tracks at the PALS laser facility when a 600 J, 350 ps (FWHM) laser pulse was focused on solid targets reaching an intensity of 3×10^{16} W/cm^2. Since the EMP affecting plasma diagnostics can be effectively detected by a simple antenna, and the recorded signal can be processed in the frequency domain [7,8], we compared the measured EMP signal with distorted parabolic tracks in order to investigate the effect of the EMP on the spectrometer, and to prove that the cause of track distortions at the PALS laser facility is the strong EMP generated in the target chamber.

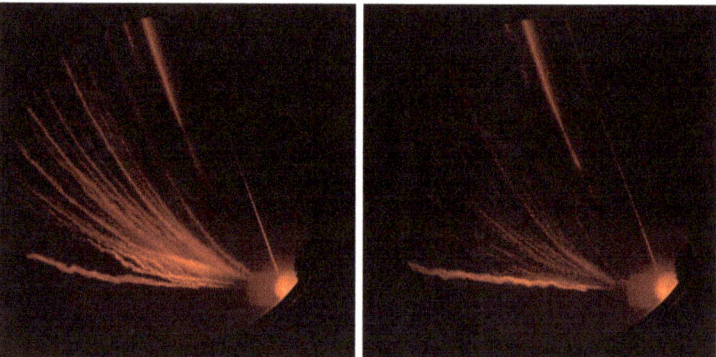

Figure 1. Typical Thomson parabola (TP) snapshots showing distorted ion tracks. Parabola parts corresponding to high-energy particles partially overlapped with each other.

2. Experimental Arrangement and Measurement

A 2 TW iodine laser system with a wavelength of 1315 nm was employed to irradiate targets composed of polymethyl methacrylate or silicon wafers doped with boron. The ions accelerated in the backward direction were detected by the TP placed at a 0° detection angle with respect to the normal target surface and at a distance of 2.17 m from the target (see Figure 2).

The spectrometer used a microchannel plate coupled to a phosphor screen and to the CCD. The strength of the TP's magnetic field was increased up to 0.12 T. A potential difference of 2.9 kV was applied across the 21.5 mm wide gap between the spectrometer electrical plates in order to reach a separation of the ion tracks on the spectrometer's detection system. The parabolic tracks on the image plane (within Cartesian coordinate system (x,y) and under nonrelativistic approximation) are described by the following equation [9]:

$$y = \frac{q}{m_0} \frac{EL_{fE}\left(\frac{L_{fE}}{2} + L_{rE}\right)}{BL_{fB}\left(\frac{L_{fB}}{2} + L_{rB}\right)} x^2, \quad (1)$$

where q is the charge of ion, m_0 is its invariant mass, E is the strength of the spectrometer's electric field, B is the strength of its magnetic field, L_{fE} (L_{fB}) is the length of the electric (magnetic) field, and L_{rE} (L_{rB}) stands for the distance between the end of the electric (magnetic) field and the recording system, respectively. The x axis was oriented in the direction of ions deflection in the magnetic field, and the y axis was oriented in the direction of their deflection in the electric field.

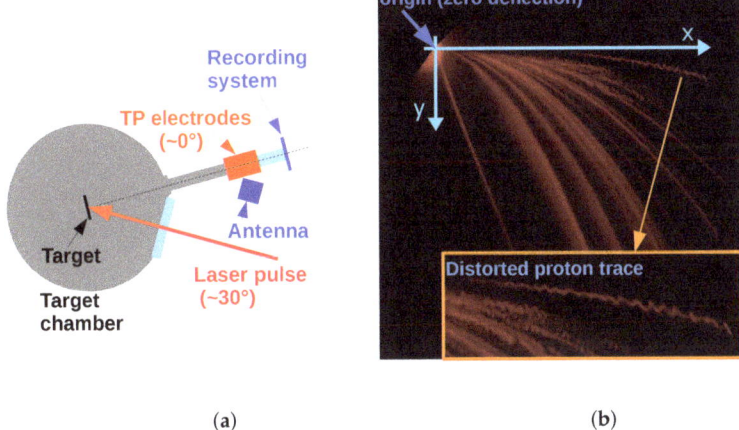

Figure 2. (a) Experimental setup at PALS laser facility showing position of the TP spectrometer and plane antenna. (b) Typical TP snapshot showing the parabolic track of protons distorted due to the electromagnetic pulse (EMP) in the Cartesian coordinate system.

Figure 2 also shows a typical TP snapshot with the Cartesian coordinate system, where the parabolic track corresponding to protons is distorted due to EMP interference. While the protons were detected by the TP, the EMP generated in the target chamber and propagated outside from it was simultaneously recorded by a plane antenna positioned directly on the TP electrodes, as can be seen in Figure 2.

3. Processing Antenna Signals and TP Snapshots

The obtained data by both the TP and the antenna were processed by a MATLAB script specifically written for this purpose. First, the parabolic curve (1) that overlapped the track of protons was plotted in the TP snapshot. In such a way, one can read the intensity of pixels associated with the parabolic curve, and plot this intensity as a function of the horizontal position x with respect to the origin of the parabola (i.e., to the zero-deflection point). Then, the velocity of ions v was derived for every point of the parabola (i.e., for each pixel) from the general equation for magnetic deflection [9]:

$$v = \frac{qBL_{fB}}{xm_0}\left(\frac{L_{fB}}{2} + L_{rB}\right), \quad (2)$$

where x stands for the distance between the origin of the parabolic track and the actual position of an ion in the detector plane due to its deflection in the magnetic field. By knowing the distance between target and recording system, the corresponding proton time of flight (TOF) was calculated. Therefore, the dependence of the pixel intensity (along the parabolic curve) on the TOF of protons was derived for each point of the parabolic track as can be seen in Figure 3. This calculation shows which part of the EMP signal influenced the TP, because the antenna (recording the EMP signal) was positioned directly on the TP electrodes. As Figure 3 shows, the signal recorded by the antenna between 0 and 243 ns (the edge of the detector) corresponds to the entire parabolic track of protons from zero-deflection point up to the edge of MCP. Since the proton signal occurred only between 120 and 243 ns in this particular measurement, only the part of the EMP signal between 120 and 243 ns was considered in further processing. This part of the signal is highlighted with red in Figure 4, showing the measured antenna signal. The EMP that affected the TP before the fastest protons (in our case, before 120 ns) can also be included in analysis. This would basically also predict the distortion of the parabolic track in the region where no protons were detected in this experiment. Nevertheless, analysis was mainly focused on the region between 120 and 243 ns because the results could be compared with the measured parabolic track of protons.

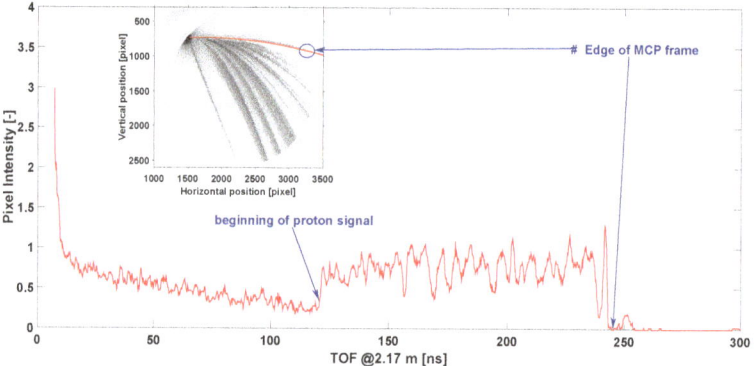

Figure 3. Intensity of pixels along the parabolic track of protons as a function of time of flight (TOF) derived from the velocity corresponding to each point of the parabolic curve. Subplot shows the TP snapshot in grayscale with the parabolic curve used for reading pixel intensity. The edge of the MCP screen is clearly visible. The TOF corresponding to the edge was taken as a point where the EMP no longer influenced the proton trajectories.

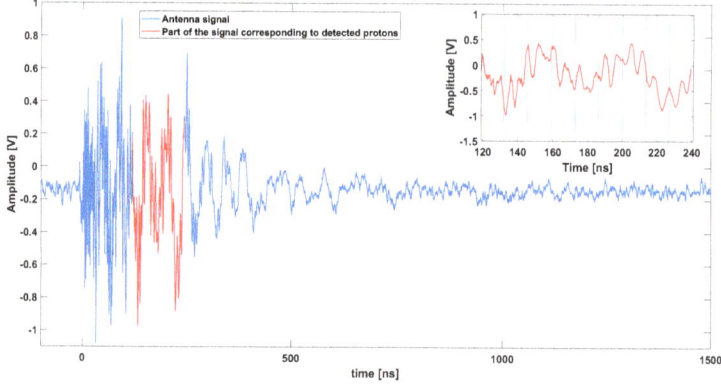

Figure 4. Detected EMP signal (blue curve). Its part highlighted with red corresponds to the TOF derived from the parabolic track of protons in Figure 3 from 120 to 243 ns; (inset) 9 samples into which the signal corresponding to TOF was divided.

The red part of the recorded EMP signal (i.e., the part corresponding to detected protons) in Figure 4 was divided into 9 samples. The length of each sample must be sufficient to retrieve its frequency spectrum using fast Fourier transform (FFT). This condition together with the length of the red part naturally led to the number of samples (in this case, N = 9). After applying the FFT on each time sample, we found 3 highest peaks corresponding to the 3 main frequencies f_i^1, f_i^2, f_i^3 included within the i-th time sample. In addition, phases $\phi_i^1, \phi_i^2, \phi_i^3$ and amplitudes A_i^1, A_i^2, A_i^3 were obtained. Lastly, this physical quantities (frequencies, phases, and amplitudes) were used to calculate the modulated electric field E_m in the model developed in MATLAB. In addition, frequencies f_i^1, f_i^2, f_i^3, which were found in time sample t_i, contributed to the modulation of the electric field only within time sample t_i, and their contribution was cancelled by setting $t_i = 0$ outside this particular time sample. In such a way, the track of protons in time sample t_i was distorted only by the electromagnetic waves that affected the TP while these protons were traversing the electric field. The other bunch of protons (e.g., related to time sample t_{i+1}) were influenced by waves that were interacting with the TP within time sample t_{i+1}. The modulation of electric field E_m can be thus expressed as a function of time corresponding to the TOF of protons. The modulation itself is considered to be a sum of sine waves because the sources of modulations are electromagnetic waves generated during laser–target interaction. Assuming the linear transfer of modulation from EMP to electric field, sinusoidal modulations with main frequencies (and corresponding phases and amplitudes) were added to the constant term of the electric field. The relation for final electric field $E(t)$ in the model may be written as

$$E(t) = E_o + K \cdot E_m(t, f_{i=1,...,9}^{j=1,...,3}, \varphi_{i=1,...,9}^{j=1,...,3}) = E_o + K \cdot \sum_{i=1}^{9} \sum_{j=1}^{3} A_i^j \cdot \sin(2\pi f_i^j t_i + \varphi_i^j), \quad (3)$$

where E_0 is the electric field applied to the electrodes, and K is the constant that may be changed in order to amplify the influence of modulation. This constant was less important, since we only investigated the similarities of the frequency. Resulting electric field $E(t)$ was no longer constant and led to the distortion of parabolic tracks on the recording system. In particular, the electric field (3) was substituted in Equation (1), which is plotted in the TP snapshot. Additionally, the captured track of protons was extracted from the snapshot by finding the maximum of intensity in a neighborhood of the parabolic track of protons. Eventually, both the extracted parabolic and the modulate track could be plotted. Both curves are shown in Figure 5 with the TP snapshot converted into grayscale in the Cartesian coordinate system.

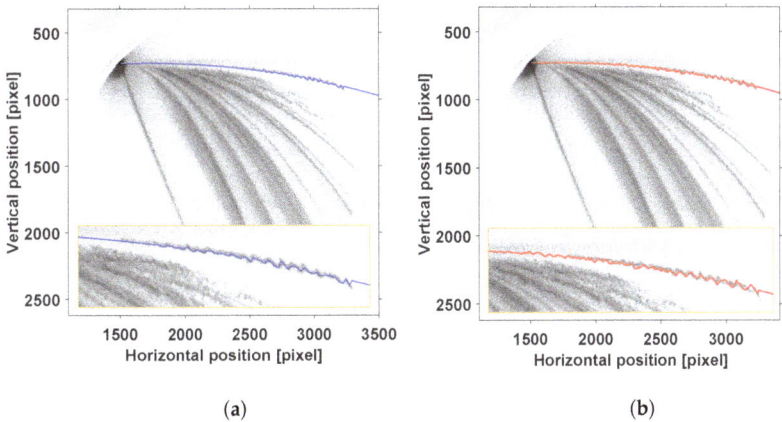

Figure 5. (**a**) Extracted parabolic track of protons as measured. (**b**) Modulated parabola plotted in MATLAB by introducing a varying electric field (3) into Equation (1).

We now demonstrate that the signal detected by the antenna was the same as the one that influenced the TP electrodes. The generated EMP on the target could propagate through the vacuum pipe connecting the TP spectrometer to the interaction chamber. Therefore, the cutoff frequency of the waveguide with a circular cross-section (radius of 50 mm) was analytically derived in order to understand whether the EMP could affect the TP electrodes from the inside. The cutoff frequency of the TE_{11} mode (the fundamental transverse electric mode of circular waveguide) was calculated as ≈1.75 GHz, which means that any electromagnetic wave of lower frequency could not propagate through the vacuum pipe towards the spectrometer. Thanks to the EMP characterization already performed at PALS, the main portion of the EMP frequency spectrum could be found below 1.5 GHz [7,10]. Hence, the antenna placed on TP electrodes recorded the EMP causing the distortion of parabolic tracks.

4. Correlation between Measured EMP and Captured Parabolic Track of Protons

In order to compare the extracted curve (blue) with the modulated one (red) in the time domain, we plotted both the extracted and the modulated parabolas as a function of TOF, as Figure 6 shows. In addition, the undistorted parabolic track is shown.

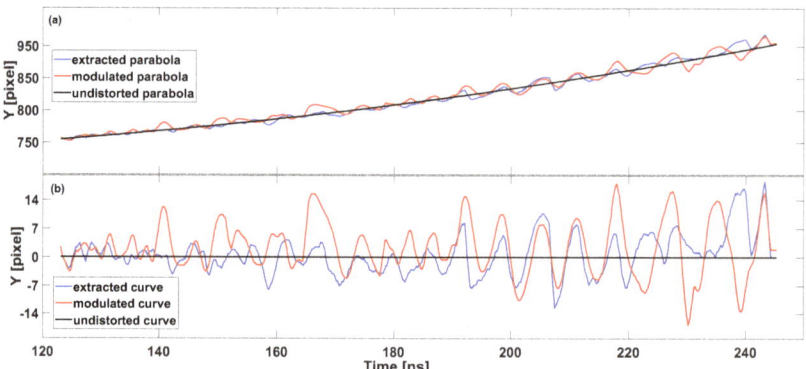

Figure 6. (**a**) Extracted (blue), modulated (red), and undistorted (black) parabolic track corresponding to protons. (**b**) Obtained curves from parabolas by subtracting parabolic dependence (1). X axis was the same in both figures. The direction of the y axis in (**a**) is the opposite with respect to Figure 2. Y axis in (**b**) shows the modulation amplitude in pixels.

This curve corresponded to the ideal parabolic track that would be plotted in the image plane if the electric field were constant. Moreover, both curves in the frequency domain could be compared. Therefore, the parabolic dependence (1) was subtracted from all curves. Figure 6 shows both curves plotted as a function of TOF. Obviously, the undistorted parabola became a constant function without any variations due to the EMP. The modulation periods of both parabolas presented similarities. In order to quantify the similarity of the two curves in Figure 6, their frequency spectra were calculated and compared to each other. As it can be observed in Figure 7, the frequency ranges are almost identical. Additionally, we found the five highest peaks occurring at the same frequencies in both spectra. The result of this procedure is shown in the inset where the frequencies at which the peaks occur are listed. Since we are interested mainly in the values of frequencies on the x axis, the y axis of both plots were normalized. Consequently, both spectra in Figure 7 were integrated using the trapezoidal rule for approximating the definite integral and the ratio of integrals was calculated to be 1.2.

Similar correlation was observed by also analyzing several additional TP snapshots and the corresponding antenna signals. The ratios between the integrals of the extracted and modulated curves were estimated to vary between 0.7 and 1.3.

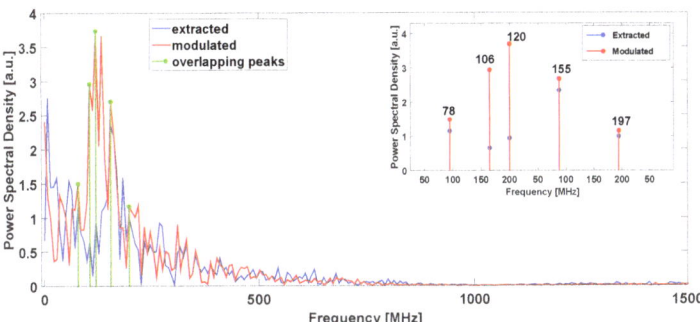

Figure 7. Frequency spectrum of extracted and modulated curves in Figure 6. Peaks occurring at the same frequencies are also plotted. Additionally, the subplot shows values of the same frequencies at which peak overlapping occurred.

5. Conclusions

Distortions of parabolic ion tracks in a TP spectrometer were reported in the literature [5,6]. Unstable ion trajectories resulting into wiggles in the detector plane were assigned to the variation of the spectrometer's electric field due to the EMP or to the pointing of the laser-accelerated proton beam itself.

On the basis of these observations, we carried out a series of measurements that showed correlation between the frequency spectrum of the EMP and the distortion of the parabolic-like tracks of protons on the recording system of the TP ion spectrometer at the PALS laser facility. In particular, frequencies extracted from the measured EMP signal were used to estimate the modulation of the electric field in our model. The parabolic tracks of protons obtained by Equation (3) and the measured ones presented similarities both in the time and the frequency domain. Frequency analysis of both the modulated and the measured parabolic curves showed that the frequency spectra had similar profiles, with peaks occurring at the same frequencies. Particularly, modulation frequencies between 50 and 200 MHz were found. In addition, the integrals of the frequency spectrum corresponding to both the modulated and the recorded parabola (i.e., the energy carried by the electrical signals) were alike. The ratios of such signal energies showed values in the range of 0.7–1.3. These observations led to the conclusion that the distortion of the spectrometer tracks detected at the PALS laser facility is caused by the EMP generated during and immediately after the high-energy laser–target interaction.

Author Contributions: Conceptualization, J.K. and A.V.; methodology, F.G., J.K., A.V., M.D.M., J.D., M.P. and D.M.; software, F.G.; validation F.G., A.V. and D.M.; formal analysis, F.G.; investigation, F.G., J.K., A.V., M.D.M., J.D., M.P. and D.M.; resources, D.M.; data curation, F.G., A.V. and M.D.M.; writing—original-draft preparation, F.G.; writing—review and editing, F.G., J.K. and D.M.; visualization, F.G.; supervision, D.M.; project administration, D.M.; funding acquisition, D.M. All authors have read and agreed to the published version of the manuscript.

Funding: This research was funded by the Ministry of Education, Youth, and Sports of the Czech Republic through the project "Advanced Research Using High-Intensity Laser-Produced Photons and Particles" (CZ.02.1.010.00.016_0190000789).

Institutional Review Board Statement: Not applicable.

Informed Consent Statement: Not applicable.

Data Availability Statement: The data that support the findings of this study are available from the corresponding author upon reasonable request.

Acknowledgments: The authors gratefully acknowledge technical support provided by PALS staff.

Conflicts of Interest: The authors declare no conflict of interest.

References

1. Olsen, J.N.; Kuswa, G.W.; Jones, E.D. Ion-expansion energy spectra correlated to laser plasma parameters. *J. Appl. Phys.* **1973**, *44*, 2275–2283. [CrossRef]
2. Brown, C.G.; Ayers, J.; Felker, B.; Ferguson, W.; Holder, J.P.; Nagel, S.R.; Piston, K.W.; Simanovskaia, N.; Throop, A.L.; Chung, M.; et al. Assessment and mitigation of diagnostic-generated electromagnetic interference at the National Ignition Facility. *Rev. Sci. Instruments* **2012**, *83*. [CrossRef] [PubMed]
3. Dubois, J.L.; Lubrano-Lavaderci, F.; Raffestin, D.; Ribolzi, J.; Gazave, J.; Fontaine, A.C.L.; D'Humières, E.; Hulin, S.; Nicolaï, P.; Poyé, A.; et al. Target charging in short-pulse-laser-plasma experiments. *Phys. Rev. E Stat. Nonlinear Soft Matter Phys.* **2014**, *89*. [CrossRef] [PubMed]
4. Consoli, F.; Tikhonchuk, V.T.; Bardon, M.; Bradford, P.; Carroll, D.C.; Cikhardt, J.; Cipriani, M.; Clarke, R.J.; Cowan, T.E.; Danson, C.N.; et al. Laser produced electromagnetic pulses: Generation, detection and mitigation. *High Power Laser Sci. Eng.* **2020**, *8*, e22. [CrossRef]
5. Carroll, D.C.; Jones, K.; Robson, L.; Mckenna, P.; Bandyopadhyay, S.; Brummitt, P.; Neely, D.; Facility, C.L.; Lindau, F.; Lundh, O. The design, development and use of a novel Thomson spectrometer for high resolution ion detection. *Cent. Laser Facil. Annu. Rep.* **2006**, *29*, 16–20.
6. Schreiber, J.; Ter-Avetisyan, S.; Risse, E.; Kalachnikov, M.; Nickles, P.; Sandner, W.; Schramm, U.; Habs, D.; Witte, J.; Schnürer, M. Pointing of laser-accelerated proton beams. *Phys. Plasmas* **2006**, *13*, 033111. [CrossRef]
7. De Marco, M.; Pfeifer, M.; Krousky, E.; Krasa, J.; Cikhardt, J.; Klir, D.; Nassisi, V. Basic features of electromagnetic pulse generated in a laser-target chamber at 3-TW laser facility PALS. *J. Phys. Conf. Ser.* **2014**, *508*, 1–5. [CrossRef]
8. Mead, M.J.; Neely, D.; Gauoin, J.; Heathcote, R.; Patel, P. Electromagnetic pulse generation within a petawatt laser target chamber. *Rev. Sci. Instruments* **2004**, *75*, 4225–4227. [CrossRef]
9. Alejo, A.; Gwynne, D.; Doria, D.; Ahmed, H.; Carroll, D.; Clarke, R.; Neely, D.; Scott, G.; Borghesi, M.; Kar, S. Recent developments in the Thomson Parabola Spectrometer diagnostic for laser-driven multi-species ion sources. *J. Instrum.* **2016**, *11*, C10005. [CrossRef]
10. De Marco, M.; Cikhardt, J.; Krása, J.; Velyhan, A.; Pfeifer, M.; Krouský, E.; Klír, D.; Řezáč, K.; Limpouch, J.; Margarone, D.; et al. Electromagnetic pulses produced by expanding laser-produced Au plasma. *Nukleonika* **2015**, *60*, 239–243. [CrossRef]

Article

Optically Switchable MeV Ion/Electron Accelerator

Itamar Cohen [1,2,*], Yonatan Gershuni [1,2], Michal Elkind [1,2], Guy Azouz [1,2], Assaf Levanon [1,2] and Ishay Pomerantz [1,2]

[1] The School of Physics and Astronomy, Tel Aviv University, Tel-Aviv 69978, Israel; gershuni@mail.tau.ac.il (Y.G.); michalelkind@mail.tau.ac.il (M.E.); guyazouz@mail.tau.ac.il (G.A.); levanonster@gmail.com (A.L.); ipom@tauex.tau.ac.il (I.P.)

[2] Center for Light-Matter Interaction, Tel Aviv University, Tel-Aviv 69978, Israel

* Correspondence: Itamarcohen1@mail.tau.ac.il

Featured Application: We demonstrate in this letter a laser-based accelerator that switches between generating beams of either multi-MeV electrons or ions by a simple optical manipulation. We analyze its applicability in terms of energy, charge, divergence, and repeatability. The versatility of this accelerator may enable various applications in industry and research, which are presented in the paper.

Abstract: The versatility of laser accelerators in generating particle beams of various types is often promoted as a key applicative advantage. These multiple types of particles, however, are generated on vastly different irradiation setups, so that switching from one type to another involves substantial mechanical changes. In this letter, we report on a laser-based accelerator that generates beams of either multi-MeV electrons or ions from the same thin-foil irradiation setup. Switching from generation of ions to electrons is achieved by introducing an auxiliary laser pulse, which pre-explodes the foil tens of ns before irradiation by the main pulse. We present an experimental characterization of the emitted beams in terms of energy, charge, divergence, and repeatability, and conclude with several examples of prospective applications for industry and research.

Keywords: laser electron acceleration; laser proton acceleration; high-intensity lasers; non-destructive testing; elemental analysis

1. Introduction

The invention of chirped pulse amplification [1], for which the 2018 Nobel Prize in Physics was awarded, introduced the era of multi-petawatt lasers [2] and led to new regimes of light–matter interaction. The most striking feature of intense laser interaction with solid targets is the emission of a variety of intense radiation types [3], including electrons, ions, x-rays, and positrons. The relatively small scale of these lasers earned these machines the moniker "tabletop accelerators" and triggered research ranging from small portable machines [4] to large facilities [5] and accelerators at the energy frontier [6].

The relatively small size and cost of laser accelerators is often promoted as their main advantage [7]. Another appealing characteristic is their ability to transport the beam over optical mirrors for most of the way [8] and generate the particle beam close to the interaction point. Consequently, radiation shielding of laser accelerators is simpler than that of conventional accelerators with comparable energies [9].

The ultrashort nature of laser-accelerated particle bunches has also been deemed advantageous for applications [10] and research [11]. This capability is further reflected by the possibility of synchronizing the particle emission with another laser or particle pulse, with sub-ps temporal jitter [12,13].

The lion's share of laser-particle acceleration research focuses on acceleration of ions and electrons. One distinct experimental difference between these two types of research is that electron acceleration usually involves gaseous targets, whereas most ion acceleration experiments are conducted by irradiation of solids.

Laser acceleration of ions to MeV level energies was introduced more than 2 decades ago [14,15] with the target-normal sheath acceleration (TNSA) [16] mechanism. Higher laser intensities and improved pulse contrast promoted more robust acceleration mechanisms, such as the breakout afterburner [17], which rely on opaque plasma becoming relativistically transparent, and radiation pressure acceleration [18] in which electrons are compressed to a highly dense layer that in turn accelerates ions.

In all these experiments, the highest energy ions are generated from sub-μm-thick foil targets. Several methods for replenishing such targets at a high rate were devised in the form of, e.g., thin sheets of liquid ethylene glycol [19] or hydrogen, which solidify when injected into vacuum [20], or with automatically positioned [21] micro-machined foil targets [22].

Gas targets are naturally easier to refresh. High-energy ion beams resulting from collisionless shockwaves induced in nearly critical gas targets were demonstrated by either using long-wavelength laser pulses [23] or with very high-density gas [12,24–26]. Tailoring the plasma profile around a solid foil target to enhance the emission of TNSA ions was also recently investigated [27].

Gaseous targets are a common choice for laser generation of high-quality electron beams. For the past 2 decades, the laser wakefield community focused on optimizing the accelerated beam quality for higher particle energy [28], sharper energy spectrum [29], higher charge [30], and improved repeatability.

A few early works identified an electron acceleration technique from solid foil targets, referred to as "the exploding foil method (EXFM)" [31]. With EXFM, low-energy light preceding the main pulse turns the foil into an expanding plume of plasma. Owing to the expansion of the plasma, the electron density falls below the critical value and becomes transparent to the main pulse, which arrives tens of ns later. The main pulse forms self-guided laser wakefield structures [32], which generates ultra-collimated, multi-MeV beams of electrons [33].

Compared to modern wakefield electron acceleration schemes, EXFM seemed non-competitive on maximum energy and a peaked spectrum. Nevertheless, the laser-to-electron energy conversion efficiency of this scheme is unprecedented, making it ideal for generating a large number of photo-nuclear reactions [11,33].

In previous studies, foil targets were exploded by pre-pulses native to the laser system, which could not be manipulated. Here we present a first experimental study in which electron beams are generated with EXFM in an *engineered* manner, i.e., with an auxiliary controlled pre-pulse. The study was enabled by the pristine intrinsic contrast of our laser system presented in Figure 1. In this letter, we show how by the mere introduction of this pre-pulse (illustrated in red in Figure 1), our setup switches from generation of TNSA ions to generating EXFM electrons.

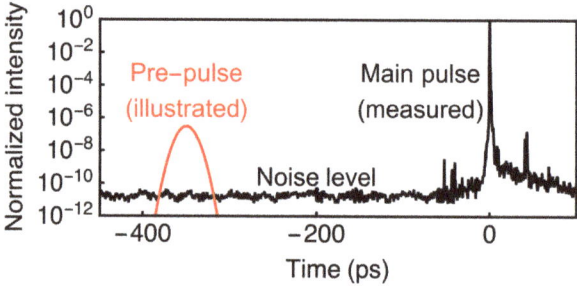

Figure 1. The temporal profile of the NePTUN laser system (black), measured with a Sequoia third-order auto-correlator [34]. The 10^{-10} background is the diagnostic noise level, forming a lower limit at t = −50 ps. The auxiliary pre-pulse is illustrated in red.

2. Experimental Setup

We performed the experiments using the NePTUN 20 TW laser system [35] at Tel Aviv University. A schematic drawing of the setup is shown Figure 2. Laser pulses of 29 fs at reduced energy of 140 mJ were focused using an f/2.5 off-axis parabolic mirror having an effective focal length of 12.7 cm unto 800 nm-thick Au foil targets. A measurement showed 70% of the laser energy to be contained within a circle of 4.1-μm diameter, which corresponds to an intensity of 1.2×10^{19} W/cm^2. The energy stability of the laser was measured to be 1.3% (RMS). The study relied on our automatic target system [21], which delivered the targets to the laser focus at a rate of 0.2 Hz.

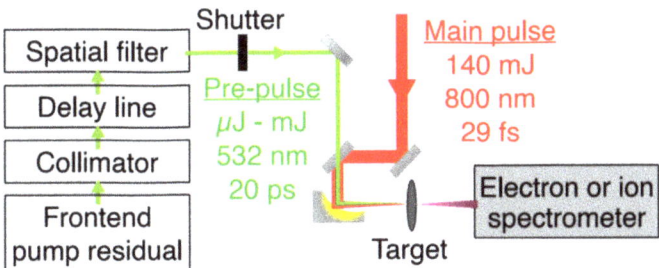

Figure 2. Schematic illustration of the irradiation setup. The main pulse (red) is focused using an off-axis parabolic mirror. The pre-pulse (green) is injected collinearly with the main pulse. Either a magnetic spectrometer or a Thomson parabola ion spectrometer is placed downstream to the generated beam.

We employ the residual energy from the frontend pump laser as the light source for the engineered pre-pulses. These λ = 532 nm, E = 30 μJ, τ = 20 ps laser pulses are optically synchronized with the main pulse. The optical period and pulse duration of these pre-pulses are much shorter than the plasma expansion time, so their exact values should not affect the plasma heating in a significant manner. Our measurements found that 70 percent of the pre-pulse energy was contained within a circle of 8.1 μm diameter, which corresponds to an intensity of 9.3×10^{11} W/cm^2. The energy stability of the pre-pulse was measured to be 1.5% (RMS). The temporal jitter between the pre- and main-pulses was measured be shorter than 20 ps. These properties correspond to a contrast ratio of 8×10^{-8} between the pre- and main-pulses. Before focusing, the pre-pulses are spatially filtered, collimated, and delayed in a variable delay line. A relative delay of 0–90 ns between the pre- and main pulses is achieved using our multi-plane "Cat's cradle" [36] delay line.

We measured the emitted electron and ion spectra for irradiation with or without auxiliary pre-pulses preceding the main pulse by 4 ns to 30 ns. Electrons were measured using a magnetic spectrometer with a field strength of 0.15 T and an angular acceptance of 0.12 msr. Ions were measured with a Thomson parabola ion spectrometer (TPIS) with a similar design to that of Morrison et al. [37], operating with an electrode voltage difference of 1 kV and having an angular acceptance of 0.10 msr. For both spectrometers, spectra were recorded by a charge-coupled device imaging a CsI(Tl) scintillator at the focal plane of the spectrometer. We obtained the absolute charge calibration of the electron spectrometer by acquiring the scintillation signal of a ^{90}Sr calibration beta emitter placed behind the scintillator, using the same imaging system.

3. Results

Recorded raw spectrograms are shown in Figure 3, for shots with and without a pre-pulse. The results feature two distinct modes of operation: for irradiation without a pre-pulse, the TPIS trace matches an ion beam with proton cut-off energy of more than 1 MeV, while a very low signal is recorded by the electron spectrometer. With pre-explosion at t = −22 ns, a beam of electrons with energies exceeding 3 MeV is recorded, and nearly no ions. The lack of TNSA ions indicates complete destruction of the target.

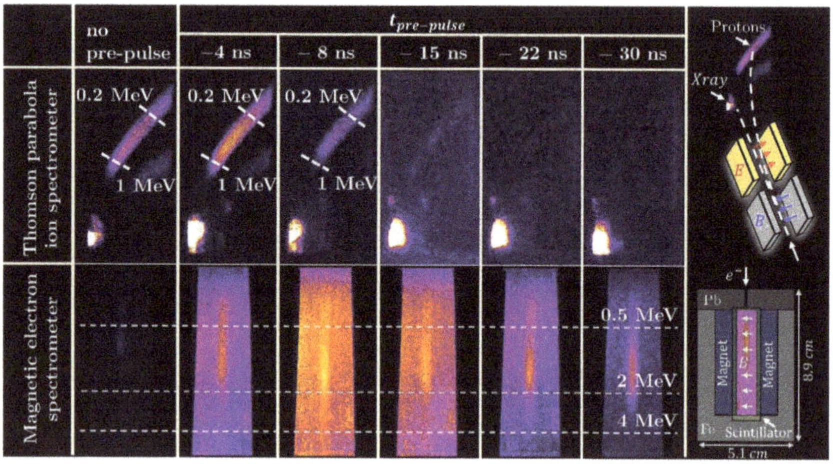

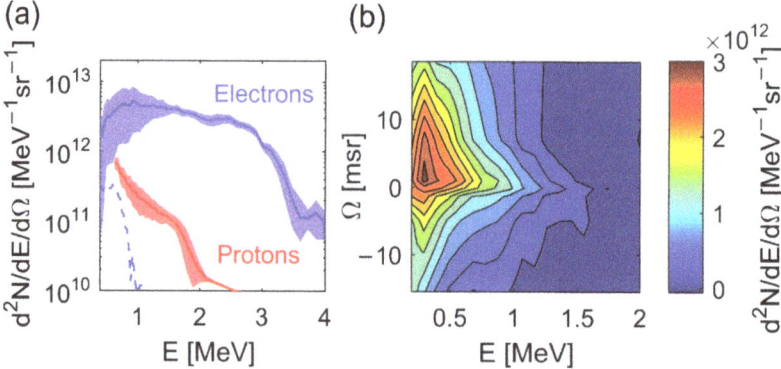

Figure 3. Raw ion (**top row**) and electron (**bottom row**) spectrograms obtained with different pre-pulse delays. The schematics of the two spectrometers are illustrated on the right.

The analyzed electron (blue) and proton (red) spectra are shown in Figure 4a. The electron spectra were recorded for shots with a relative delay of t = −22 ns. The shaded areas represent the standard deviation between 11 consecutive shots for the electrons and 14 consecutive shots for the protons. The electron spectrum recorded on a shot without a pre-pulse is shown in dashed blue. The total electron charge is more than an order of magnitude lower than the proton number and has a cutoff energy of about 1 MeV.

Figure 4. (**a**) Proton spectra from 14 consecutive shots without pre-pulse (red) and electron spectra from 11 consecutive shots with t = −22 ns pre-pulses (blue). The shaded area represents the standard deviation between shots. The recorded electron spectrum of a shot without a pre-pulse is shown in dashed blue. (**b**) Charge spatial-spectral distribution of the electron beam.

We measured the electron divergence by translating the electron spectrometer across the beam in 7 different positions. The result, presented in Figure 4b, features an average divergence of 10 msr.

4. Discussion

Several potential applications may benefit from this irradiation scheme. Energy-dispersive x-ray (EDX) [38] spectroscopy and particle-induced x-ray emission (PIXE) [39] are two powerful techniques for material analysis. They are widely used in the semiconductor industry [40,41] and in biomedical applications [42,43]. EDX reveals the elemental composition of solid samples, while PIXE resolves ~µm-deep stratigraphic structures. Both methods rely on measuring x-rays emitted from a sample, following its irradiation with particle beams in the keV-to-MeV energy range. Laser-driven EDX was recently demonstrated [44], using a mixed beam of laser-accelerated electrons and protons emitted from irradiated solid foils. Laser-driven PIXE was demonstrated on the same setup, by sweeping out the electrons with a magnetic field. Our acceleration scheme, which would amount to adding the controlled pre-pulse to this setup, can enable EDX with a 1000 times brighter beam of electrons in the MeV range (compare dashed to solid blue curves in Figure 4a). If necessary, removal of these excess electrons using magnetic deflection may be applied to this setup as well. Proton energies of over 3 MeV, which are the requirement for conducting PIXE, may be obtained using a 100 TW-class laser system.

Particle beams in the MeV energy range are also used for conducting non-destructive testing (NDT). Example applications include the investigation of trucks and cargo containers [45] for detecting the contraband of explosives [46], narcotics [47], and special nuclear materials [48]. The use of γ-rays has already reached commercial maturity [49], but the applicability of other beam types is limited by the titanic dimensions of conventional particle accelerators.

With shadowgraphy, the simplest form of NDT, information is revealed by the fraction of particles transmitted through the interrogated sample. Using multiple types of radiation may reveal details that are not obtained by each beam type by itself [50]. We illustrate this idea in Figure 5, which shows the simulated transmission of 10 MeV protons (left) and electrons (right) through a sample of 600 µm thick coaxial cylinders made of Al, W, and Cu.

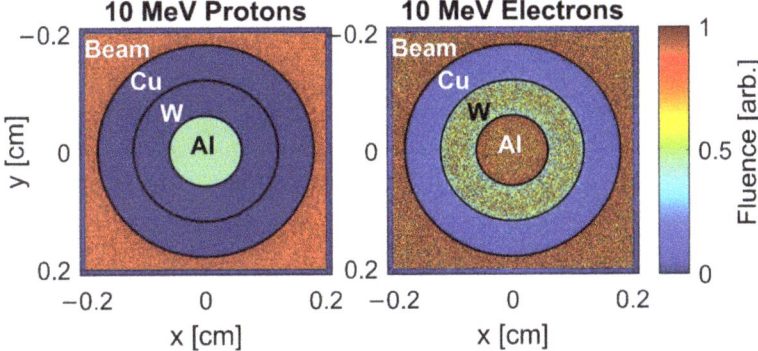

Figure 5. Particle transport simulation of the transmission of 10 MeV proton (**left**) and electron (**right**) beams passing through a sample of 600 µm thick Al, W, and Cu. The color scale is normalized to the beam fluence.

The simulation was conducted with the FLUKA particle transport simulation code [51]. Figure 5 shows that the Al casts a ~50% shadow on the proton beam, whereas the W and Cu shadows are absolute and indistinguishable. The electron beam, however, reveals a difference between the two heavier metals, but the Al is nearly 100% transparent.

For nuclear physics research, the ability to switch between beams of electrons and ions within >1 Hz may be applied to study $^AZ(p,x)$ reactions, on isotopes with O (1 s) lifetimes. A sample of long-lived ^{A+1}Z isotope, e.g., ^{56}Ni, may be irradiated with MeV electrons to induce the ^{56}Ni$(\gamma,n)^{55}$Ni reaction by bremsstrahlung. The resulting ^{55}Ni has a half-life of $T_{1/2}$ = 204 ms [52]. Measurements of the ^{55}Ni(p,γ) reaction, which is important for determining whether the rp-process bypasses the ^{56}Ni waiting point [53], may then be made in situ.

5. Conclusions

In this letter, we reported on the *applicable* aspects of a laser particle acceleration scheme, in which beams of either MeV electrons or ions are chosen by opening or closing an optical shutter. The plasma dynamics governing EXFM has rich dependence on the pre-pulse energy and delay, and on the target material and thickness. One aspect which is important for applications, is the scaling of the electron energy with higher laser intensities and the required pre-pulse parameters. On a Petawatt laser, for example, we generated electron beams with a temperature of 10.5 MeV by irradiating plastic target foils with laser energy of E = 90 J, pulse duration of 150 fs and an intrinsic pre-pulse energy of about 1 µJ preceding the main pulse by 60 ns [11]. An investigation of these aspects will be the subject of a future publication.

Author Contributions: Conceptualization, I.P.; methodology, I.C., Y.G. and M.E.; software, G.A.; validation, Y.G. and M.E.; formal analysis, I.C. and Y.G.; writing—original draft preparation, I.C.; writing—review and editing, I.P. and I.C.; supervision, I.P. and A.L.; project administration, A.L.; funding acquisition, I.P. All authors have read and agreed to the published version of the manuscript.

Funding: The study was supported by Israel Ministry of Energy grant no. 220-11-054 and by the Zuckerman STEM Leadership Program. I.C. acknowledges support by the Jabotinsky Fellowship of the Ministry of Science and Technology, Israel.

Data Availability Statement: The data that support the findings of this study are available from the corresponding author upon reasonable request.

Acknowledgments: We acknowledge aid in target fabrication from the Tel Aviv University Center for Nanoscience and Nanotechnology.

Conflicts of Interest: The authors declare no conflict of interest.

References

1. Strickland, D.; Mourou, G. Compression of amplified chirped optical pulses. *Opt. Commun.* **1985**, *56*, 219–221. [CrossRef]
2. Lureau, F.; Matras, G.; Chalus, O.; Derycke, C.; Morbieu, T.; Radier, C.; Casagrande, O.; Laux, S.; Ricaud, S.; Rey, G.; et al. High-energy hybrid femtosecond laser system demonstrating 2 × 10 PW capability. *High Power Laser Sci. Eng.* **2020**, *8*, 43. [CrossRef]
3. Daido, H.; Nishiuchi, M.; Pirozhkov, A.S. Review of laser-driven ion sources and their applications. *Rep. Prog. Phys.* **2012**, *75*, 56401. [CrossRef] [PubMed]
4. Wille, H.; Rodríguez, M.; Kasparian, J.; Mondelain, D.; Yu, J.; Mysyrowicz, A.; Sauerbrey, R.; Wolf, J.P.; Wöste, L. Teramobile: A mobile femtosecond-terawatt laser and detection system. *Eur. Phys. J. Appl. Phys.* **2002**, *20*, 183–190. [CrossRef]
5. Le Garrec, B.; Sebban, S.; Margarone, D.; Precek, M.; Weber, S.; Klimo, O.; Korn, G.; Rus, B. ELI-beamlines: Extreme light infrastructure science and technology with ultra-intense lasers. In Proceedings of the High Energy/Average Power Lasers and Intense Beam Applications VII, San Francisco, CA, USA, 2–4 February 2014; Davis, S.J., Heaven, M.C., Schriempf, J.T., Eds.; SPIE: Washington, DC, USA, 2014; Volume 8962, p. 89620.
6. Gschwendtner, E.; Adli, E.; Amorim, L.; Apsimon, R.; Assmann, R.; Bachmann, A.M.; Batsch, F.; Bauche, J.; Berglyd Olsen, V.K.; Bernardini, M.; et al. AWAKE, The Advanced Proton Driven Plasma Wakefield Acceleration Experiment at CERN. *Nucl. Instrum. Methods Phys. Res. Sect. A Accel. Spectrom. Detect. Assoc. Equip.* **2016**, *829*, 76–82. [CrossRef]
7. Martin, M. Laser accelerated radiotherapy: Is it on its way to the clinic? *J. Natl. Cancer Inst.* **2009**, *101*, 450–451. [CrossRef]
8. Ledingham, K.W.D.; Bolton, P.R.; Shikazono, N.; Ma, C.-M.C. Towards Laser Driven Hadron Cancer Radiotherapy: A Review of Progress. *Appl. Sci.* **2014**, *4*, 402–443. [CrossRef]
9. Fan, J.; Luo, W.; Fourkal, E.; Lin, T.; Li, J.; Veltchev, I.; Ma, C.-M. Shielding design for a laser-accelerated proton therapy system. *Phys. Med. Biol.* **2007**, *52*, 3913–3930. [CrossRef] [PubMed]
10. Bayart, E.; Flacco, A.; Delmas, O.; Pommarel, L.; Levy, D.; Cavallone, M.; Megnin-Chanet, F.; Deutsch, E.; Malka, V. Fast dose fractionation using ultra-short laser accelerated proton pulses can increase cancer cell mortality, which relies on functional PARP1 protein. *Sci. Rep.* **2019**, *9*. [CrossRef]
11. Pomerantz, I.; McCary, E.; Meadows, A.R.; Arefiev, A.; Bernstein, A.C.; Chester, C.; Cortez, J.; Donovan, M.E.; Dyer, G.; Gaul, E.W.; et al. Ultrashort Pulsed Neutron Source. *Phys. Rev. Lett.* **2014**, *113*, 184801. [CrossRef]
12. Chen, S.N.; Negoita, F.; Spohr, K.; d'Humières, E.; Pomerantz, I.; Fuchs, J. Extreme brightness laser-based neutron pulses as a pathway for investigating nucleosynthesis in the laboratory. *Matter Radiat. Extrem.* **2019**, *4*, 054402. [CrossRef]

13. Nakatsutsumi, M.; Appel, K.; Baehtz, C.; Chen, B.; Cowan, T.E.; Göde, S.; Konopkova, Z.; Pelka, A.; Priebe, G.; Schmidt, A.; et al. Femtosecond laser-generated high-energy-density states studied by x-ray FELs. *Plasma Phys. Control. Fusion* **2017**, *59*, 14028. [CrossRef]
14. Snavely, R.A.; Key, M.H.; Hatchett, S.P.; Cowan, T.E.; Roth, M.; Phillips, T.W.; Stoyer, M.A.; Henry, E.A.; Sangster, T.C.; Singh, M.S. Intense high-energy proton beams from petawatt-laser irradiation of solids. *Phys. Rev. Lett.* **2000**, *85*, 2945. [CrossRef]
15. Hatchett, S.P.; Brown, C.G.; Cowan, T.E.; Henry, E.A.; Johnson, J.S.; Key, M.H.; Koch, J.A.; Langdon, A.B.; Lasinski, B.F.; Lee, R.W. Electron, photon, and ion beams from the relativistic interaction of Petawatt laser pulses with solid targets. *Phys. Plasmas* **2000**, *7*, 2076. [CrossRef]
16. Roth, M.; Schollmeier, M. Ion Acceleration: TNSA. In *Laser-Plasma Interactions and Applications*; Springer: Heidelberg, Germany, 2013; pp. 303–350.
17. Hegelich, B.M.; Pomerantz, I.; Yin, L.; Wu, H.C.; Jung, D.; Albright, B.J.; Gautier, D.C.; Letzring, S.; Palaniyappan, S.; Shah, R.; et al. Laser-driven ion acceleration from relativistically transparent nanotargets. *New J. Phys.* **2013**, *15*, 85015. [CrossRef]
18. Henig, A.; Steinke, S.; Schnürer, M.; Sokollik, T.; Hörlein, R.; Kiefer, D.; Jung, D.; Schreiber, J.; Hegelich, B.M.; Yan, X.Q.; et al. Radiation-Pressure Acceleration of Ion Beams Driven by Circularly Polarized Laser Pulses. *Phys. Rev. Lett.* **2009**, *103*, 245003. [CrossRef] [PubMed]
19. Morrison, J.T.; Feister, S.; Frische, K.D.; Austin, D.R.; Ngirmang, G.K.; Murphy, N.R.; Orban, C.; Chowdhury, E.A.; Roquemore, W.M. MeV proton acceleration at kHz repetition rate from ultra-intense laser liquid interaction. *New J. Phys.* **2018**, *20*, 22001. [CrossRef]
20. Gauthier, M.; Curry, C.B.; Göde, S.; Brack, F.E.; Kim, J.B.; MacDonald, M.J.; Metzkes, J.; Obst, L.; Rehwald, M.; Rödel, C.; et al. High repetition rate, multi-MeV proton source from cryogenic hydrogen jets. *Appl. Phys. Lett.* **2017**, *111*, 114102. [CrossRef]
21. Gershuni, Y.; Roitman, D.; Cohen, I.; Porat, E.; Danan, Y.; Elkind, M.; Levanon, A.; Louzon, R.; Reichenberg, D.; Tsabary, A.; et al. A gatling-gun target delivery system for high-intensity laser irradiation experiments. *Nucl. Instrum. Methods Phys. Res. Sect. A Accel. Spectrom. Detect. Assoc. Equip.* **2019**, *934*, 58–62. [CrossRef]
22. Gershuni, Y.; Elkind, M.; Cohen, I.; Tsabary, A.; Sarkar, D.; Pomerantz, I. Automated Delivery of Microfabricated Targets for Intense Laser Irradiation Experiments. *J. Vis. Exp.* **2021**, e61056. [CrossRef]
23. Haberberger, D.; Tochitsky, S.; Fiuza, F.; Gong, C.; Fonseca, R.A.; Silva, L.O.; Mori, W.B.; Joshi, C. Collisionless shocks in laser-produced plasma generate monoenergetic high-energy proton beams. *Nat. Phys.* **2012**, *8*, 95–99. [CrossRef]
24. Puyuelo-Valdes, P.; Henares, J.L.; Hannachi, F.; Ceccotti, T.; Domange, J.; Ehret, M.; D'humieres, E.; Lancia, L.; Marquès, J.-R.; Ribeyre, X.; et al. Proton acceleration by collisionless shocks using a supersonic H 2 gas-jet target and high-power infrared laser pulses articles you may be interested in Proton acceleration by collisionless shocks using a supersonic H 2 gas-jet target and high-power infra. *Phys. Plasmas* **2019**, *26*, 123109. [CrossRef]
25. Sylla, F.; Flacco, A.; Kahaly, S.; Veltcheva, M.; Lifschitz, A.; Malka, V.; D'Humières, E.; Andriyash, I.; Tikhonchuk, V. Short intense laser pulse collapse in near-critical plasma. *Phys. Rev. Lett.* **2013**, *110*. [CrossRef]
26. Henares, J.L.; Puyuelo-Valdes, P.; Hannachi, F.; Ceccotti, T.; Ehret, M.; Gobet, F.; Lancia, L.; Marquès, J.R.; Santos, J.J.; Versteegen, M.; et al. Development of gas jet targets for laser-plasma experiments at near-critical density. *Rev. Sci. Instrum.* **2019**, *90*. [CrossRef]
27. Levy, D.; Bernert, C.; Rehwald, M.; Andriyash, I.A.; Assenbaum, S.; Kluge, T.; Kroupp, E.; Obst-Huebl, L.; Pausch, R.; Schulze-Makuch, A.; et al. Laser-plasma proton acceleration with a combined gas-foil target. *New J. Phys.* **2020**, *22*, 103068. [CrossRef]
28. Leemans, W.P.; Gonsalves, A.J.; Mao, H.S.; Nakamura, K.; Benedetti, C.; Schroeder, C.B.; Toth, C.; Daniels, J.; Mittelberger, D.E.; Bulanov, S.S.; et al. Multi-GeV Electron Beams from Capillary-Discharge-Guided Subpetawatt Laser Pulses in the Self-Trapping Regime. *Phys. Rev. Lett.* **2014**, *113*, 245002. [CrossRef] [PubMed]
29. Faure, J.; Rechatin, C.; Norlin, A.; Lifschitz, A.; Glinec, Y.; Malka, V. Controlled injection and acceleration of electrons in plasma wakefields by colliding laser pulses. *Nature* **2006**, *444*, 737–739. [CrossRef] [PubMed]
30. Cecchetti, C.A.; Betti, S.; Gamucci, A.; Giulietti, A.; Giulietti, D.; Koester, P.; Labate, L.; Patak, N.; Vittori, F.; Ciricosta, O.; et al. High-charge, multi-MeV electron bunches accelerated in moderate laser-plasma interaction regime. In *AIP Conference Proceedings*; AIP Publishing LLC: New York, NY, USA, 2010; Volume 1209, pp. 19–22. [CrossRef]
31. Giulietti, D.; Galimberti, M.; Giulietti, A.; Gizzi, L.; Borghesi, M.; Balcou, P.; Rousse, A.; Rousseau, J. High-energy electron beam production by femtosecond laser interactions with exploding-foil plasmas. *Phys. Rev. E* **2001**, *64*, 15402. [CrossRef]
32. Kneip, S.; Nagel, S.R.; Martins, S.F.; Mangles, S.P.D.; Bellei, C.; Chekhlov, O.; Clarke, R.J.; Delerue, N.; Divall, E.J.; Doucas, G.; et al. Near-GeV acceleration of electrons by a nonlinear plasma wave driven by a self-guided laser pulse. *Phys. Rev. Lett.* **2009**, *103*, 035002. [CrossRef]
33. Giulietti, D.; Galimberti, M.; Giulietti, A.; Gizzi, L.A.; Numico, R.; Tomassini, P.; Borghesi, M.; Malka, V.; Fritzler, S.; Pittman, M.; et al. Production of ultracollimated bunches of multi-MeV electrons by 35 fs laser pulses propagating in exploding-foil plasmas. *Phys. Plasmas* **2002**, *9*, 3655. [CrossRef]
34. Sequoia HD, Amplitude Tech. Available online: https://amplitude-technologies.pagesperso-orange.fr/sequoia.htm (accessed on 7 June 2021).
35. Porat, E.; Levanon, A.; Roitman, D.; Cohen, I.; Louzon, R.; Pomerantz, I. Towards direct-laser-production of relativistic surface harmonics. In *Relativistic Plasma Waves and Particle Beams as Coherent and Incoherent Radiation Sources III*; SPIE: Prague, Czech Republic, 2019; p. 17.

36. Cohen, I.; Levanon, A.; Roitman, D.; Shohat, D.; Urisman, E.; Pomerantz, I. Cat's cradle: A compact, 3D mounted, 90-ns optical delay-line for laser-electron acceleration. *Laser Accel. Electrons Protons Ions V* **2019**, *11037*, 38. [CrossRef]
37. Morrison, J.T.; Willis, C.; Freeman, R.R.; van Woerkom, L. Design of and data reduction from compact Thomson parabola spectrometers. *Rev. Sci. Instrum.* **2011**, *82*, 33506. [CrossRef] [PubMed]
38. Bell, D.; Garratt-Reed, A. Energy Dispersive X-ray Analysis in the Electron Microscope. Garland Science: New York, NY, USA, 2003.
39. Gonsior, B. Chapter 3 Particle Induced X-Ray Emission (PIXE). In *Techniques and Instrumentation in Analytical Chemistry*; Elsevier: Amsterdam, The Netherlands, 1988; Volume 8, pp. 123–179.
40. Karydas, A.G.; Streeck, C.; Bogdanovic Radovic, I.; Kaufmann, C.; Rissom, T.; Beckhoff, B.; Jaksic, M.; Barradas, N.P. Ion beam analysis of Cu(In,Ga)Se 2 thin film solar cells. *Appl. Surf. Sci.* **2015**, *356*, 631–638. [CrossRef]
41. Nam, D.; Opanasyuk, A.S.; Koval, P.V.; Ponomarev, A.G.; Jeong, A.R.; Kim, G.Y.; Jo, W.; Cheong, H. Composition variations in Cu2ZnSnSe4 thin films analyzed by X-ray diffraction, energy dispersive X-ray spectroscopy, particle induced X-ray emission, photoluminescence, and Raman spectroscopy. *Thin Solid Films* **2014**. [CrossRef]
42. Wyroba, E.; Suski, S.; Miller, K.; Bartosiewicz, R. Biomedical and agricultural applications of energy dispersive X-ray spectroscopy in electron microscopy. *Cell. Mol. Biol. Lett.* **2015**, *20*, 488–509. [CrossRef]
43. Sharmila, P.P.; Tharayil, N.J. DNA Assisted Synthesis, Characterization and Optical Properties of Zinc Oxide Nanoparticles. *Int. J. Mater. Sci. Eng.* **2014**. [CrossRef]
44. Mirani, F.; Maffini, A.; Casamichiela, F.; Pazzaglia, A.; Formenti, A.; Dellasega, D.; Russo, V.; Vavassori, D.; Bortot, D.; Huault, M.; et al. Integrated quantitative PIXE analysis and EDX spectroscopy using a laser-driven particle source. *Sci. Adv.* **2021**, *7*. [CrossRef]
45. Runkle, R.C.; White, T.A.; Miller, E.A.; Caggiano, J.A.; Collins, B.A. Photon and neutron interrogation techniques for chemical explosives detection in air cargo: A critical review. *Nucl. Instrum. Methods Phys. Res. Sect. A Accel. Spectrom. Detect. Assoc. Equip.* **2009**, *603*, 510–528. [CrossRef]
46. Overley, J.C.; Chmelik, M.S.; Rasmussen, R.J.; Schofield, R.M.S.; Lefevre, H.W. Explosives detection through fast-neutron time-of-flight attenuation measurements. *Nucl. Instrum. Methods Phys. Res. Sect. B Beam Interact. Mater. Atoms* **1995**, *99*, 728–732. [CrossRef]
47. Fink, C.L.; Micklich, B.J.; Yule, T.J.; Humm, P.; Sagalovsky, L.; Martin, M.M. Evaluation of neutron techniques for illicit substance detection. *Nucl. Instrum. Methods Phys. Res. Sect. B Beam Interact. Mater. Atoms* **1995**, *99*, 748–752. [CrossRef]
48. Rynes, J.; Bendahan, J.; Gozani, T.; Loveman, R.; Stevenson, J.; Bell, C. Gamma-ray and neutron radiography as part of a pulsed fast neutron analysis inspection system. *Nucl. Instrum. Methods Phys. Res. Sect. A Accel. Spectrom. Detect. Assoc. Equip.* **1999**, *422*, 895–899. [CrossRef]
49. Rapiscan Systems. Available online: https://www.rapiscansystems.com/en/products/cvi (accessed on 7 June 2021).
50. Eberhardt, J.E.; Rainey, S.; Stevens, R.J.; Sowerby, B.D.; Tickner, J.R. Fast neutron radiography scanner for the detection of contraband in air cargo containers. *Appl. Radiat. Isot.* **2005**, *63*, 179–188. [CrossRef] [PubMed]
51. Battistoni, G.; Muraro, S.; Sala, P.R.; Cerutti, F.; Ferrari, A. Others The FLUKA code: Description and benchmarking. In *AIP Conference Proceedings*; AIP Publishing LLC: New York, NY, USA, 2007; AIP Publishing LLC: New York, NY, USA, 2007; Volume 896, pp. 31–49.
52. Reusen, I.; Andreyev, A.; Andrzejewski, J.; Bijnens, N.; Franchoo, S.; Huyse, M.; Kudryavtsev, Y.; Kruglov, K.; Mueller, W.F.; Piechaczek, A.; et al. β-decay study of [54,55] Ni produced by an element-selective laser ion source. *Phys. Rev. C Nucl. Phys.* **1999**, *59*, 2416–2421. [CrossRef]
53. Ong, W.J.; Langer, C.; Montes, F.; Aprahamian, A.; Bardayan, D.W.; Bazin, D.; Brown, B.A.; Browne, J.; Crawford, H.; Cyburt, R.; et al. Low-lying level structure of Cu 56 and its implications for the rp process. *Phys. Rev. C* **2017**, *95*, 055806. [CrossRef]

Review

Multi-GeV Laser Wakefield Electron Acceleration with PW Lasers

Hyung Taek Kim [1,*], Vishwa Bandhu Pathak [2], Calin Ioan Hojbota [2], Mohammad Mirzaie [2], Ki Hong Pae [1,2], Chul Min Kim [1,2], Jin Woo Yoon [1,2], Jae Hee Sung [1,2] and Seong Ku Lee [1,2]

[1] Advanced Photonics Research Institute, Gwangju Institute of Science and Technology (GIST), Gwangju 61005, Korea; khpae1@gist.ac.kr (K.H.P.); chulmin@gist.ac.kr (C.M.K.); yoonjw@gist.ac.kr (J.W.Y.); sungjh@gist.ac.kr (J.H.S.); lsk@gist.ac.kr (S.K.L.)

[2] Center for Relativistic Laser Science, Institute for Basic Science (IBS), Gwangju 61005, Korea; vishwabandhu@ibs.re.kr (V.B.P.); calinh@ibs.re.kr (C.I.H.); mirzaie@ibs.re.kr (M.M.)

* Correspondence: htkim@gist.ac.kr

Featured Application: Compact electron accelerators, Compact synchrotron source, Radiography.

Abstract: Laser wakefield electron acceleration (LWFA) is an emerging technology for the next generation of electron accelerators. As intense laser technology has rapidly developed, LWFA has overcome its limitations and has proven its possibilities to facilitate compact high-energy electron beams. Since high-power lasers reach peak power beyond petawatts (PW), LWFA has a new chance to explore the multi-GeV energy regime. In this article, we review the recent development of multi-GeV electron acceleration with PW lasers and discuss the limitations and perspectives of the LWFA with high-power lasers.

Keywords: petawatt laser; laser plasma; laser wakefield acceleration; compact electron accelerator; GeV electron beam

1. Introduction

Laser wakefield acceleration (LWFA) has attracted much attention since it was proposed in 1979 by T. Tajima and J. Dawson [1] due to its possibility to provide a huge acceleration field for electron acceleration. Thus, LWFA can realize table-top high-energy electron accelerators and be the next generation of electron accelerators with extremely high energy over 100 GeV. However, the proposal was pending for a long time because it required too high a performance for the high-power lasers at the time. As the chirped pulse amplification (CPA) technology [2] initiated the rapid progress of high-power lasers in the 1990s, the short-pulse high-power lasers led to the realization of laser electron accelerations [3–5], albeit the quality of the electron beam was not good enough for applications. In 2004, a milestone was laid in LWFA research: a mono-energetic collimated electron beam was achieved in the bubble regime by using an intense femtosecond laser [6–8]. Since then, LWFA has been intensively investigated with high-power femtosecond lasers to provide high-quality electron beams and radiation sources [9] for practical applications to non-destructive inspections, ultrafast x-ray spectroscopy, and x-ray microscopy.

Even though LWFA can provide a huge acceleration field, some scientific and technological problems need to be solved for practical applications. First of all, LWFA uses complex nonlinear dynamics of plasma media [10], and its acceleration structure has the dimensions of tens of microns in space and hundreds of femtoseconds in time. Secondly, an intense laser pulse is modified significantly during the propagation through the plasma medium, and the modification of the laser pulse alters the plasma medium and acceleration process as a feedback loop. In addition, the electron injection into the plasma wave

spontaneously happens in the plasma, which is called self-injection. Therefore, the whole acceleration process is highly nonlinear and unstable, limiting the electron energy [11,12], beam quality and stability [13,14]. Many studies are ongoing to solve these problems to improve the performance of LWFA.

The advancement of high-power laser technology is essential for the enhancement of LWFA performance. Enormous efforts have been exerted to increase the laser's peak power and they consequently succeeded in building petawatt (PW) lasers [15]. The development of PW lasers provided a chance to explore a new regime of laser particle accelerations and relativistic laser–plasma interactions. In the last decade, several types of PW lasers have been used in LWFA experiments. A PW laser was demonstrated in Texas university, Austin, by adapting the CPA to an Nd:Glass laser [16]. This hybrid laser had a very low repetition rate, below one shot/hour. The most successful demonstration of PW lasers was based on Ti:Sapphire CPA lasers. These lasers can provide laser energy over 30 J, pulse duration of about 30 fs, and a repetition rate of over 0.1 shot/second [17]. Ti:Sapphire lasers with peak power over PW have been commercialized and installed in several research institutes for relativistic laser–plasma science. As the laser power increases, the achievable electron energy by LWFA has increased by more than an order of magnitude, compared to the first demonstration of the bubble-regime LWFA in 2004. Recently, multi-GeV electron beams were obtained with a centimeter-long medium [11,18,19]; the conventional radio-frequency (RF) acceleration technology requires a few hundred meters for such beams. In addition, many applications of LWFA or radiation sources from LWFA have been demonstrated in the last decade. Therefore, LWFA has the potential for compact linear accelerators and x-ray sources as the next generation of electron accelerators.

In this paper, we review several exemplary experiments on LWFA with PW lasers. The large-scale laser facilities are installing or recently installed multi-PW lasers, e.g., the three pillars of extreme light infrastructures (ELI) [20], the Zetawatt-Equivalent Ultrashort Pulse Laser System (ZEUS) [21], the Exawatt Center for Extreme Light Studies (XCELS) [22], the Shanghai Superintense Ultrafast Laser Facility (SULF) [23], the Apollon laser [24], and the Center for Relativistic Laser Science (CoReLS) [25]. Thus, this review on the prominent experimental results on LWFA with PW lasers can be a valuable guide for the LWFA with the emerging high-power lasers.

This article is organized into five sections, as follows. We explain the fundamental physics of the LWFA process briefly in Section 2 and address the representative experimental results on multi-GeV LWFA with PW lasers in Section 3. We discuss the perspective of LWFA with PW lasers in Section 4, then we conclude.

2. Basic Physics of LWFA

In this section, we will describe the basic physical process and energy scalings of LWFA. LWFA can be realized by focusing a high-power laser pulse at a relativistic intensity above 10^{18} W/cm^2 onto a gaseous medium, as shown in Figure 1. When such an intense laser pulse interacts with a gaseous medium, the atoms in the medium are ionized at the rising edge of the pulse to turn into an underdense plasma. Thus, the main peak of the laser pulse interacts with an underdense plasma. At the laser intensity in the relativistic regime, where the normalized vector potential $a_0 > 1$, electrons in the plasma acquire a relativistic quiver velocity in the laser field. The normalized vector potential a_0 is defined as $eE_0/(m_e c \omega_0)$, where E_0, ω_0, e, m_e, and c is the laser electric field amplitude, the laser angular frequency, the electron charge, the electron rest mass, and the speed of light, respectively. When a_0 is comparable to or larger than unity, the maximum quiver velocity of a classically oscillating electron in the laser field is close to the speed of light. As the intense laser pulse interacts with the plasma, the electrons are pushed away from the laser propagation axis by ponderomotive force originated from the laser-intensity gradient of a tightly focused laser pulse. Because the electrons are expelled from the laser axis, leaving much heavier ions behind, an extremely high electrostatic field is induced by the charge separation, which acts as a restoring force for the displaced electrons. As the electrons are expelled and return to the laser axis repeatedly, periodic modulations of electron density following the laser pulse, known as a plasma wave or Langmuir wave, are created [10], as shown in Figure 1. The shape of the plasma wave can be a spherical shell [26,27], called a plasma bubble, when the a_0 is sufficiently higher than 1, and the pulse duration is shorter than half the plasma period. If an electron bunch happens to roll into the bubble by self-injection, the bunch can be rapidly accelerated in the laser propagation direction by the enormous electric field in the bubble: this field is usually stronger by three orders of magnitude than that of the conventional RF linear accelerators. As a comparison, while the current state-of-the-art linac can be driven by S-band RF having 0.1 GV/m [28], the electric field gradients from LWFA can reach as high as 200 GeV/m with a centimeter-scale plasma medium having an electron density of about 10^{18} electrons/cm^3 driven by PW laser pulses.

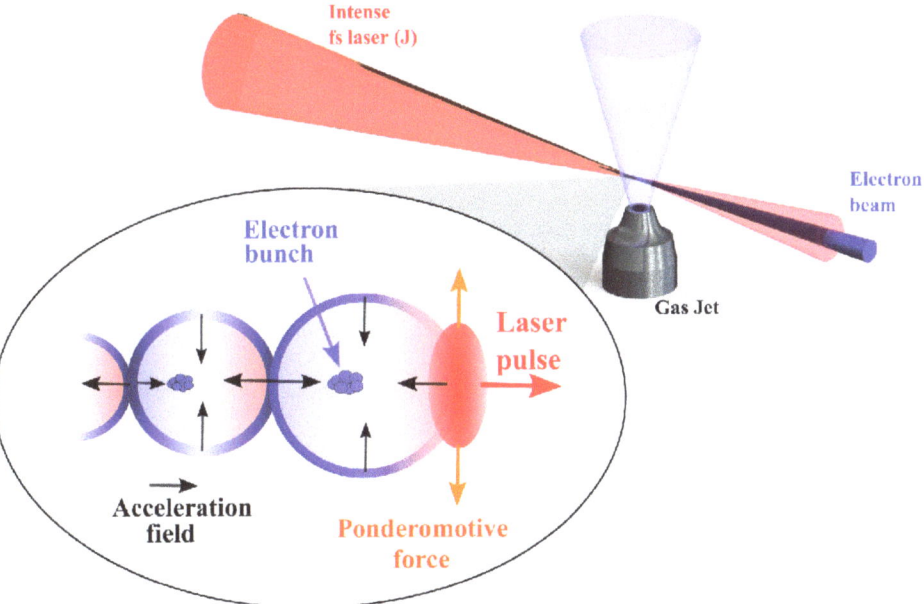

Figure 1. Schematic of LWFA process.

One of the most critical issues in LWFA is to enhance the electron energy for given laser parameters. The electron energy is limited by the effective acceleration length and the average acceleration field strength. The effective acceleration length is determined either by the laser etching (depletion) length $L_{etch} \approx (\omega_0/\omega_p)^2 c\tau_L$ or by the dephasing length $L_d = (4/3)\left(\omega_0^2/\omega_p^2\right)\sqrt{a_0}c/\omega_p$, where τ_L is the laser pulse duration, and $\omega_p = \sqrt{4\pi n_0 e^2/m_e}$ is the plasma frequency with n_0 being the plasma density. The etching length (or depletion length) denotes the distance limit of laser propagation by the loss of laser energy in plasma media. The dephasing length is the maximum acceleration length for electrons to overtake the accelerating phase of the wakefield. For a non-evolving plasma-bubble in the blowout regime, the average acceleration field strength approximately corresponds to $\sqrt{a_0}/2$ when the dephasing length is larger than the etching length, and a_0 is sufficiently larger than 1. Therefore, the achievable energy gain in LWFA for given laser power and plasma density can be given as [29]

$$\triangle E[\text{GeV}] \approx 1.7 \left(\frac{P_L[\text{TW}]}{100}\right)^{\frac{1}{3}} \left(\frac{10^{18}}{n_0[\text{cm}^{-3}]}\right)^{\frac{2}{3}} \left(\frac{0.8}{\lambda_0[\mu m]}\right)^{\frac{4}{3}} \tag{1}$$

where P_L is the peak laser power in terawatt (TW). Thus, the electron energy can be enhanced by increasing the laser power and decreasing the plasma density. However, the self-injection of electron bunches into the bubble can be prohibited when the plasma density is low, and thus, the achievable electron energy is limited at low plasma densities. In addition, the defects of the laser pulse and plasma medium can terminate the acceleration process through nonlinear processes, which are usually stronger at a higher laser power. Therefore, enhancing the electron energy by controlling laser power and plasma density is not a straightforward task.

3. Multi-GeV LWFA with PW-Class Lasers

In this section, we review several exemplary experimental results on the energy enhancement of LWFA with PW lasers. Since high-quality electron beams have been produced in the bubble or blowout regime, significant efforts have been focused on increasing the energy of the electron beam. As PW lasers are developed, the energy of the laser-driven electron beam dramatically increased to a multi-GeV regime, as shown in this section.

3.1. LWFA with Texas PW Laser

The PW laser at the University of Texas at Austin was developed by implementing the hybrid OPCPA scheme with Nd:glass laser amplifiers and had a pulse duration of 140 fs and pulse energy of 140 J [16]. The laser has been used for various laser–plasma experiments such as electron acceleration, ion acceleration, and neutron generation. Especially, the electron energy of 2 GeV was successfully demonstrated [11]. The experiment was performed by focusing the PW laser pulses with a spherical mirror having an f-number of 47 onto a 7-cm-long helium gas cell. The accelerated electron beam was dispersed by a 6.7-cm-long dipole magnet having a field strength of 1.1 T. Fiducial arrays made of tungsten wires were inserted between the magnet and the detection screens to measure the electron energy correctly. The beam cross-section at the focus was not optimal: the intensity profile was asymmetric and had several spots.

The experimental results showed that the PW laser pulses produced electron beams with energy over 2 GeV, as shown in Table 1. According to the energy formula (1), the electron energy of 2 GeV is expected for the PW laser's power and a plasma density of 5×10^{17} electrons/cm^{-3}. The electron energy was lower at lower plasma densities, which is opposite to the prediction from (1). This behavior can be attributed to the poor focal spot. A low-quality focal spot with internal structures may be beneficial to induce self-injection in such a low-density plasma but deteriorates the laser propagation and electron acceleration. It was pointed out that the spatial shaping of the PW laser pulse is necessary to enhance the electron energy.

3.2. Dual-Stage LWFA with PW Laser at UQBF

In this section, we review the dual-stage LWFA with the PW lasers at the Ultrashort Quantum Beam Facility (UQBF), Advanced Photonics Research Institute (APRI), GIST. The APRI group successfully constructed two PW beamlines in 2012 by using the CPA scheme and Ti:Sapphire amplification media. The first beamline produced energy of 30 J and a pulse duration of 30 fs [17], and the second beamline did 45 J [30] and the same pulse duration. The PW laser at UQBF was used for LWFA experiments to produce multi-GeV electron beams. As discussed in Section 2, the achievable electron energy can be increased by increasing the laser power and lowering plasma density. However, the self-injection of electron bunches into plasma waves can be prohibited by reducing the plasma density. Thus, the plasma medium density and profile should be carefully designed to maximize the electron energy: the acceleration length should be maximized while keeping self-injection occurring. One solution can be to combine gas media of different lengths and densities called dual-stage or cascaded acceleration.

The dual-stage LWFA experiments were performed by focusing the PW laser onto a dual gas jet medium consisting of 4-mm and 10-mm helium gas jets [18]. The first 4-mm helium jet acted as an injector stage, and the second 10-mm jet boosted electron energy. Laser pulses with an energy of 25 J were focused with a 4-m long concave spherical mirror, as shown in Figure 2a. The wavefront aberration of the laser pulse was corrected using a deformable mirror installed before the compressor. The laser pulse was stretched to 60 fs with a positive chirp by detuning the compressor grating.

Table 1. Experimental results for three different laser shots from the Texas PW laser [11]. Reproduced with permission from [Xiaoming Wang], [*Nat. Commun*]; published by [macmillan Publishers Limited], [2013].

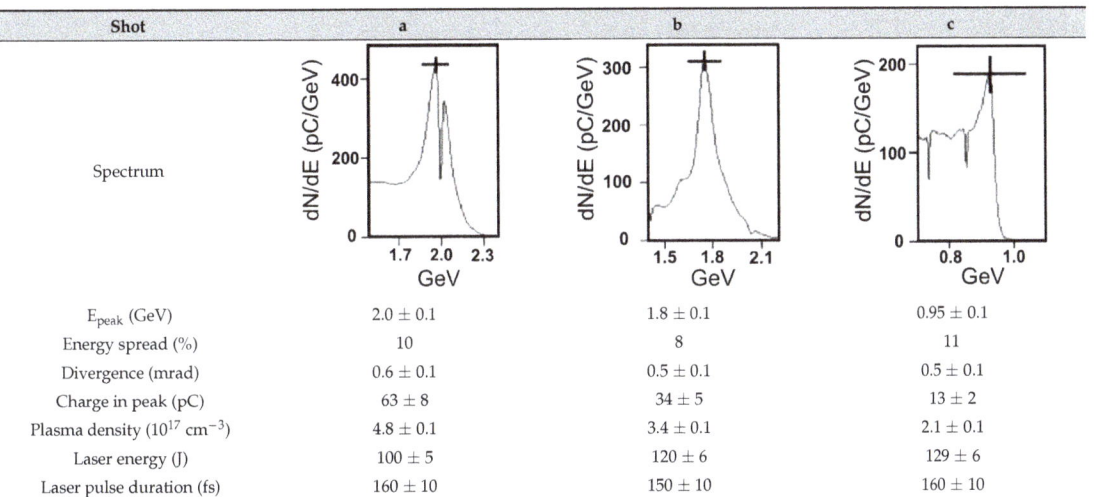

Shot	a	b	c
Spectrum			
E_{peak} (GeV)	2.0 ± 0.1	1.8 ± 0.1	0.95 ± 0.1
Energy spread (%)	10	8	11
Divergence (mrad)	0.6 ± 0.1	0.5 ± 0.1	0.5 ± 0.1
Charge in peak (pC)	63 ± 8	34 ± 5	13 ± 2
Plasma density (10^{17} cm^{-3})	4.8 ± 0.1	3.4 ± 0.1	2.1 ± 0.1
Laser energy (J)	100 ± 5	120 ± 6	129 ± 6
Laser pulse duration (fs)	160 ± 10	150 ± 10	160 ± 10

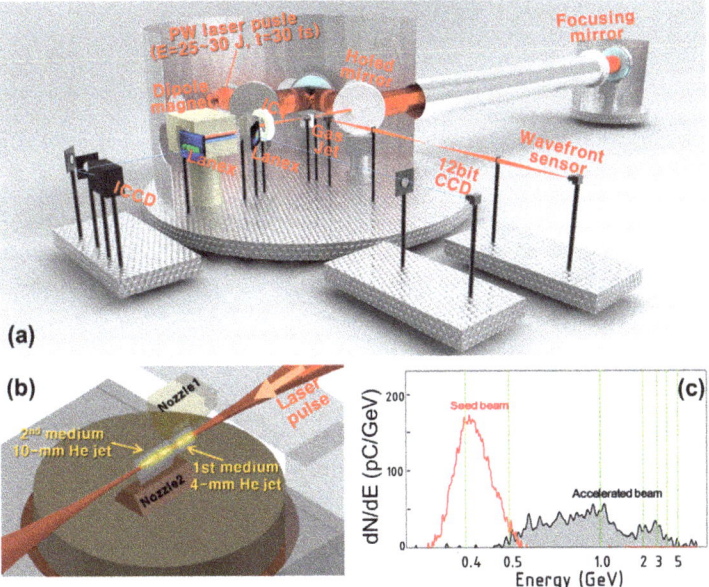

Figure 2. (**a**) Experimental layout for dual-stage LWFA with a PW laser pulse, (**b**) schematic drawing of the dual-stage target, and (**c**) the experimental result with the dual-stage target [18]. In figure (**c**), the red line shows the electron spectrum from the first target, and the black line shows the spectrum after the second target.

In the dual-stage LWFA, several issues should be properly treated to obtain a high-energy electron beam. Firstly, a self-injection should happen in the first medium, and the resulting electron bunch should have sufficient energy when entering the plasma wave in the second medium. Secondly, the electron beam and driving laser pulses should be properly coupled into the second medium. Thirdly, the electron beam should be accelerated in the second medium without an additional electron injection. The first 4-mm helium gas jet was optimized to obtain a 400 MeV electron beam by tuning the gas pressure to have an electron density of 2×10^{18} electrons/cm^3. No electron beam signal was observed when the second jet was used alone with densities below 1×10^{18} electrons/cm^3. A significant enhancement of electron energy was observed with the dual gas jet target having electron densities of 2×10^{18} electrons/cm^3 for the 4-mm jet and 0.8×10^{18} electrons/cm^3 for the 10-mm jet. The gap between the two jets was about 2 mm, and the laser focus was at the middle of the gap. At this condition, the electron bunch from the first jet could be successfully coupled to the second target because the low plasma density in the second jet enlarged the plasma wavelength to have a higher chance to catch the electron bunch from the first target. In addition, the second target having a lower density than the self-injection threshold can prohibit continuous self-injection that can reduce the acceleration field strength. When the plasma densities of the two jets were independently controlled, the electron energy was over 3 GeV. At this condition, the electron beam has a charge of about 10 pC over 2 GeV energy, energy spread about 50%, and beam divergence of about 4 mrad.

The dual-stage acceleration can be a simple solution to obtain a high-energy electron beam. Recently, a dual-stage acceleration with two driving laser pulses was demonstrated by using capillary discharge media [31]. Even though we can expect an energy gain at each stage in a staged acceleration, precise control of each stage for stability is challenging. In the dual gas jet target, the turbulence between the targets can also make the electron beam unstable. Thus, the method to handle the qualities of the accelerated electron beam should be investigated by manipulating the driving laser pulse and plasma medium. In addition, the electron energy with dual-stage LWFA was still much less than the 10 GeV that is expected for PW lasers because the laser propagation is limited to be an order of 1 cm. For increasing the electron energy further, an external guiding structure for PW laser pulses should be applied to keep the laser intensity over 10 cm.

In the dual-stage acceleration, the PW laser pulse was stretched to be positively chirped with a duration of 60 fs. It was stretched to control the acceleration gradient of LWFA by manipulating the pulse's spectral phase [32]; such a control method was demonstrated experimentally at UQBF [13,33]. In particular, positive group-delay dispersion (GDD) enhanced the energy and charge of the electron beam, and third-order dispersion (TOD) improved the energy further and the stability of the beams. The combination of a dual-stage target and careful control of laser pulse properties can be an effective way to shape the electron beams and control the acceleration process.

3.3. LWFA with Capillary Discharge Plasmas at LBNL

Laser propagation through a plasma medium is a highly complicated process. To increase the electron energy for a given laser power, the elongation of laser propagation is a critical issue in LWFA research. Most experiments were performed with self-guiding schemes that provide a much longer propagation length than the Rayleigh range by balancing relativistic self-focusing and diffraction. For increasing the electron energy, the plasma density should be lower, and the medium length should be longer. However, the elongation of laser-propagation length by relativistic self-guiding is getting more difficult as plasma density is lowered because the critical power for self-guiding increases as the plasma density decreases. Thus, the elongation of the laser propagation through the plasma medium is an essential technique to increase electron energy with PW laser pulses. One of the solutions is guiding the laser pulse with a plasma channel. The plasma channel guiding utilizes a refractive index gradient in the transverse direction like optical fibers.

It can contain high-intensity laser pulses in the relativistic regime due to the extremely high-intensity limit of the plasma medium. Several groups developed plasma channel technology [34–36], and the research group at Lawrence Berkley National Laboratory successfully applied the plasma channel to enhance the electron energy [16,32,33].

The first successful application of a plasma channel to LWFA demonstrated 1 GeV electron acceleration by focusing a 40 TW laser pulse to a 3.3 cm plasma channel [37]. The plasma channel was formed in a pre-ionized hydrogen plasma confined in a capillary tube. The capillary tube was fabricated on a sapphire block by laser machining: two gas inlets and a central tube with a few-hundred-microns diameter. The hydrogen gas was fully ionized by a high-voltage electric pulse applied to the electrodes at both ends of the capillary tube. The pre-formed plasma had a hyperbolic electron density profile in the transverse direction that can guide an intense laser pulse. The capillary discharge medium has an obvious advantage of elongated laser propagation through the plasma medium. Table 2 summarizes the successful demonstrations of electron energy enhancement with capillary discharge plasma channels and sub-PW [19] and PW lasers [12].

Table 2. Characteristics of electron beams from capillary discharge plasma channel and experimental condition for three different experiments with laser power of 40 TW [37], 300 TW [19], and 850 TW [12]. Reproduced with permission from [Leemans, W.P], [*Nat. Phys*]; published by [Nature Publishing Group], [2006].

	Experiment 1	Experiment 2	Experiment 3
Spectrum			
Channel length (cm)	3.3	9	20
Plasma density (10^{17} cm^{-3})	43	7	3.4
Laser power (TW)	40	300	850
Laser pulse duration (fs)	40	40	40
E_{peak} (GeV)	1	4.2	7.8
Energy spread (%)	1.6 (r.m.s.)	6 (r.m.s.)	~10 (FWHM)
Divergence (mrad)	1.6 (r.m.s.)	0.3 (r.m.s.)	0.2 (FWHM)
Charge in peak (pC)	~30	6	5

The enhancement of electron energy with the laser power is not straightforward, even though the plasma channel can guide the driving laser pulse to a long distance. Since 1-GeV electron beam was produced with a laser power below 100-TW, as seen in experiment 1 in Table 2, a 1-PW laser pulse should have the capability to generate a 10-GeV electron beam. Despite the use of sub-PW laser pulses, a 4.2-GeV electron beam was produced with a 9 cm capillary discharge plasma channel because of the nonlinear evolution of laser pulses with a top-hat profile. The nonlinear propagation in the plasma can assist the self-injection process but disturb smooth laser propagation in the plasma channel. For increasing electron energy in LWFA further, a longer laser propagation through a plasma with a lower plasma density is essential. However, the nonlinear laser propagation can prohibit the increase of electron energy by limiting long and smooth laser propagation through a plasma medium with an extremely low electron density below 5×10^{17} electrons/cm^3. Although experiment 2 in Table 2 was performed with an almost perfectly focused laser beam of Strehl ratio of about 0.8, the top-hat laser profile in the near field, ordinarily formed by the laser amplification, induced a nonlinear laser propagation and hindered the additional increase of electron energy.

The nonlinear laser propagation problem has been mitigated by steepening the transversal electron density gradient of the plasma channel. A nanosecond laser, focused on the axis of the discharge capillary plasma channel, heated through inverse bremsstrahlung the core of the capillary discharge plasma channel and created a deeper electron density valley that could guide a PW laser pulse efficiently. Thus, the effect of the nonlinear laser propagation could be mitigated, and the laser pulse could propagate tens of centimeters in a plasma channel with an electron density of 3×10^{17} electrons/cm^3. This improvement of laser propagation by a steepened plasma channel made it possible to generate the most energetic electron beam of about 8 GeV from LWFA (experiment 3 in Table 2). This result implies that engineering the plasma medium is a key to realizing the maximum electron energy expected by the power-scaling of the electron energy. Consequently, more and more efforts should be exerted to control the plasma medium, not only to increase laser power but also to find suitable electron acceleration conditions for high-energy electron beams by LWFA.

4. Perspective of LWFA with PW Lasers

In this section, we will discuss the current difficulties of LWFA with PW lasers and the future perspective of LWFA with upcoming multi-PW lasers. We reviewed several experimental results on LWFA with PW laser pulses. Overall, PW lasers demonstrated multi-GeV LWFA in the energy range from 2–8 GeV with divergence of about 1 mrad, the beam charge in the order of 10 pC, and energy spread of about 10%. The rapid progress of high-power lasers enabled the development of high-energy electron beams with high bunch charge and small beam emittance. Although PW lasers began to appear a decade ago, and the expectations on LWFA have been quite promising, experimental results were relatively rare. The advancement of LWFA with PW lasers was retarded due to the technological difficulties in operating PW lasers and the growing complexity of experimental setups. LWFA uses highly nonlinear processes in a plasma medium with micrometer scale acceleration structures. Thus, tiny defects of laser pulses and the plasma media can significantly deteriorate the acceleration processes. As laser power and system size increase, the elimination of the flaws is getting more difficult.

The recent development of high-power laser reached 10 PW peak powers [38], and 100-GeV electron acceleration with LWFA is not an absurd goal. However, the massive scale of the LWFA experimental system with the 10-PW lasers can make it challenging to realize a 100-GeV electron beam. From the estimation with Equation (1), a 10-PW laser with 250 J energy can produce a 100 GeV electron beam by focusing the laser pulse with F/# > 150 onto a 10-m length plasma medium with an electron density of about 10^{16} electrons/cm^3. If the beam size of the 10 PW laser is about half a meter, then the LWFA experimental system, including the focusing system, acceleration medium, and detection system, should be more than 100 m to achieve 100 GeV. The 10 PW laser should have the beam pointing stability below 1 μrad before the focusing mirror for its pulse to be properly guided along the 10-m plasma channel. The plasma medium also has to be well designed and fabricated to be transversally profiled for a deep electron density gradient to guide the 10-PW laser pulse with a longitudinal uniformity over 10 m. For that reason, engineering efforts should be devoted to constructing more stable 10-PW lasers with a clean focal spot as well as a long plasma channel medium with substantially profiled electron density distribution.

The electron injection at such a low electron density is problematic. The self-injection process occurs when the laser intensity and the plasma density are high enough to induce the wave breaking of the plasma wave. The self-injection, empirically, happens when the laser power is higher than the critical power, $P_c \approx 17 \left(\frac{\omega_0}{\omega_p}\right)^2$ GW [29]; that is, the laser power where relativistic self-focusing dominates over diffraction. For the plasma with an electron density of 10^{16} electrons/cm^3, the critical power is about 3 PW. However, the laser pulse duration should be stretched to be more than 150 fs to prevent too quick etching, and the laser power on target would be below 2 PW. At this condition, self-injection is not possible. Recently, electron injection mechanisms, such as ionization injection [39–41], density shock injection [42,43], and nanoparticle insertion [44,45], have been proposed and demonstrated. Because the laser should propagate 10 m for 100 GeV acceleration, the electron injection process should not degrade laser properties and should occur only at the beginning of the medium. Thus, the electron injection mechanism for 100 GeV LWFA should be chosen carefully to maintain the laser quality and induce localized injection at the beginning.

The nanoparticle insertion method can be promising as an injection method for achieving 100 GeV by LWFA because nanoparticles can induce an electron bunch with a sufficient charge at extremely low plasma density close to 10^{16} electrons/cm^3 while making negligible effects on laser propagation due to its tiny size, much smaller than the laser wavelength. A nanoparticle in plasma medium for LWFA can induce a highly localized injection, leading to an electron beam with a small emittance. A numerical study showed that a nanoparticle in plasma could facilitate a controllable injection to produce a high-quality 5-GeV electron beam with a 0.5-PW laser pulse [44]. Furthermore, a recent experimental study demonstrated nanoparticle-assisted laser wakefield acceleration with a nanoparticle-mixed helium gas jet [45]. Although controlling precisely the location of nanoparticles in plasma is challenging, the nanoparticle injection method can be a promising method to realize a 100-GeV electron beam with 10-PW-class lasers.

An alternative way to increase the energy gain of LWFA is to use an intense two-color laser pulse [46]. A recent numerical study with particle-in-cell simulations showed the feasibility of all-optical staging of LWFA using a two-color laser pulse train: a fundamental laser pulse induces an electron injection, and the subsequent second harmonic pulse accelerates the injected electron bunch to high energy. The theoretical study showed the possibility of achieving 10 GeV with a-few-PW lasers and a-few-centimeter-long plasmas. It was suggested that the two-color scheme might achieve 100 GeV with the near-future state-of-the-art lasers having power in the range of 10 PW.

In addition to control of injection and increasing the laser power, other technical challenges of plasma media and laser controls need to be addressed. The structure of the acceleration medium needs careful consideration, thus shaping the density profile over long distances is required. For example, the use of density up-ramp medium [47] or multi-jets configuration [48] has been recently employed, albeit they have been done in a low laser power regime and with short distance. The careful shaping of the profile can produce beams with energy spread below 1% [49]. We, thus, foresee that longitudinal control of the plasma density profile over a wide density range (10^{14}–10^{19} cm^{-3}) is a necessity for improving the energy and quality of electron beams produced with multi-PW lasers. While longitudinal control of the density profile seems the major challenge for improving PW-laser-based acceleration, advances in various guiding methods and technologies will provide additional improvement of the acceleration process. Besides the challenge of producing stable long-distance channels [50], curved channel technology will provide a useful method to control the directionality of electron beams and laser pulses [51]. In addition, recent theoretical and numerical studies proposed to overcome the dephasing length of LWFA, so-called phase-locked [52] or dephasingless [53] LWFA, by adapting the superluminal velocity of focal spot movement [54], which can be a way to maximize electron energy for given laser power.

LWFA is considered a promising electron acceleration technology that may overcome the limitations of the current RF linear accelerators, despite the drawbacks such as the bulky systems of lasers with peak powers beyond PW and sophisticated acceleration processes. Upcoming laser systems having a peak power beyond 10 PW have the potentials to enhance the electron energy more than an order of magnitude, even close to TeV electron energy, which can initiate a new horizon of fundamental physics. For a new era of particle physics with LWFA, developments of two technologies are essential; one is precise control with sub-micron accuracy of the upcoming high-power lasers with peak power of 10–100 PW, and the other is profiled plasma channels over 10 m. In addition, proposing and demonstrating new schemes of electron injection and acceleration processes, such as nanoparticle injection, two-color LWFA, and dephasingless LWFA, should be pursued.

5. Conclusions

We reviewed the progress of LWFA with PW lasers in the last decade. The Texas PW laser was successfully applied to LWFA and produced 2 GeV electron beams, while the acceleration was limited due to the poor focal spot. The PW laser at UQBF demonstrated a 3-GeV electron beam by a dual-stage acceleration scheme. The electron energy in the dual-stage LWFA was still below what is expected for PW lasers due to short laser propagation without a guiding structure. The most successful experimental results of LWFA with PW lasers have been obtained by using a capillary discharge plasma channel by the Berkeley group. Although the plasma channel can guide a PW laser pulse, the nonlinear laser propagation in the plasma channel can limit the acceleration length and electron energy. The nonlinearity in laser propagation was suppressed by deepening the plasma channel by collisional heating of the plasma channel core with a nanosecond laser. As a result, a 7.8-GeV electron beam was produced with a PW laser pulse and the capillary discharge plasma channel. In the last decade, the advent of PW lasers brought the expectations of rapid progress in LWFA research, but the development of LWFA in this new regime has been retarded by technological barriers. In the upcoming decade, 10–100 PW lasers will be constructed and used for electron acceleration by LWFA. Suppose the plasma medium and the laser propagation are controlled over about 10 m along the propagation direction and at the precision of micrometers in the transverse direction. In that case, the LWFA with PW lasers will break the limit of the conventional RF accelerations.

Author Contributions: H.T.K. wrote the draft. H.T.K., V.B.P., C.I.H., M.M., K.H.P., C.M.K., J.W.Y., J.H.S. and S.K.L. reviewed and edited the manuscript. All authors have read and agreed to the published version of the manuscript.

Funding: This research was supported by the GIST Research Institute (GRI) grant funded by the GIST in 2021, Ultrashort Quantum Beam Facility (UQBF) operation program (140011) through APRI-GIST, the National Research Foundation of Korea (NRF) grant funded by the Korea gov-ernment (MSIT) Grant No. NRF-2020R1F1A1070538, and the Institute for Basic Science, Korea (IBS-R012-D1).

Institutional Review Board Statement: Not applicable.

Informed Consent Statement: Not applicable.

Data Availability Statement: Not applicable.

Conflicts of Interest: The authors declare no conflict of interest.

References

1. Tajima, T.; Dawson, J.M. Laser Electron Accelerator. *Phys. Rev. Lett.* **1979**, *43*, 267–270. [CrossRef]
2. Strickland, D.; Mourou, G. Compression of amplified chirped optical pulses. *Opt. Commun.* **1985**, *56*, 219–221. [CrossRef]
3. Nakajima, K.; Fisher, D.; Kawakubo, T.; Nakanishi, H.; Ogata, A.; Kato, Y.; Kitagawa, Y.; Kodama, R.; Mima, K.; Shiraga, H.; et al. Observation of Ultrahigh Gradient Electron Acceleration by a Self-Modulated Intense Short Laser Pulse. *Phys. Rev. Lett.* **1995**, *74*, 4428–4431. [CrossRef] [PubMed]
4. Coverdale, C.A.; Darrow, C.B.; Decker, C.D.; Mori, W.B.; Tzeng, K.C.; Marsh, K.A.; Clayton, C.E.; Joshi, C. Propagation of intense subpicosecond laser pulses through underdense plasmas. *Phys. Rev. Lett.* **1995**, *74*, 4659–4662. [CrossRef] [PubMed]
5. Umstadter, D.; Chen, S.Y.; Maksimchuk, A.; Mourou, G.; Wagner, R. Nonlinear optics in relativistic plasmas and laser wake field acceleration of electrons. *Science* **1996**, *273*, 472–475. [CrossRef] [PubMed]
6. Faure, J.; Glinec, Y.; Pukhov, A.; Kiselev, S. A laser–plasma accelerator producing monoenergetic electron beams. *Nature* **2004**, *431*, 541–544. [CrossRef] [PubMed]
7. Geddes, C.G.R.; Van Tilborg, J.; Esarey, E.; Schroeder, C.B.; Bruhwiler, D.; Nieter, C.; Cary, J.; Leemans, W.P. High-quality electron beams from a laser wakefield accelerator using plasma-channel guiding. *Nature* **2004**, *431*, 538–541. [CrossRef]
8. Mangles, S.; Murphy, C.; Najmudin, Z. Monoenergetic beams of relativistic electrons from intense laser–plasma interactions. *Nature* **2004**, *431*, 535–538. [CrossRef]
9. Albert, F.; Thomas, A.G.R. Applications of laser wakefield accelerator-based light sources. *Plasma Phys. Control. Fusion* **2016**, *58*, 103001. [CrossRef]
10. Esarey, E.; Schroeder, C.; Leemans, W. Physics of laser-driven plasma-based electron accelerators. *Rev. Mod. Phys.* **2009**, *81*, 1229–1285. [CrossRef]

11. Wang, X.; Zgadzaj, R.; Fazel, N.; Li, Z.; Yi, S.; Zhang, X.; Henderson, W.; Chang, Y.-Y.; Korzekwa, R.; Tsai, H.-E.; et al. Quasi-monoenergetic laser-plasma acceleration of electrons to 2 GeV. *Nat. Commun.* **2013**, *4*, 1988. [CrossRef]
12. Gonsalves, A.J.; Nakamura, K.; Daniels, J.; Benedetti, C.; Pieronek, C.; De Raadt, T.C.H.; Steinke, S.; Bin, J.H.; Bulanov, S.S.; Van Tilborg, J.; et al. Petawatt Laser Guiding and Electron Beam Acceleration to 8 GeV in a Laser-Heated Capillary Discharge Waveguide. *Phys. Rev. Lett.* **2019**, *122*, 084801. [CrossRef]
13. Kim, H.T.; Pathak, V.B.; Hong Pae, K.; Lifschitz, A.; Sylla, F.; Shin, J.H.; Hojbota, C.; Lee, S.K.; Sung, J.H.; Lee, H.W.; et al. Stable multi-GeV electron accelerator driven by waveform-controlled PW laser pulses. *Sci. Rep.* **2017**, *7*, 1–8. [CrossRef]
14. Maier, A.R.; Delbos, N.M.; Eichner, T.; Hübner, L.; Jalas, S.; Jeppe, L.; Jolly, S.W.; Kirchen, M.; Leroux, V.; Messner, P.; et al. Decoding Sources of Energy Variability in a Laser-Plasma Accelerator. *Phys. Rev. X* **2020**, *10*. [CrossRef]
15. Danson, C.; Hillier, D.; Hopps, N.; Neely, D. Petawatt class lasers worldwide. *High Power Laser Sci. Eng.* **2021**, *3*, 3. [CrossRef]
16. Gaul, E.W.; Martinez, M.; Blakeney, J.; Jochmann, A.; Ringuette, M.; Hammond, D.; Borger, T.; Escamilla, R.; Douglas, S.; Henderson, W.; et al. Demonstration of a 1.1 petawatt laser based on a hybrid optical parametric chirped pulse amplification/mixed Nd:glass amplifier. *Appl. Opt.* **2010**, *49*, 1676–1681. [CrossRef]
17. Sung, J.H.; Lee, S.K.; Yu, T.J.; Jeong, T.M.; Lee, J. 0.1 Hz 1.0 PW Ti:sapphire laser. *Opt. Lett.* **2010**, *35*, 3021–3023. [CrossRef]
18. Kim, H.T.; Pae, K.H.; Cha, H.J.; Kim, I.J.; Yu, T.J.; Sung, J.H.; Lee, S.K.; Jeong, T.M.; Lee, J. Enhancement of Electron Energy to the Multi-GeV Regime by a Dual-Stage Laser-Wakefield Accelerator Pumped by Petawatt Laser Pulses. *Phys. Rev. Lett.* **2013**, *111*, 165002. [CrossRef]
19. Leemans, W.P.; Gonsalves, A.J.; Mao, H.-S.; Nakamura, K.; Benedetti, C.; Schroeder, C.B.; Tth, C.; Daniels, J.; Mittelberger, D.E.; Bulanov, S.S.; et al. Multi-GeV Electron Beams from Capillary-Discharge-Guided Subpetawatt Laser Pulses in the Self-Trapping Regime. *Phys. Rev. Lett.* **2014**, *113*, 245002. [CrossRef]
20. Mourou, G.A.; Korn, G.; Sandner, W.; Collier, J.L. *Science and Technology with Ultra-Intense Lasers ELI-Extreme Light Infrastructure WHITEBOOK*; THOSS Media GmbH: Berlin, Germany, 2011.
21. Zettawatt-Equivalent Ultrashort pulse laser System (ZEUS)—Home for Zettawatt-Equivalent Ultrashort pulse laser System (ZEUS). Available online: https://zeus.engin.umich.edu/ (accessed on 24 May 2021).
22. Exawatt Center for Extreme Light Studies (XCELS). Available online: https://xcels.ipfran.ru/img/site-XCELS.pdf (accessed on 22 June 2021).
23. Liang, X.; Leng, Y.; Li, R.; Xu, Z. Recent progress on the shanghai superintense ultrafast laser facility (SULF) at SIOM. In *High Intensity Lasers and High Field Phenomena*; Optical Society of America: Washington, DC, USA, 2020; p. HTh2B.2.
24. Papadopoulos, D.N.; Le Blanc, C.; Chériaux, G.; Georges, P.; Zou, J.P.; Mennerat, G.; Druon, F.; Pellegrina, A.; Ramirez, P.; Giambruno, F.; et al. The apollon-10P project: Design and current status. In *Advanced Solid State Lasers*; Optical Society of America: Washington, DC, USA, 2013; p. ATu3A.43.
25. Sung, J.H.; Lee, H.W.; Yoo, J.Y.; Yoon, J.W.; Lee, C.W.; Yang, J.M.; Son, Y.J.; Jang, Y.H.; Lee, S.K.; Nam, C.H. 4.2 PW, 20 fs Ti:sapphire laser at 0.1 Hz. *Opt. Lett.* **2017**, *42*, 2058. [CrossRef]
26. Lu, W.; Huang, C.; Zhou, M.; Mori, W.B.; Katsouleas, T. Nonlinear theory for relativistic plasma wakefields in the blowout regime. *Phys. Rev. Lett.* **2006**, *10*, 165002. [CrossRef] [PubMed]
27. Pukhov, A.; Meyer-ter-Vehn, J. Laser wake field acceleration: The highly non-linear broken-wave regime. *Appl. Phys. B Lasers Opt.* **2002**, *74*, 355–361. [CrossRef]
28. Faillace, L.; Agustsson, R.; Frigola, P.; Murokh, A.; Rosenzweig, J. Ultra-High Gradient Compact S-Band Linac for Laboratory and Industrial Applications. In Proceedings of the 1st International Particle Accelerator Conference: IPAC'10, Kyoto, Japan, 23–28 May 2010.
29. Lu, W.; Tzoufras, M.; Joshi, C.; Tsung, F.; Mori, W.; Vieira, J.; Fonseca, R.; Silva, L. Generating multi-GeV electron bunches using single stage laser wakefield acceleration in a 3D nonlinear regime. *Phys. Rev. Spec. Top. Accel. Beams* **2007**, *10*, 061301. [CrossRef]
30. Yu, T.J.; Lee, S.K.; Sung, J.H.; Yoon, J.W.; Jeong, T.M.; Lee, J. Generation of high-contrast, 30 fs, 1.5 PW laser pulses from chirped-pulse amplification Ti:sapphire laser. *Opt. Express* **2012**, *20*, 10807–10815. [CrossRef]
31. Steinke, S.; Van Tilborg, J.; Benedetti, C.; Geddes, C.G.R.; Schroeder, C.B.; Daniels, J.; Swanson, K.K.; Gonsalves, A.J.; Nakamura, K.; Matlis, N.H.; et al. Multistage coupling of independent laser-plasma accelerators. *Nature* **2016**, *530*, 190–193. [CrossRef]
32. Pathak, V.B.; Vieira, J.; Fonseca, R.A.; Silva, L.O. Effect of the frequency chirp on laser wakefield acceleration New Journal of Physics Effect of the frequency chirp on laser wakefield acceleration. *New J. Phys.* **2012**, *14*, 23057–23070. [CrossRef]
33. Shin, J.; Kim, H.T.; Pathak, V.B.; Hojbota, C.; Lee, S.K.; Sung, J.H.; Lee, H.W.; Yoon, J.W.; Jeon, C.; Nakajima, K.; et al. Quasi-monoenergetic multi-GeV electron acceleration by optimizing the spatial and spectral phases of PW laser pulses. *Plasma Phys. Control. Fusion* **2018**, *60*, 064007. [CrossRef]
34. Spence, D.J.; Butler, A.; Hooker, S.M. Gas-filled capillary discharge waveguides. *J. Opt. Soc. Am. B* **2003**, *20*, 138. [CrossRef]
35. Lu, H.; Liu, M.; Wang, W.; Wang, C.; Liu, J.; Deng, A.; Xu, J.; Xia, C.; Li, W.; Zhang, H.; et al. Laser wakefield acceleration of electron beams beyond 1 GeV from an ablative capillary discharge waveguide. *Appl. Phys. Lett.* **2011**, *99*, 091502. [CrossRef]
36. Jang, D.G.; Kim, M.S.; Nam, I.H.; Uhm, H.S.; Suk, H. Density evolution measurement of hydrogen plasma in capillary discharge by spectroscopy and interferometry methods. *Appl. Phys. Lett.* **2011**, *99*, 141502. [CrossRef]
37. Leemans, W.P.; Nagler, B.; Gonsalves, A.J.; Tóth, C.; Nakamura, K.; Geddes, C.G.R.; Esarey, E.; Schroeder, C.B.; Hooker, S.M. GeV electron beams from a centimetre-scale accelerator. *Nat. Phys.* **2006**, *2*, 696–699. [CrossRef]

38. Li, W.; Gan, Z.; Yu, L.; Wang, C.; Liu, Y.; Guo, Z.; Xu, L.; Xu, M.; Hang, Y.; Xu, Y.; et al. 339 J high-energy Ti:sapphire chirped-pulse amplifier for 10 PW laser facility. *Opt. Lett.* **2018**, *43*, 5681. [CrossRef]
39. Pak, A.; Marsh, K.A.; Martins, S.F.; Lu, W.; Mori, W.B.; Joshi, C. Injection and Trapping of Tunnel-Ionized Electrons into Laser-Produced Wakes. *Phys. Rev. Lett.* **2010**, *104*, 025003. [CrossRef]
40. Clayton, C.E.; Ralph, J.E.; Albert, F.; Fonseca, R.A.; Glenzer, S.H.; Joshi, C.; Lu, W.; Marsh, K.A.; Martins, S.F.; Mori, W.B.; et al. Self-guided laser wakefield acceleration beyond 1 GeV using ionization-induced injection. *Phys. Rev. Lett.* **2010**, *105*, 105003. [CrossRef]
41. Mirzaie, M.; Li, S.; Zeng, M.; Hafz, N.A.M.; Chen, M.; Li, G.Y.; Zhu, Q.J.; Liao, H.; Sokollik, T.; Liu, F.; et al. Demonstration of self-truncated ionization injection for GeV electron beams. *Sci. Rep.* **2015**, *5*, 14659. [CrossRef]
42. Thaury, C.; Guillaume, E.; Lifschitz, A.; Ta Phuoc, K.; Hansson, M.; Grittani, G.; Gautier, J.; Goddet, J.-P.; Tafzi, A.; Lundh, O.; et al. Shock assisted ionization injection in laser-plasma accelerators. *Sci. Rep.* **2015**, *5*, 16310. [CrossRef]
43. Götzfried, J.; Döpp, A.; Gilljohann, M.F.; Foerster, F.M.; Ding, H.; Schindler, S.; Schilling, G.; Buck, A.; Veisz, L.; Karsch, S. Physics of High-Charge Electron Beams in Laser-Plasma Wakefields. *Phys. Rev. X* **2020**, *10*, 041015. [CrossRef]
44. Cho, M.H.; Pathak, V.B.; Kim, H.T.; Nam, C.H. Controlled electron injection facilitated by nanoparticles for laser wakefield acceleration. *Sci. Rep.* **2018**. [CrossRef]
45. Aniculaesei, C.; Pathak, V.B.; Oh, K.H.; Singh, P.K.; Lee, B.R.; Hojbota, C.I.; Pak, T.G.; Brunetti, E.; Yoo, B.J.; Sung, J.H.; et al. Proof-of-Principle Experiment for Nanoparticle-Assisted Laser Wakefield Electron Acceleration. *Phys. Rev. Appl.* **2019**, *12*, 044041. [CrossRef]
46. Pathak, V.B.; Kim, H.T.; Vieira, J.; Silva, L.O.; Nam, C.H. All optical dual stage laser wakefield acceleration driven by two-color laser pulses. *Sci. Rep.* **2018**, *8*, 11772. [CrossRef]
47. Aniculaesei, C.; Pathak, V.B.; Kim, H.T.; Oh, K.H.; Yoo, B.J.; Brunetti, E.; Jang, Y.H.; Hojbota, C.I.; Shin, J.H.; Jeon, J.H.; et al. Electron energy increase in a laser wakefield accelerator using up-ramp plasma density profiles. *Sci. Rep.* **2019**, *9*, 1–7. [CrossRef]
48. Tomkus, V.; Girdauskas, V.; Dudutis, J.; Gečys, P.; Stankevič, V.; Račiukaitis, G.; Gallardo González, I.; Guénot, D.; Svensson, J.B.; Persson, A.; et al. Laser wakefield accelerated electron beams and betatron radiation from multijet gas targets. *Sci. Rep.* **2020**, *10*, 1–17. [CrossRef] [PubMed]
49. Ke, L.T.; Feng, K.; Wang, W.T.; Qin, Z.Y.; Yu, C.H.; Wu, Y.; Chen, Y.; Qi, R.; Zhang, Z.J.; Xu, Y.; et al. Near-GeV Electron Beams at a Few Per-Mille Level from a Laser Wakefield Accelerator via Density-Tailored Plasma. *Phys. Rev. Lett.* **2021**, *126*, 214801. [CrossRef] [PubMed]
50. Miao, B.; Feder, L.; Shrock, J.E.; Goffin, A.; Milchberg, H.M. Optical Guiding in Meter-Scale Plasma Waveguides. *Phys. Rev. Lett.* **2020**, *125*, 074801. [CrossRef] [PubMed]
51. Ehrlich, Y.; Cohen, C.; Zigler, A.; Krall, J.; Sprangle, P.; Esarey, E. Guiding of high intensity laser pulses in straight and curved plasma channel experiments. *Phys. Rev. Lett.* **1996**, *77*, 4186–4189. [CrossRef] [PubMed]
52. Caizergues, C.; Smartsev, S.; Malka, V.; Thaury, C. Phase-locked laser-wakefield electron acceleration. *Nat. Photonics* **2020**, *14*, 475–479. [CrossRef]
53. Palastro, J.P.; Shaw, J.L.; Franke, P.; Ramsey, D.; Simpson, T.T.; Froula, D.H. Dephasingless Laser Wakefield Acceleration. *Phys. Rev. Lett.* **2020**, *124*, 134802. [CrossRef]
54. Froula, D.H.; Turnbull, D.; Davies, A.S.; Kessler, T.J.; Haberberger, D.; Palastro, J.P.; Bahk, S.W.; Begishev, I.A.; Boni, R.; Bucht, S.; et al. Spatiotemporal control of laser intensity. *Nat. Photonics* **2018**, *12*, 262–265. [CrossRef]

Article

A Few MeV Laser-Plasma Accelerated Proton Beam in Air Collimated Using Compact Permanent Quadrupole Magnets

Fernando Brandi [1,*], Luca Labate [1,2,*], Daniele Palla [1,†], Sanjeev Kumar [1,†,‡], Lorenzo Fulgentini [1], Petra Koester [1], Federica Baffigi [1], Massimo Chiari [3], Daniele Panetta [4] and Leonida Antonio Gizzi [1,2]

[1] Consiglio Nazionale delle Ricerche, Istituto Nazionale di Ottica, 56124 Pisa, Italy; daniele.palla@ino.cnr.it (D.P.); sanjeev.physicsdavv@gmail.com (S.K.); lorenzo.fulgentini@ino.cnr.it (L.F.); petra.koester@ino.cnr.it (P.K.); federica.baffigi@ino.cnr.it (F.B.); leonidaantonio.gizzi@cnr.it (L.A.G.)
[2] Istituto Nazionale di Fisica Nucleare (INFN), Sezione di Pisa, 56127 Pisa, Italy
[3] Istituto Nazionale di Fisica Nucleare (INFN), Sezione di Firenze, 50019 Sesto Fiorentino, Italy; chiari@fi.infn.it
[4] Consiglio Nazionale delle Ricerche, Istituto di Fisiologia Clinica, 56124 Pisa, Italy; daniele.panetta@ifc.cnr.it
* Correspondence: fernando.brandi@ino.cnr.it (F.B.); Luca.labate@ino.cnr.it (L.L.)
† These authors contributed equally to this work.
‡ Current address: Accelerator Physics Group, Cockcroft Institute, Department of Physics and Astronomy, The University of Manchester, Manchester M13 9PL, UK.

Abstract: Proton laser-plasma-based acceleration has nowadays achieved a substantial maturity allowing to seek for possible practical applications, as for example Particle Induced X-ray Emission with few MeV protons. Here we report about the design, implementation, and characterization of a few MeV laser-plasma-accelerated proton beamline in air using a compact and cost-effective beam transport line based on permanent quadrupole magnets. The magnetic beamline coupled with a laser-plasma source based on a 14-TW laser results in a well-collimated proton beam of about 10 mm in diameter propagating in air over a few cm distance.

Keywords: laser-plasma accelerator; TNSA; laser-accelerated protons; magnetic beamline; Particle Induced X-ray Emission

1. Introduction

After decades of fundamental research in laser-plasma particle acceleration, nowadays this novel acceleration technique is experiencing a great impulse towards implementation for practical applications. The possibility to achieve laser-based particle acceleration with a compact setup is a very appealing factor for the development of high-quality electron [1] and proton/ion [2] accelerators. Specifically concerning protons, a few to hundreds of MeV particle energy can be achieved via laser-based acceleration [3,4]. Some examples of envisaged or already implemented practical applications of laser-accelerated protons are radiotherapy with tens to hundreds of MeV protons [4,5], as well as the radiography of laser directly-driven implosions [6] and imaging of fast laser-generated magnetic fields [7–9] with tens of MeV protons. Concerning lower energy beams, a few MeV protons can be used for material characterization and surface/superficial processes [10], like Particle-Induced X-ray Emission (PIXE). PIXE is a high-sensitivity non-destructive analysis technique that enables to perform quantitative characterization of the surface elemental composition of materials by measuring the characteristic X-ray emission induced by proton irradiation [11]. PIXE is typically implemented using 2 to 3 MeV proton beams from classical electrostatic accelerators.

Pulsed proton beams with a few MeV particle energy can indeed be efficiently generated with laser intensities of about 10^{19} W/cm^2 via the so-called Target Normal Sheath Acceleration (TNSA) process [3,4,12–15]. Briefly, in the TNSA process, an ultraintense laser beam is focused on a thin solid target creating a hot plasma; the fast electrons thereby generated are ejected, inducing a strong electric field normal to the rear surface of the

TNSA target; protons and ions are then accelerated by such a high field. Intensities needed to trigger the TNSA process are routinely achieved using laser systems with a peak power of tens of TW which can run at a repetition rate up to 10 Hz, and are nowadays available in many research laboratories worldwide as well as commercially available as standard products [16,17].

The implementation of laser-plasma accelerated proton beams for PIXE application have been recently investigated [18–23], mainly with modeling and simulations. In [18], a detailed analysis is performed by a Monte Carlo simulation of PIXE measurements using a realistic laser-driven few MeV proton source with broad band energy spectrum and a single photon counting CCD camera for spectral analysis of the X-ray emission from the irradiated sample. Interestingly, it was shown that implementing measurements with different energy distributions, i.e., cut-off energy, can allow to extract quantitative information of inhomogeneous samples, i.e., with a depth-dependent elemental composition, performing the so-called "Differential PIXE" measurements [24]. Indeed, the cut-off energy of laser-accelerated protons can be tuned by adjusting the laser-plasma interaction conditions, as for example the position of the TNSA target with respect to the laser focus. In [19], a Monte Carlo simulation of laser-driven PIXE experiments using few MeV laser-accelerated protons is presented, showing the feasibility of measurements on materials of importance for the cultural heritage context. Of particular importance, in [20], the effect of the TNSA fast electrons on the PIXE signal have been analyzed and quantified. Simulations showed that the contribution of such fast electrons is not negligible, and therefore their removal from the beam path is mandatory. In [21], measurements are reported of the characteristics X-ray emission from samples in vacuum after single pulse irradiation with laser-accelerated particles generated using the very powerful TITAN laser of the Jupiter Laser facility at Lawrence Livermore National Laboratory. In [22], a detailed study is reported on the design of a magnetic beamline for laser-accelerated proton energy up to 20 MeV and the final spot of about 10 mm^2, comprised of focusing with magnetic quadrupoles and energy selection with a magnetic chicane. In [23], a detailed experimental investigation on the use of a laser-driven particle source for quantitative PIXE analysis and EDX spectroscopy in vacuum is reported.

In general, a key and very appealing characteristic when using few MeV protons for practical applications is the possibility of having access to the particle beam in ambient atmosphere, i.e., with external beam [25]. This allows one to easily irradiate a sample in atmospheric conditions, which is necessary when the sample cannot be placed in vacuum (e.g., biological specimen and samples containing volatile components [26–28]), or when many samples have to be analyzed in a limited period of time avoiding sample exchange in vacuum (e.g., aerosol samples [29,30]). Although the proton beam accelerated via TNSA propagates mainly towards the direction normal to the rear side of the laser-plasma target, it has a divergence of typically 10° to 15° half-angle [31–34]. Therefore, for practical use of the laser-accelerated protons, a magnetic transport beamline has to be implemented in order to transfer the protons from the TNSA source to the application site [22,31,35,36]. Moreover, the magnetic beamline (MBL) can remove the unwanted fast electrons created during TNSA.

Here we report about the design, implementation, and characterization of a few MeV laser-plasma-accelerated proton beamline in air using a compact and cost-effective proton transport based on permanent quadrupole magnets. The MBL is coupled with a TNSA laser-plasma proton source based on a 14-TW laser, resulting in a collimated few MeV proton beam of about 10 mm in diameter propagating in air over a few cm distance.

2. Results and Discussion

2.1. Magnetic Beamline Design

The MBL is specifically designed to achieve a few MeV proton beam of about a 10-mm diameter collimated over a few centimeters in length when propagating in air.

The MBL consists of magnetic quadrupoles comprising standard neodymium-based commercial permanent magnets of $25 \times 12 \times 4$ mm^3 dimensions that are embedded in a soft iron supporting cage, as shown schematically in Figure 1a. The simple design and components of the developed permanent quadrupoles results in a compact and cost-effective beamline.

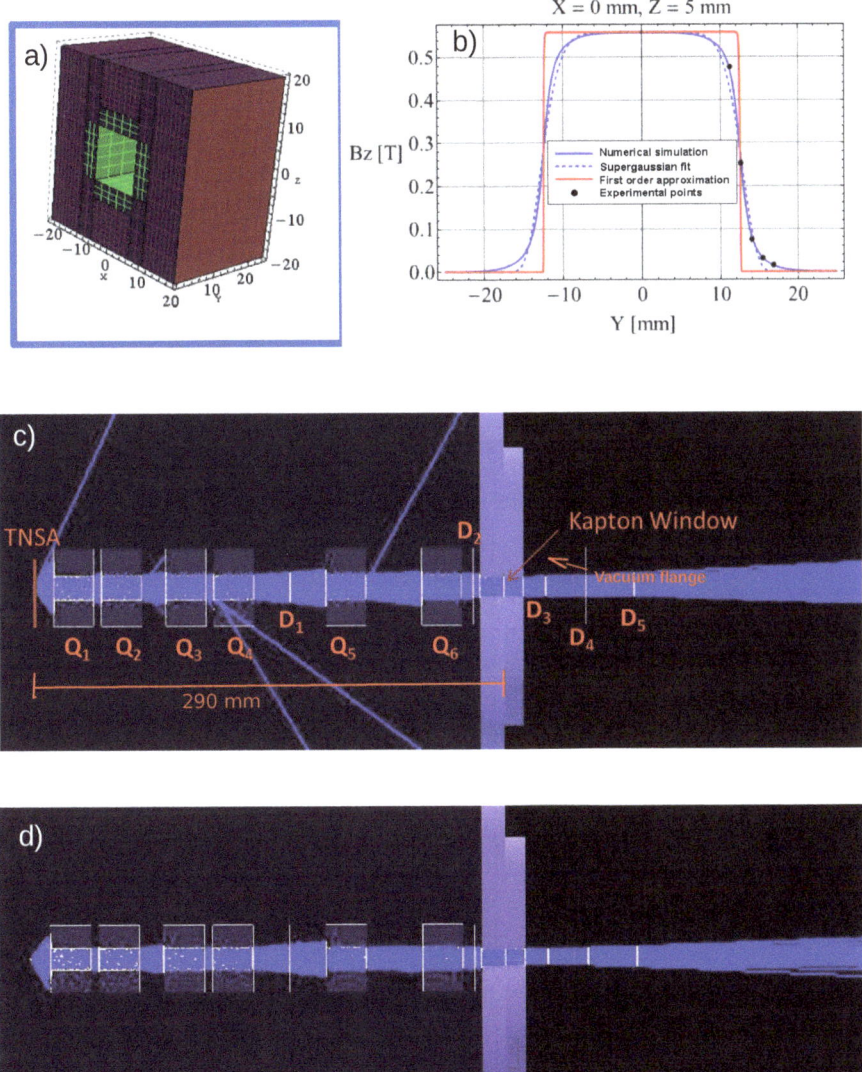

Figure 1. Design of the magnetic beamline: (**a**) Schematic of the quadrupoles, the green shows the four permanent magnets, the brown shows the supporting soft-iron structure, dimensions in mm; (**b**) magnetic field in the quadrupole measured at position x = 0 close to the permanent magnet surface: Measured values (black points), numerically reconstructed field (blue line), supergaussian fit (blue dashed line), truncated ideal quadrupole field (red line); (**c**) vertical cross section of the MBL simulation (Q_i are the quadrupoles and D_i the virtual detectors used in the simulation); and (**d**) horizontal cross section of the MBL simulation.

The transport of the laser-accelerated protons through the MBL is studied using the Monte Carlo GEANT4 toolkit [37] (see Methods for details). An analytical function for the magnetic field of the quadrupoles is used in the GEANT4 simulations. Such a function is obtained by fitting the magnetic field numerically, reconstructed from actual measurements, of which an example is reported in Figure 1b (see Materials and Methods for details). In Figure 1b, the truncated ideal quadrupole magnetic field is also reported as a reference for comparison. The aim of the simulation is to find a configuration of the MBL that efficiently transfers the few MeV divergent proton beam from the TNSA source to a collimated beam in air. The proton beam exits the vacuum chamber through a Kapton window of a 10-mm diameter and 13-μm thickness, which sustains a vacuum to the 10^{-4} mbar level. The compact MBL set-up comprises six quadrupole magnets placed with alternating field orientation and gaps of 5 mm, 15 mm, 5 mm, 45 mm, and 35 mm between each other starting from the TNSA source side. The total length of the MBL is 255 mm. The first quadrupole is placed at 12.5 mm from the TNSA source and the overall distance between the Kapton window and the TNSA source is measured to be 290(5) mm. In Figure 1c,d the schematics of the two orthogonal transverse cross sections of the MBL are shown along with the simulated proton beam trajectories (see Materials and Methods).

The characteristics of the proton beam transported in air is evaluated in details by performing simulations at an initial proton energy in narrow ranges. In Figure 2a, the particle distribution and the final energy obtained in air at 1 cm after the Kapton window are reported for initial energy in the ranges 2.4 to 2.6 MeV, 2.9 to 3.1 MeV, and 3.4 to 3.6 MeV. To compare with the experimental measurements, the time-of-flight (ToF) of the protons as a function of the initial energy is also evaluated. The graph reported in Figure 2b shows the ToF as well as the final energy considering the transport through the MBL, the Kapton window, and 1 cm of air at ambient conditions.

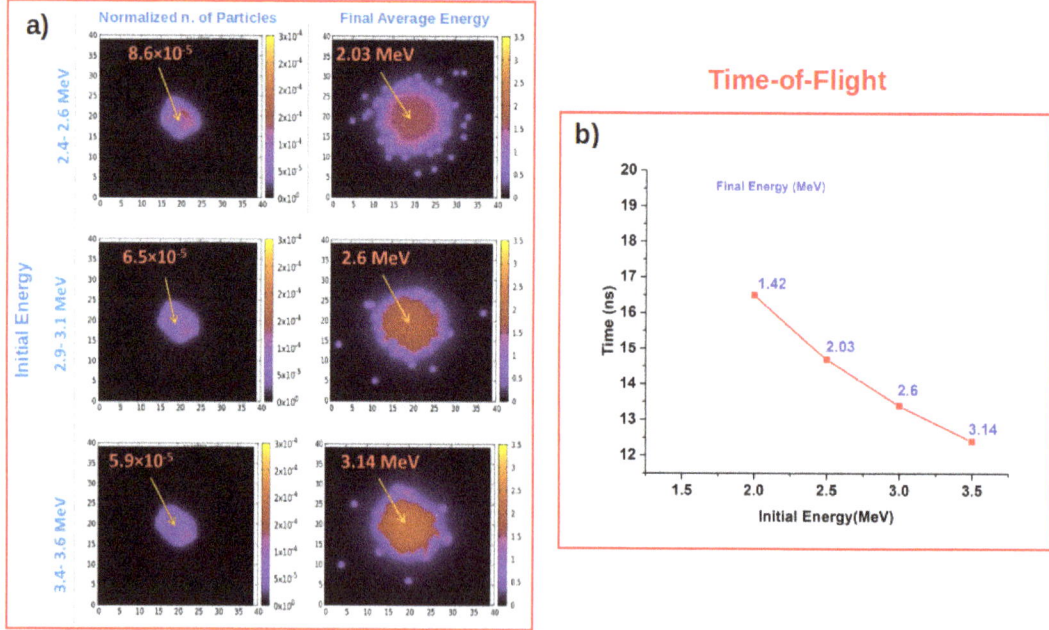

Figure 2. Proton beam characteristics at 1 cm after Kapton windows. (**a**) Proton particles distribution and final energy at various initial energy ranges calculated over an area of 40 mm × 40 mm centred on the MBL axis at position (20 mm, 20 mm); the highlighted numbers represents the values on the MBL axis; (**b**) graph of the ToF as function of the initial proton energy, with final energy also indicated.

The properties of the proton beam when propagating in air are analyzed using the software SRIM [38]. Figure 3a reports the proton trajectory for an initial point-like beam with a flat energy spectrum, from 4.0 to 1.7 MeV, impinging normally to the 13-μ Kapton window and propagating through 4 cm of air. The resulting final spread of the beam in the transverse direction is in the order of a few mm. The graph in Figure 3b shows the final energy distribution after propagation through the Kapton window and the 4 cm path in air, with a sloping down trailing energy tail to zero energy, due to convolution with energy straggling effects and partial stopping of the lower energy protons (the range of 1.7 MeV protons in air, after losing energy in passing through the Kapton window, is 3.9 cm).

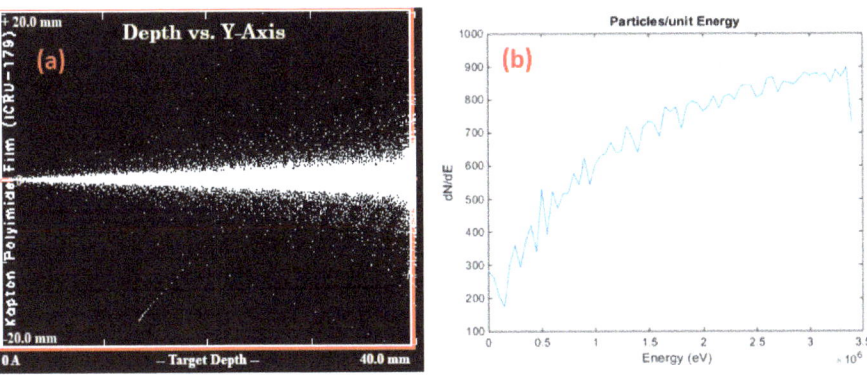

Figure 3. SRIM calculations of the few MeV proton beam propagation through the Kapton window and the 4-cm path in air: (**a**) Ensemble of the protons trajectories; (**b**) final proton energy distribution assuming an initial flat distribution of 1000 protons per unit energy.

In order to evaluate the effect of the MBL on the fast electrons produced during the TNSA process, a GEANT4 simulation assuming a flat energy distribution between 0.1 and 1 MeV is performed. The result of such a simulation experiment is reported in Figure 4 and clearly shows that the fast electrons are very efficiently filtered out by the MBL.

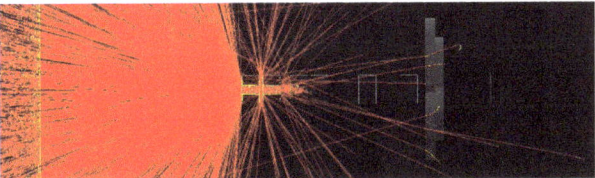

Figure 4. The effect of the magnetic Beamline on the TNSA fast electrons.

2.2. Experiments

A schematic representation of the compact laser-based accelerator realized and tested is reported in Figure 5. The laser system used is the TW laser beamline at the Intense Laser Irradiation Laboratory of the CNR-INO in Pisa [39]. The laser beam is guided by multiple steering mirrors to an off-axis parabolic (AOP) mirror. The intensity in the focus is estimated to be several times 10^{19} W/cm^2 (see Materials and Methods). The TNSA laser target used is a 5-micrometer thick titanium foil, whose position is controlled by a three-axis motorized stage with micrometer resolution. An optical camera is used to image the laser target in order to control the position of the laser focus on the titanium foil.

In Figure 6, the picture of the actual compact laser accelerator is reported, showing the laser beam transport line, the OAP mirror, the TNSA laser target, the MBL, and the

Kapton window. The MBL is supported by a motorized linear stage that can be remotely controlled to insert and remove the MBL from the proton beam path.

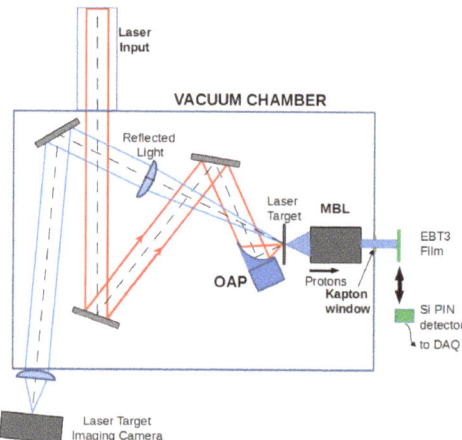

Figure 5. Schematic of the experimental setup, showing the laser-plasma target, the compact magnetic beamline, and the proton beam diagnostics after the Kapton window, alternatively the EBT3 radiochromic film or the Si PIN diode for Time of Flight measurements.

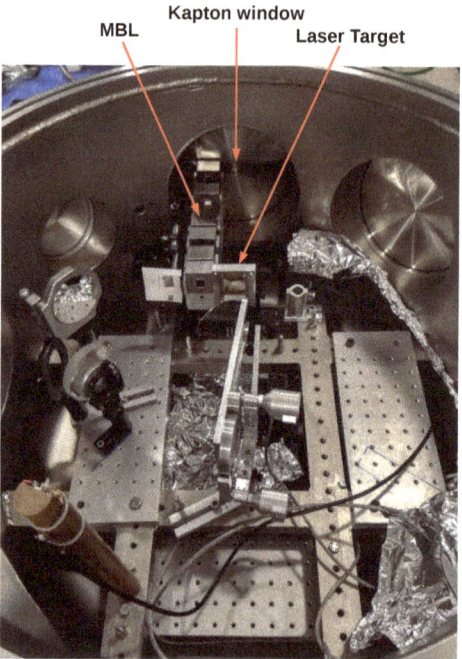

Figure 6. Picture of the actual compact accelerator, highlighting the TNSA laser target, the compact magnetic beamline, and the Kapton window to let the proton beam exit in air. In the picture, the MBL has been removed from the proton beam propagation direction using the dedicated motorized stage for better visualization.

The energy of the laser-generated proton beam is characterized with ToF measurements with the particle detector placed in air at 1 cm after the Kapton window. In Figure 7, the typical ToF traces measured with and without the MBL are shown. These data represent the maximum cut-off energy which is achieved when optimizing the TNSA process. When the TNSA target is moved out from the optimal position, proton beams with lower cut-off energy are obtained.

The actual cut-off energy value is inferred from the ToF data by the onset of the steep rising edge of the proton signal relative to the reference time corresponding to the laser-plasma interaction on the titanium foil target (t = 0). Such a reference time is set at 1.0 ns before the onset of the first ToF peak which is due mainly to the fast electrons with a contribution from X-rays from the laser-plasma (see Material and Methods Experiments section for details). The maximum cut-off proton energy achieved is ≈3 MeV in agreement with reported scaling law for the TNSA process [34,40]. The uncertainty on the cut-off proton energy determined by ToF measurements is estimated to be 0.2 MeV (see the Material and Methods Experiments section for details). Importantly, the first peak in the ToF traces is suppressed when using the MBL, confirming that fast electrons are removed from the proton beam path.

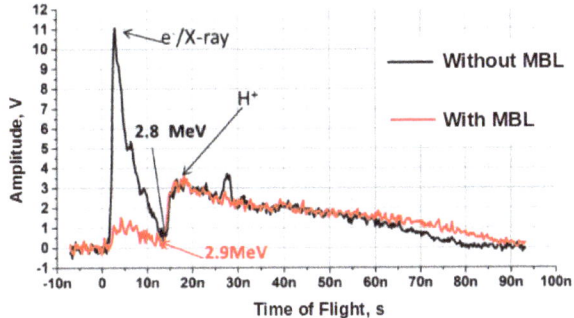

Figure 7. Time-of-flight measurements with and without the MBL: The first peak is due to fast electrons and X-rays, and the second peak is due to protons (cut-off energy highlighted).

Radiochromic EBT3 films [41] are used to characterize the spatial distribution of the proton beam in air and to perform dosimetry. The results from EBT3 film irradiation experiments are reported in Figure 8. For direct and easier comparison between simulations and experiments, Figure 8a shows the particle distribution from GEANT4 simulation at 1 cm after the Kapton window considering a beam with a flat initial energy distribution from 1.7 MeV to 3.5 MeV. In Figure 8b, the image of the EBT3 film at 1 cm after the Kapton window irradiated by 8 shots is reported. In Figure 8c, the image of the EBT3 film at 4 cm after the Kapton window irradiated by 15 shots is reported showing slight ellipticity of the proton beam due to the MBL. The experimental measurements show a good agreement with the simulated beam reported in Figure 8a. The proton beam after 4-cm propagation in air shows a smoother profile with a few mm gradient region at the edge of the beam in agreement with the SRIM calculations. These results confirm that the MBL is producing a well-collimated proton beam for several centimeters in the air.

The delivered dose is evaluated from the optical density of the scanned EBT3 radiochromic film and the calibrations reported for mono-energetic protons [42,43]. Thus the calculated average dose is 1 Gy/shot and 0.4 Gy/shot after propagating in air for 1 cm and 4 cm respectively with an uncertainty estimated to be in the order of 20% (see the Material and Methods Experiments section). The reduced dose measured further away from the Kapton window reflects the loss of lower energy protons in air, as from the calculations reported in Figure 3b. The proton particle fluence per shot after propagating 4 cm in the air is estimated to be 3×10^7 cm^{-2}.

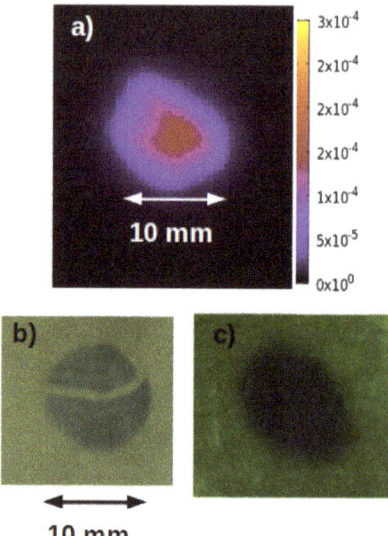

Figure 8. Measurements with EBT3 radiochromic films and comparison with simulation: (**a**) Proton beam cross section calculated with a GEANT4 toolkit: (**b**) EBT3 measurement at 1 cm from Kapton window (8 shots); (**c**) EBT3 measurement at 4 cm after the Kapton window (15 shots). The lower scale bar applies to both EBT3 film images. In (**b**), the shadow from a metal wire is present. The contrast in (**c**) has been altered for better visualization of the image.

3. Conclusions

A laser-accelerated proton beamline delivering 3-MeV particle energy has been conceived, designed, realized, and tested, aimed at practical applications, like PIXE measurements. The proton source used is based on the TNSA process and implemented using a 14 TW laser system. Quadrupole permanent magnets are used to transport the protons from the TNSA source to the sample site in air through a thin Kapton window. The magnetic beamline design is compact and cost-effective and has been defined using Monte Carlo simulations in order to achieve a collimated proton beam over several cm in length, as well as to remove unwanted fast electrons from the beam path.

From dosimetry measurements, the number of few MeV protons after propagating 4 cm in air is estimated to be 2×10^9 in 100 shots, which is on the same order as the number of protons impinging on the PIXE sample used in the simulation experiments reported in [18,19]. This finding indicates that PIXE measurements are feasible with the presented laser-plasma accelerated proton beamline within tens of seconds assuming a 10-Hz repetition rate operation. Finally, it is noted that the energy spectrum of the laser-accelerated proton beam can be easily tuned (by moving the TNSA target with respect to the laser focus) in order to have different cut-off energies, therefore allowing to implement differential PIXE measurements of in-homogeneous samples in depth [18].

4. Materials and Methods

4.1. Quadrupole Magnets

Each magnetic quadrupole comprises 4 permanent neodymium-based magnets of a $25 \times 12 \times 4$ mm^3 dimension with a nominal surface field of 1.2 T. The magnets are arranged with the field alternatively oriented in a soft iron frame of a $40 \times 40 \times 25$ mm^3 dimension to gives a quadrupole field at the first order. This represents the simplest quadrupole design allowing, at the same time, for the largest effective free aperture. However, in the case of a square aperture bounded of permanent magnets, the quadrupole field cannot be approximated as an ideal field as the equipotential surfaces are not hyperbolic. For this reason, the actual field has been carefully measured and then simulated to obtain a proper approximation of the relative multipole field expansion.

The orthogonal component of the magnetic field has been measured using a Hall probe along parallel paths taken at different distances from the entrance. Using these results as matching points, the complete 3D field has been simulated using Radia [44,45], a software package build in C++ and interfaced with Mathematica (Wolfram Research). The focusing/defocusing properties of each device has been preliminary calculated using [46]:

$$f_c = 1/k \sin(kL) \simeq 8.4 \text{ cm}, \qquad f_d = -1/k \sinh(kL) \simeq -7.4 \text{ cm} \qquad (1)$$

for focusing and defocusing length respectively, where $k = (q \partial_x B_x / p)^{1/2}$ was calculated for 3-MeV protons with q and p the proton charge and momentum, respectively. The considered transverse gradient was $\partial_x B_x$ = 110 T/m while L = 25 mm is the longitudinal quadrupole length. In terms of these parameters, the whole design of the magnetic line, which is made of six elements, has been roughly defined according to the classical thick lens equation. The preliminary design takes into account that it is possible (in ideal conditions) to focalize a monoenergetic bunch in the same point in both orthogonal planes using a combination of identical devices. This properties follows from $(kL)^2 \simeq 0.35 \ll 1$, which implies remarkably different focal lengths $f_c \neq -f_d$ (see Equation (1)). Clearly, the whole guiding system remains intrinsically astigmatic as the case of the thin lens approximation. Finally, the fine optimization has been obtained through several tests performed with GEANT4, in which an analytical model for the 3D magnetic field has been implemented to take into account the fringe field. An analytical approximation has been chosen instead of the complete Radia fields in order to drastically speed up the simulation process. No relevant differences has been observed in the final results considering a realistic protons bunch. In more detail, the transverse component of the field was used $B_\perp = A(B_x, 0, B_z)$, where A is a supergaussian amplitude, while the $B_{x,z}$ components are given by:

$$B_x = \left(K_0 - \frac{K_1}{2}z^4\right)x + \left(K_1 z^2 - \frac{K_1}{10}x^2\right)x^3,$$

$$B_z = -\left(K_0 - \frac{K_1}{2}x^4\right)z - \left(K_1 x^2 - \frac{K_1}{10}z^2\right)z^3, \qquad (2)$$

where k_0 and k_1 are free fit parameters. Expressions (2) can be directly obtained trough a Taylor's expansions considering a square symmetry and the divergenceless and irrotational conditions on the fields.

4.2. Monte Carlo Simulations of the Quadrupole Beamline

The entire quadrupole beamline was designed and simulated using a code developed on purpose using the GEANT4 library toolkit [47,48]. In particular, all the volumes/materials making up the quadrupole structure were taken into account (as it can be realized looking at Figures 1 and 4), as well as the detailed vacuum flange and Kapton window structures. The expressions given in Equation (2) were used for the magnetic fields. The G4EmPenelopePhysics physics list was used. For each run, a total number of 2.5×10^7 primary protons (or electrons, in the case shown in Figure 4) was used. The angle ϑ between the original direction of each primary particle and the symmetry axis of the system is distributed according to a gaussian function, i.e., $P(\vartheta) \propto exp(-\vartheta^2/\sigma_\vartheta^2)$, with $\sigma_\vartheta \simeq 13°$. According to the existing literature, this is a typical value for few MeV TNSA protons [31–34]. For each run, the total number, mean energy, r.m.s. energy, and average arrival times of the particles of interest (protons or electrons) were sampled on one (or more) virtual plane ("detectors") perpendicular to the main symmetry axis; this plane was sampled using "virtual pixels" with a typical size of 0.5–1 mm.

4.3. Experiments

For the experiment reported here, the 800-nm Ti:Sapphire "TW" laser beamline at the Intense Laser Irradiation Laboratory of the CNR-INO in Pisa was employed. This laser beamline provides a 30 fs duration, 450 mJ energy pulses, with an M^2 factor close to 1.5. The laser beam was focused on the TNSA target foil with a 15° angle of incidence using an $f/\approx 1.5$ Off-Axis Parabola (Thorlabs Model MPD229-M03: Gold coating—focal length 50.8 mm—90° off-axis angle, reflected wavefront error $<\lambda/2$ at 633 nm). The final intensity on the target is estimated to be about 7–8 $\times 10^{19}$ based on the optical quality of the low-cost OAP.

The ToF measurements were performed in air using a Si PIN diode biased with a voltage of about 80 Volt as the particle detector. An oscilloscope (Lecroy-Waverunner 64Xi, 600-MHz bandwidth, and 5-GS/s sampling rate) is used to acquire the ToF detector signal. The time "zero" on the ToF traces is set relative to the X-ray/fast electrons peak that is 1.00(2) ns (given a target to Si PIN detector distance of 300(5) mm) after the proton starting time which coincides on a picosecond time-scale with the laser pulse arrival time. The uncertainty on the time difference between the X-ray/fast electrons and the cut-off proton arrival time on the particle detector is limited basically by the sampling rate. As a conservative time accuracy estimate, we can assume two times the sampling rate which results in 0.2 MeV uncertainty in the 2 to 3 MeV cut-off energy range.

For radiochromic measurements in air, the first polyester supporting layer have been removed from the EBT3 films prior to irradiation in order for the few MeV laser-accelerated protons to reach the active layer of the film. Dosimetry evaluations are performed from the net optical density of the scanned films based on the calibration reported for EBT3 film using mono-energetic 4 and 5 MeV protons [42,43]. By performing SRIM calculations for different discrete input energy with and without the first supporting layer the uncertainty on our estimates is about 20%.

Author Contributions: Conceptualization, F.B. (Fernando Brandi), L.L., M.C, and L.A.G.; methodology, F.B. (Fernando Brandi), and L.L.; software, L.L., D.P. (Daniele Palla), and S.K.; validation, F.B. (Fernando Brandi), L.L.; formal analysis, L.L., D.P. (Daniele Palla), and S.K.; investigation, F.B. (Fernando Brandi), L.L., D.P. (Daniele Palla), S.K., L.F., P.K., and F.B. (Federica Baffigi); resources, F.B. (Fernando Brandi), L.L., and M.C.; data curation, F.B. (Fernando Brandi), L.L., D.P. (Daniele Palla), and S.K.; writing—original draft, F.B. (Fernando Brandi), L.L., D.P. (Daniele Palla), and S.K.; writing—review and editing, F.B. (Fernando Brandi), L.L., D.P. (Daniele Palla), and S.K.; visualization, F.B. (Fernando Brandi), L.L., D.P. (Daniele Palla), and S.K.; supervision, F.B. (Fernando Brandi), L.L., M.C., and L.A.G.; project administration, F.B. (Fernando Brandi), L.L., and L.A.G.; funding acquisition, F.B. (Fernando Brandi), L.L., M.C., D.P. (Daniele Panetta), and L.A.G. All authors have read and agreed to the published version of the manuscript.

Funding: This research was co-funded by Regione Toscana (POR FSE 2014-2020) and VCS srl (Parma, Italy) with the grant "LaserPIXE" within the programme ARCO-CNR. This project has also received funding from the CNR-funded Italian research Network ELI-Italy (D.M. No. 631 08.08.2016).

Institutional Review Board Statement: Not applicable.

Informed Consent Statement: Not applicable.

Data Availability Statement: Data are avilable from the corresponding authors upon reasonable request.

Acknowledgments: The authors wish to thank Fabio Di Martino of the U. O. di Fisica Sanitaria, Azienda Ospedaliero-Universitaria Pisana (Pisa, Italy) for support with the analysis of the irradiated EBT3 radiochromic films. The authors acknowledge the useful contributions of Claudia Ciraci and Gabriele Messina.

Conflicts of Interest: The authors declare no conflict of interest.

References

1. Assmann, R.W.; Weikum, M.K.; Akhter, T.; Alesini, D.; Alexandrova, A.S.; Anania, M.P.; Andreev, N.E.; Andriyash, I.; Artioli, M.; Aschikhin, A.; et al. EuPRAXIA Conceptual Design Report. *Eur. Phys. J. Spec. Top.* **2020**, *229*, 3675–4284. [CrossRef]
2. Margarone, D.; Cirrone, G.A.P.; Cuttone, G.; Amico, A.; Andò, L.; Borghesi, M.; Bulanov, S.S.; Bulanov, S.V.; Chatain, D.; Fajstavr, A.; et al. ELIMAIA: A Laser-Driven Ion Accelerator for Multidisciplinary Applications. *Quantum Beam Sci.* **2018**, *2*, 8. [CrossRef]
3. Snavely, R.A.; Key, M.H.; Hatchett, S.P.; Cowan, T.E.; Roth, M.; Phillips, T.W.; Stoyer, M.A.; Henry, E.A.; Sangster, T.C.; Singh, M.S.; et al. Intense High-Energy Proton Beams from Petawatt-Laser Irradiation of Solids. *Phys. Rev. Lett.* **2000**, *85*, 2945–2948. [CrossRef] [PubMed]
4. Daido, H.; Nishiuchi, M.; Pirozhkov, A.S. Review of laser-driven ion sources and their applications. *Rep. Prog. Phys.* **2012**, *75*, 056401. [CrossRef] [PubMed]
5. Giulietti, A. (Ed.) *Laser-Driven Particle Acceleration Towards Radiobiology and Medicine*; Springer International Publishing: Cham, Switzerland 2016.
6. Zylstra, A.B.; Li, C.K.; Rinderknecht, H.G.; Séguin, F.H.; Petrasso, R.D.; Stoeckl, C.; Meyerhofer, D.D.; Nilson, P.; Sangster, T.C.; Le Pape, S.; et al. Using high-intensity laser-generated energetic protons to radiograph directly driven implosions. *Rev. Sci. Instrum.* **2012**, *83*, 013511. [CrossRef]
7. Liao, G.; Li, Y.; Zhu, B.; Li, Y.; Li, F.; Li, M.; Wang, X.; Zhang, Z.; He, S.; Wang, W.; et al. Proton radiography of magnetic fields generated with an open-ended coildriven by high power laser pulses. *Matter Radiat. Extremes* **2016**, *1*, 187–191. [CrossRef]
8. Gao, L.; Ji, H.; Fiksel, G.; Fox, W.; Evans, M.; Alfonso, N. Ultrafast proton radiography of the magnetic fields generated by a laser-driven coil current. *Phys. Plasmas* **2016**, *23*, 043106. [CrossRef]
9. Law, K.F.F.; Bailly-Grandvaux, M.; Morace, A.; Sakata, S.; Matsuo, K.; Kojima, S.; Lee, S.; Vaisseau, X.; Arikawa, Y.; Yogo, A.; et al. Direct measurement of kilo-tesla level magnetic field generated with laser-driven capacitor-coil target by proton deflectometry. *Appl. Phys. Lett.* **2016**, *108*, 091104. [CrossRef]
10. Schreiber, J.; Bolton, P.R.; Parodi, K. "Hands-on" laser-driven ion acceleration: A primer for laser driven source development and potential applications. *Rev. Sci. Instrum.* **2016**, *87*, 071101. [CrossRef]
11. Ishii, K. PIXE and Its Applications to Elemental Analysis. *Quantum Beam Sci.* **2019**, *3*, 12. [CrossRef]
12. Wilks, S.C.; Langdon, A.B.; Cowan, T.E.; Roth, M.; Singh, M.; Hatchett, S.; Key, M.H.; Pennington, D.; MacKinnon, A.; Snavely, A.R. Energetic proton generation in ultra-intense laser—Solid interactions. *Phys. Plasmas* **2001**, *8*, 542. [CrossRef]
13. Gizzi, L.A.; Giove, D.; Altana, C.; Brandi, F.; Cirrone, P.; Cristoforetti, G.; Fazzi, A.; Ferrara, P.; Fulgentini, L.; Koester, P.; et al. A New Line for Laser-Driven Light Ions Acceleration and Related TNSA Studies. *Appl. Sci.* **2017**, *7*, 984. [CrossRef]
14. Gizzi, L.A.; Baffigi, F.; Brandi, F.; Bussolino, G.; Cristoforetti, G.; Fazzi, A.; Fulgentini, L.; Giove, D.; Koester, P.; Labate, L.; et al. Light Ion Accelerating Line (L3IA): Test experiment at ILIL-PW. *Nucl. Instrum. Methods Phys. Res. A* **2018**, *909*, 160–163. [CrossRef]
15. Gizzi, L.A.; Boella, E.; Labate, L.; Baffigi, F.; Bilbao, P.J.; Brandi, F.; Cristoforetti, G.; Fazzi, A.; Fulgentini, L.; Giove, D.; et al. Enhanced laser-driven proton acceleration via improved fast electron heating in a controlled pre-plasma. *Sci. Rep.* **2021**, *11*, 13728. [CrossRef] [PubMed]
16. Available online: https://amplitude-laser.com/ (accessed on 7 July 2021).
17. Available online: https://www.thalesgroup.com/en/markets/market-specific-solutions/lasers (accessed on 7 July 2021).
18. Passoni, M.; Fedeli, L.; Mirani, F. Superintense laser-driven ion beam analysis. *Sci. Rep.* **2019**, *9*, 9202. [CrossRef] [PubMed]
19. Barberio, M.; Antici, P. Laser-PIXE using laser-accelerated proton beams. *Sci. Rep.* **2019**, *9*, 6855. [CrossRef] [PubMed]
20. Passoni, M.; Arioli, F.M.; Cialfi, L.; Dellasega, D.; Fedeli, L.; Formenti, A.; Giovannelli, A.C.; Maffini, A.; Mirani, F.; Pazzaglia, A.; et al. Advanced laser-driven ion sources and their applications in materials and nuclear science. *Plasma Phys. Control. Fusion* **2020**, *62*, 014022. [CrossRef]
21. Barberio, M.; Veltri, S.; Scisciò, M.; Antici, P. Laser-Accelerated Proton Beams as Diagnostics for Cultural Heritage. *Sci. Rep.* **2017**, *7*, 40415. [CrossRef] [PubMed]
22. Scisciò, M.; Migliorati, M.; Palumbo, L.; Antici, P. Design and optimization of a compact laser-driven proton beamline. *Sci. Rep.* **2018**, *8*, 6299. [CrossRef]
23. Mirani, F.; Maffini, A.; Casamichiela, F.; Pazzaglia, A.; Formenti, A.; Dellasega, D.; Russo, V.; Vavassori, D.; Bortot, D.; Huault, M.; et al. Integrated quantitative PIXE analysis and EDX spectroscopy using a laser-driven particle source. *Sci. Adv.* **2021**, *7*, eabc8660. [CrossRef]
24. Enguita, O.; Climent-Font, A.; García, G.; Montero, I.; Fedi, M.E.; Chiari, M.; Lucarelli, F. Characterization of metal threads using differential PIXE analysis. *Nucl. Instrum. Methods Phys. Res. B* **2002**, *189*, 328–333. [CrossRef]
25. William, E.T. Pixe analysis with external beams: Systems and applications. *Nucl. Instrum. Methods Phys. Res. B* **1984**, *3*, 211–219. [CrossRef]
26. Maeda, K.; Hasegawa, K.; Hamanaka, H.; Ogiwara, K. Development of an in-air high-resolution PIXE system. *Nucl. Instrum. Methods Phys. Res. B* **1998**, *134*, 418–426. [CrossRef]
27. Sakai, T.; Oikawa, M.; Sato, T.; Nagamine, T.; Moon, H.D.; Nakazato, K.; Suzuki, K. New in-air micro-PIXE system for biological applications. *Nucl. Instrum. Methods Phys. Res. B* **2005**, *231*, 112. [CrossRef]
28. Menu, M. External beam applications to painting materials. *Nucl. Instrum. Methods Phys. Res. B* **1993**, *75*, 469–475. [CrossRef]

29. Lucarelli, F.; Calzolai, G.; Chiari, M.; Giannoni, M.; Mochi, D.; Nava, S.; Carraresi, L. The upgraded external-beam PIXE/PIGE set-up at LABEC for very fast measurements on aerosol samples. *Nucl. Instrum. Methods Phys. Res. B* **2014**, *318*, 55–59. [CrossRef]
30. Lucarelli, F.; Calzolai, G.; Chiari, M.; Nava, S.; Carraresi, L. Study of atmospheric aerosols by IBA techniques: The LABEC experience. *Nucl. Instrum. Methods Phys. Res. B* **2018**, *417*, 121. [CrossRef]
31. Nishiuchi, M.; Daito, I.; Ikegami, M.; Daido, H.; Mori, M.; Orimo, S.; Ogura, K.; Sagisaka, A.; Yogo, A.; Pirozhkov, A.S.; et al. Focusing and spectral enhancement of a repetition-rated, laser-driven, divergent multi-MeV proton beam using permanent quadrupole magnets. *Appl. Phys. Lett.* **2009**, *94*, 061107. [CrossRef]
32. Groza, A.; Chirosca, A.; Stancu, E.; Butoi, B.; Serbanescu, M.; Dreghici, D.B.; Ganciu, M. Assessment of Angular Spectral Distributions of Laser Accelerated Particles for Simulation of Radiation Dose Map in Target Normal Sheath Acceleration Regime of High Power Laser-Thin Solid Target Interaction—Comparison with Experiments. *Appl. Sci.* **2020**, *10*, 4390. [CrossRef]
33. Mancic, A.; Robiche, J.; Antici, P.; Audebert, P.; Blancard, C.; Combis, P.; Dorchies, F.; Faussurier, G.; Fourmaux, S.; Harmand, M.; et al. Isochoric heating of solids by laser-accelerated protons: Experimental characterization and self-consistent hydrodynamic modeling. *High Energy Density Phys.* **2010**, *6*, 21–28. [CrossRef]
34. Fuchs, J.; Antici, P.; d'Humières, E.; Lefebvre, E.; Borghesi, M.; Brambrink, E.; Cecchetti, C.A.; Kaluza, M.; Malka, V.; Manclossi, M.; et al. Laser-driven proton scaling laws and new paths towards energy increase. *Nat. Phys.* **2006**, *2*, 48–54. [CrossRef]
35. Cirrone, G.A.P.; Cuttone, G.; Romano, F.; Schillaci, F.; Scuderi, V.; Amato, A.; Candiano, G.; Costa, M.; Gallo, G.; Larosa, G.; et al. Design and Status of the ELIMED Beam Line for Laser-Driven Ion Beams. *Appl. Sci.* **2015**, *5*, 427–445. [CrossRef]
36. Scuderi, V.; Amato, A.; Amico, A.G.; Borghesi, M.; Cirrone, G.A.P.; Cuttone, G.; Fajstavr, A.; Giuffrida, L.; Grepl, F.; Korn, G.; et al. Diagnostics and Dosimetry Solutions for Multidisciplinary Applications at the ELIMAIA Beamline. *Appl. Sci.* **2018**, *8*, 1415. [CrossRef]
37. Available online: https://geant4.web.cern.ch/ (accessed on 7 July 2021).
38. Available online: http://www.srim.org/ (accessed on 7 July 2021).
39. Gizzi, L.A.; Labate, L.; Baffigi, F.; Brandi, F.; Bussolino, G.; Fulgentini, L.; Koester, P.; Palla, D. Overview and specifications of laser and target areas at the Intense Laser Irradiation Laboratory. *High Power Laser Sci. Eng.* **2021**, *9*, E10. [CrossRef]
40. Zeil, K.; Kraft, S.D.; Bock, S.; Bussmann, M.; Cowan, T.E.; Kluge, T.; Metzkes, J.; Richter, T.; Sauerbrey, R.; Schramm, U. The scaling of proton energies in ultrashort pulse laser plasma acceleration. *New J. Phys.* **2010**, *12*, 045015. [CrossRef]
41. EBT3 Specification Data Sheet. Available online: http://www.gafchromic.com/documents/EBT3_Specifications.pdf (accessed on 7 July 2021).
42. Reinhardt, S.; Würl, M.; Greubel, C.; Humble, N.; Wilkens, J.J.; Hillbr, ; M.; Mairani, A.; Assmann, W.; Parodi, K. Investigation of EBT2 and EBT3 films for proton dosimetry in the 4–20 MeV energy range. *Radiat. Environ. Biophys.* **2015**, *54*, 71–79. [CrossRef]
43. Vadrucci, M.; Esposito, G.; Ronsivalle, C.; Cherubini, R.; Marracino, F.; Montereali, R.M.; Picardi, L.; Piccinini, M.; Pimpinella, M.; Vincenti, M.A.; et al. Calibration of GafChromic EBT3 for absorbed dose measurements in 5 MeV proton beam and 60 Co γ-rays. *Med. Phys.* **2015**, *42*, 4678. [CrossRef]
44. Elleaume, P.; Chubar, O.; Chavanne, J. Computing 3D magnetic fields from insertion devices, In Proceedings of the 1997 Particle Accelerator Conference (Cat. No.97CH36167), Vancouver, BC, Canada, 16 May 1997; Volume 3, pp. 3509–3511.
45. Chubar, O.; Elleaume, P.; Chavanne, J. A three-dimensional magnetostatics computer code for insertion devices. *J. Synchrotron Radiat.* **1998**, *5*, 481. [CrossRef]
46. Penner, S. Calculations of Properties of Magnetic Deflection Systems. *Rev. Sci. Instrum.* **1961**, *32*, 150. [CrossRef]
47. Agostinelli, S.; Allisonas, J.; Amakoe, K.; Apostolakisa, J.; Araujoaj, H.; Arcelmxa, P.; Asaigai, M.; Axenit, D.; Banerjeebil, S.; Barrandan, G.; et al. Geant4—A simulation toolkit. *Nucl. Instrum. Meth. Phys. Res. A* **2003**, *506*, 250–303. [CrossRef]
48. Allison, J.; Amako, K.; Apostolakis, J.; Arce, P.; Asai, M.; Aso, T.; Baglih, E.; Bagulyai, A.; Banerjeej, S.; Barrand, G.; et al. Recent developments in Geant4. *Nucl. Instrum. Meth. Phys. Res. A* **2016**, *835*, 186–225. [CrossRef]

Article

Spectroscopic Studies of Laser-Based Far-Ultraviolet Plasma Light Source

Majid Masnavi [1,2,*] and Martin Richardson [2]

1. Department of Sciences, Valencia College, Orlando, FL 32825, USA
2. Laser Plasma Laboratory, Center for Directed Energy Systems, College of Optics and Photonics, University of Central Florida, Orlando, FL 32816, USA; mcr@creol.ucf.edu
* Correspondence: majidmasnavi@creol.ucf.edu

Abstract: A series of experiments is described which were conducted to measure the absolute spectral irradiances of laser plasmas created from metal targets over the wavelength region of 123–164 nm by two separate 1.0 µm lasers, i.e., using 100 Hz, 10 ns, 2–20 kHz, 60–100 ns full-width-at-half-maximum pulses. A maximum radiation conversion efficiency of $\approx 3\%/2\pi$sr is measured over a wavelength region from ≈ 125 to 160 nm. A developed collisional-radiative solver and radiation-hydrodynamics simulations in comparison to the spectra detected by the Seya–Namioka-type monochromator reveal the strong broadband experimental radiations which mainly originate from bound–bound transitions of low-ionized charges superimposed on a strong continuum from a dense plasma with an electron temperature of less than 10 eV.

Keywords: laser-produced plasma; plasma light source; far-ultraviolet spectroscopy; Seya–Namioka monochromator; radiation-hydrodynamics; collisional-radiative model

Citation: Masnavi, M.; Richardson, M. Spectroscopic Studies of Laser-Based Far-Ultraviolet Plasma Light Source. *Appl. Sci.* **2021**, *11*, 6919. https://doi.org/10.3390/app11156919

Academic Editor: Anming Hu

Received: 30 June 2021
Accepted: 26 July 2021
Published: 27 July 2021

Publisher's Note: MDPI stays neutral with regard to jurisdictional claims in published maps and institutional affiliations.

Copyright: © 2021 by the authors. Licensee MDPI, Basel, Switzerland. This article is an open access article distributed under the terms and conditions of the Creative Commons Attribution (CC BY) license (https://creativecommons.org/licenses/by/4.0/).

1. Introduction

The vacuum-ultraviolet (VUV, with the wavelength $\lambda \approx 10$–200 nm) [1], the extreme-ultraviolet (EUV, $\lambda \approx 10$–121 nm) and X-ray (XR, $\lambda \approx 0.01$–10 nm) spectral bands of the electromagnetic radiation have the potential for important applications, especially in the semiconductor industry for high volume manufacturing lithography (HVML) [2–5], metrology tools [6–11], and material sciences [12–14]. Usually, for laboratory applications, a part of the VUV radiation, the so-called far-ultraviolet (FUV), in the energy range from ≈ 6 to 10 eV (the corresponding wavelength region of $\lambda \approx 122$–200 nm) is obtained from discharge lamps or excimer lasers. The former has drawbacks regarding achievable irradiances, whereas the latter are restricted to a few specific wavelengths. Nowadays, the pulsed-power generator-based Z-pinch type plasmas and the laser-produced plasmas (LPPs) are practical high-power radiation sources in the EUV to XR spectrum regions. LPPs have been increasingly considered as bright, broadband light sources, due to their intense radiative emission and their small plasma sizes. Particularly, LPPs generate spectral emission that includes both various line radiations due to bound–bound transitions of ion charge states and continuum components, extending from the visible to the XR regions and can be selected by the choice of the target material and laser irradiation conditions. To date, the most industrial development of LPPs sources has concentrated on microlithography applications in the EUV and XR regions.

In this study, we present calibrated spectral irradiances and the measured radiation conversion efficiencies (CEs) over the wavelength region from ≈ 123 to 164 nm created by a LPP source with a few solid planar targets. Additionally, a relativistic configuration-interaction flexible atomic code (FAC) [15], a developed non-local thermodynamic equilibrium (non-LTE) population kinetics code, the so-called collisional-radiative (CR) model [16–18], and two-dimensional radiation-hydrodynamics FLASH code [19] were used to investigate the silicon (Si) plasma dynamics created by a 1.064 µm, 10 ns full-width-at-half-maximum (FWHM) laser pulse with planar solid target. This study enabled investigating the plasma spectral features of low-ionized charge states of various elements and the CEs, especially in a high-repetition rate low-laser irradiance LPP source, as well as to benchmark the computational model.

2. Experimental Setup

We described the experimental setup employed in this study, as done in previous publications, which can be seen for example in Refs. [4,6,17,20,21]. Briefly, in the present study, two 1.0 µm lasers were used separately, a Q-switched Nd:YAG solid-state laser producing 10 ns FWHM pulses at 100 Hz repetition rate and a fiber laser operating with adjustable pulse width and repetition rate, e.g., 60–100 ns FWHM and 2–20 kHz, respectively. The output of these laser pulses was focused in vacuum by a 25.4 mm diameter, 60 mm focal length lens onto fast moving planar solid targets to create plasmas. The laser spot size diameters on the target for the 10 ns and 60–100 ns FWHM pulses were measured to be ≈120 µm ($1/e^2$ width ≈200 µm for an ideal Gaussian pulse) and 80 µm ($1/e^2$ width ≈135 µm), respectively. The focused beam of these two lasers generated plasmas in a pressure of ≈1.3×10^{-4} Pa vacuum chamber from a rotating target having a rotational speed of ≈5 RPM. The surface of each target was aligned to the focal plane of the laser with a combination of translation and rotation stages. Linear and rotational motion was in the plane of the target surface to provide a new target surface for each laser shot. However, the target rotational speed was not fast enough to provide a fresh sample in each laser shot for the 60–100 ns beam having a 2–20 kHz repetition rate. The plasma spectral features recorded at an angle $\leq 15°$ from the target's normal were characterized using an aberration corrected 234/302 McPherson Seya–Namioka style spectrometer, with a 1200 groove/mm grating, 200 mm focal length, 0.1 nm achievable spectral resolution (tested at the wavelength of ≈185 nm with the 10 µm wide slit), and 4 nm/mm dispersion. The spectrometer was customized with a fiber optic face plate, coupled micro-channel plate (MCP), with a cesium iodide (CsI) photocathode at the output image plane. This photocathode limits the spectral response of the spectrometer to the wavelengths shorter than ≈164 nm. A chilled charged-couple-device (CCD) array (169 µm^2 1024-pixel detector) with a fiber optic face plate was coupled to the MCP's fiber optic face plate.

The spectrometer and its optical system were calibrated with a standard Deuterium (D_2) lamp (X2D2, L9841 Hamamatsu) over an equivalent distance between the source and the slit. The lamp provides the absolute calibrated irradiance data 100 cm from the lamp over the wavelength region from ≈115 to 300 nm. Furthermore, the wavelength of the spectrometer is calibrated using the spectral features of the standard D_2 lamp. The spectral irradiance of the standard lamp is shown in Figure 1 (right ordinate in units of µW cm^{-2} nm^{-1}) over the wavelength region of 120–170 nm. Using the lamp data, the instrument response correction, the so-called, "absolute radiometric response correction curve" is tabulated. An absolutely calibrated Si plasma radiation created by the 10 ns FWHM, 100 Hz laser pulse at the irradiance (I) of ≈2.5×10^{11} W cm^{-2} is also shown in Figure 1 (left ordinate in units of µW cm^{-2} nm^{-1}). The Si spectra were obtained by accumulating 12,000 laser shots, each on a fresh target, i.e., the acquisition time was 120 s. In all calibration processes and laser plasma experiments, the background noise signal is subtracted from the real data. It should be emphasized that the background noise signal was recorded for each experiment over the same acquisition time. This means that the noise signal is recorded over the same acquisition time in the absence of plasma. The spectral features of the calibrated Si spectrum may be identified (Figure 1 and Table 1) using the atomic database on the National Institute of Standards and Technology (NIST) website [22]. It has to be noted that the resolution of the spectrometer was not enough to resolve all weak spectral features as listed in the NIST database. The main spectral features of Si plasma emission mainly originated from doubly and triply ionized charge states (Si III–Si IV). Particularly, two strong spectral peaks about the wavelength of 140 nm are produced by two resonance transitions between the ground and singly excited states of $2p^6$ 3s (J = 1/2)

− 2p⁶ 3p (J = 3/2) (the wavelength of $\lambda \approx 140$ nm) and 2p⁶ 3s (J = 1/2) − 2p⁶ 3p (J = 1/2) ($\approx$140.5 nm) in Si IV. Here, the J is the total angular momentum.

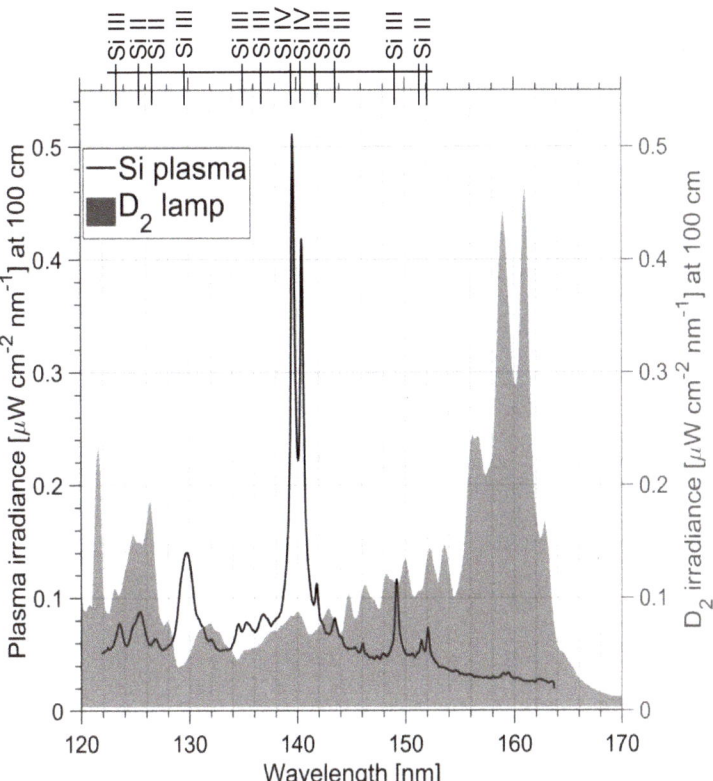

Figure 1. Comparison of the spectral irradiance of the standard Deuterium (D$_2$) lamp (gray shaded area, right-hand scale) with a typical recorded calibrated spectral irradiance of a Si plasma at a distance of 100 cm from the target over the $\approx$123–164 nm wavelength region generated by 1.064 µm laser, 10 ns FWHM pulses at 100 Hz repetition rates (black line, left-hand scale). The laser irradiance was $\approx 2.5 \times 10^{11}$ W cm^{-2} (the laser energy $\approx$230 mJ). The strong Si spectral lines are identified using the NIST atomic database [22] as listed in Table 1.

Table 1. The observed Si spectral lines (Figure 1) according to the NIST database [22].

States	Transitions (Lower–Upper Levels)	Observed Wavelengths (nm)	Transition Probabilities (1/s)
Si II	$3s^2 3p + 3s3p^2 - 3p^3 + 3s^2 3d$	125.1–126.5	$(0.47–3) \times 10^9$
	$3s^2 3p - 3s^2 4s$	152.6–153.3	$(0.4–0.8) \times 10^9$
Si III	$3p^2 - 3s6p$	123.5	2.77×10^9
	$3s3p - 3p^2$	128–130.3	$(0.5–2.1) \times 10^9$
	$3s3d - 3p3d$	134–134.3	$(0.7–0.9) \times 10^9$
	$3s4s + 3s3d - 3p4s + 3p3d$	136.1–136.7	$(0.8–1) \times 10^9$
	$3s3p - 3p^2$	141.7	2.2×10^9
	$3s4p + 3s3d + 3s4s - 3p4p + 3p3d + 3p4s$	143.3–143.6	$(0.4–0.9) \times 10^9$
	$3s3d - 3s4f$	150–150.2	$(1.7–2.1) \times 10^9$
Si IV	$2p^6 3s - 2p^6 3p$	139.4	0.88×10^9
	$2p^6 3s - 2p^6 3p$	140.3	0.86×10^9

3. Computational Model

To theoretically investigate the spectral characteristics of plasma radiation, we constructed a CR balance-rate equation, including excited states in a detail-level accounting approach [6,16,18,21]. The CR model includes all of the important atomic processes in a typical LPP light source, such as the auto-ionization from the doubly excited states and dielectronic recombination, electron impact ionization and three-body recombination, electron impact excitation and deexcitation, photo-ionization and radiative recombination, photo-excitation and photo-deexcitation. The effect of photo-absorption on a level population is calculated by reducing the radiative decay rate by a factor equal to the escape probability factor. A frequency-averaged escape probability formalism is employed for the Voigt spectral line radiation. Due to the lack of public and validated atomic physics data necessary for solving the CR model, see for example, the NIST database [22], the calculations of the atomic cross-sections and rates for any chosen element were performed using the FAC code [15]. The FAC solves the relativistic Dirac equation, using a single central parametric potential to compute the orbitals. Radiative decay, collisional excitation, and ionization, auto-ionization and photo-ionization cross sections, and rates are computed within the distorted wave approximation. To study the plasma dynamics in LPPs, a radiation-hydrodynamics code FLASH, is used [19]. The FLASH is a three-temperature (electron, ion, and radiation) state-of-the-art radiation-hydrodynamics solver, including the thermal conduction, multi-group radiation diffusion, tabulated equations-of-states (EOS), and laser ray-tracing model. For a given target material, the constructed CR is used to calculate a necessary non-LTE EOS database, including the spectral emissivity and spectral absorption coefficients on a density–temperature grid. In the present study, the calculations were carried only out for an Si plasma. To identify the Si ion charge states responsible for the experimental Si spectral emission in Figure 1 and also to verify the calculated spectral line positions by the FAC code, calculations were done using the CR solver for a homogeneous plasma. In this work, the CR model for Si includes a total of 1050 levels of the neutral to fully ionized Si charge states as listed in Table 2. For simplicity, the CR solver includes main spectral transitions among responsible low-ionized charge states for plasma FUV emission.

Table 2. The CR model for Si plasma includes all of the ground states from the neutral (Si I) through fully ionized charge states, and particularly, the important transitions from Si I through Si IX. Here, n and l are, respectively, the principal and orbital quantum numbers. The total levels in the CR is 1050.

States	Configurations
Si I	$1s^22s^22p^63s^23p^2$, $1s^22s^22p^63s^13p^3$, $1s^22s^22p^63s^23p^1 nl$ $(n = 4,5)$ $(l < n)$, $1s^22s^22p^63s^23p^1 nl$ $(n = 6,7)$ $(l < 3)$, $1s^22s^22p^63p^4$
Si II	$1s^22s^22p^63s^23p^1$, $1s^22s^22p^63s^13p^2$, $1s^22s^22p^63s^2 nl$ $(n = 4)$ $(l < n)$, $1s^22s^22p^63s^2 nl$ $(n = 5,6,7)$ $(l < 3)$, $1s^22s^22p^63p^3$
Si III	$1s^22s^22p^63s^2$, $1s^22s^22p^63s^13p^1$, $1s^22s^22p^63s^1 nl$ $(n = 4)$ $(l < n)$, $1s^22s^22p^63s^1 nl$ $(n = 5,6,7)$, $(l < 3)$, $1s^22s^22p^63p^2$
Si IV	$1s^22s^22p^63s^1$, $1s^22s^22p^63p^1$, $1s^22s^22p^6 nl$ $(n = 4)$ $(l < n)$, $1s^22s^22p^6 nl$ $(n = 5,6,7)$ $(l < 3)$
Si V	$1s^22s^22p^6$, $1s^22s^22p^5 nl$ $(n = 3)$ $(l < n)$, $1s^22s^22p^5 nl$ $(n = 4,5,6,7)$ $(l < 3)$
Si VI	$1s^22s^22p^5$, $1s^22s^22p^4 nl$ $(n = 3)$ $(l < n)$, $1s^22s^22p^4 nl$ $(n = 4,5,6,7)$ $(l < 3)$
Si VII	$1s^22s^22p^4$, $1s^22s^22p^3 nl$ $(n = 3)$ $(l < n)$, $1s^22s^22p^3 nl$ $(n = 4,5)$ $(l < 3)$
Si VIII	$1s^22s^22p^3$, $1s^22s^22p^2 nl$ $(n = 3)$ $(l < n)$, $1s^22s^22p^2 nl$ $(n = 4,5)$ $(l < 3)$
Si IX	$1s^22s^22p^2$, $1s^22s^22p^1 nl$ $(n = 3)$ $(l < n)$, $1s^22s^22p^1 nl$ $(n = 4,5)$ $(l < 3)$

Figure 2a presents a typical non-LTE spectral emissivity (in units of W cm^{-3} nm^{-1} sr^{-1}) and the opacity coefficients ($=\kappa/\rho$, where κ is the spectral absorption coefficient in units of cm^{-1} and ρ is the density in units of g cm^{-3}) in the tabulated EOS Si database over the wavelength region of 120–170 nm for an artificial homogeneous plasma at $\rho \approx 10^{-4}$ g cm^{-3} and a temperature of kT $\approx$ 5 eV. The CR model depends on three different temperatures for the electron (T_e), ion (T_i), and the radiation field (T_r). Here, it is assumed that $T_e = T_i = $ kT $\approx$ 5 eV and $T_r = 0.2 \times T_e$. It is found that the effect of T_r on the spectral emissivity and opacity coefficient (Figure 2a) is negligible at this condition. Throughout this study, the spectral emissivity and opacity coefficients include the bound–bound, bound–free and free–free processes. Figure 2b presents the spectral radiance (in units of W cm^{-2} nm^{-1} sr^{-1}) of an artificial homogeneous Si plasma at $\rho \approx 10^{-4}$ and $\approx 4 \times 10^{-4}$ g cm^{-3}, kT $\approx$ 5 eV, and the photon path length (e.g., the plasma radius) of d $\approx$ 350 µm. An inspection of Figures 1 and 2b reveal the calibrated Si spectra is more and less in agreement with the calculated spectral radiance, especially at $\rho \approx 10^{-4}$ g cm^{-3}. Note that in the FAC code, the accuracy of the wavelengths and transition rates for VUV and visible lines that usually result from the transitions within the same configurations from near-neutral ions can be limited, especially for transition metals with incomplete d-shell. Although it is possible to adjust the energy levels, however, the detailed investigation on the spectral line positions was beyond the scope of the present study. The calculations in Figure 2b demonstrate the spectral radiations from two Si III and Si IV charge states are main contributors for measured calibrated FUV emission in Figure 1. Note that the time-space integrated spectral irradiance (Figure 1) can be estimated using the CR solver coupled to hydrodynamics code. However, a very crude approximation may be made as follows. The spectral irradiance (M_λ, in units of W cm^{-2} nm^{-1}) is linked to the spectral radiance (L_λ, in units of W cm^{-2} nm^{-1} sr^{-1}) by the Lambert's cosine law [23], i.e., $M_\lambda = \pi L_\lambda$. This irradiance is inversely proportional to the square of the distance from the plasma, that is, the inverse square law. Suppose a spherical plasma with a radius d $\approx$ 350 µm (somewhat larger than the laser spot size), a plasma emission duration $\Delta\tau \approx$ 20 ns (i.e., 2 $\times$ FWHM laser pulse), and the laser repetition-rates v = 100 Hz. With these assumptions, Figure 2b gives approximately the measured irradiance in Figure 1. For example, for strong spectral lines about the wavelength 140 nm (with the radiance of $\approx 4 \times 10^4$ W cm^{-2} nm^{-1} in Figure 2b), the irradiance at 100 cm from the target is $\approx (4 \times 10^4 \times 10^6) \pi A_s \Delta\tau v/100^2 \approx 0.4$ µW cm^{-2} nm^{-1}. Here, the A_s is the plasma area. Indeed, in transient, non-LTE plasmas with strong temperature and density gradients generated in LPP sources, the plasma parameters such as the temperature and density, plasma size, and the integrated spectral emission are space- and time-dependent and cannot be simulated under the assumption of the perfect homogeneity of the plasma (e.g., Figure 2b). Consequently, there are a few discrepancies between the calculated spectral radiance (Figure 2b) and measured spectral irradiance (Figure 1). For example, the calculation cannot reproduce the measured intensity ratio of two strong Si IV lines around 140 nm. In addition, a comparison among the corresponding spectral emissivities and opacities of these lines (Figure 2a), the spectral radiance (Figure 2b) and the measured spectral irradiance reveals that the ratio approaches the black-body limit due to the opacity effect. Thus, the calculation may reproduce the measured Si IV line intensity ratio at different plasma conditions, e.g., from an optically thinner plasma.

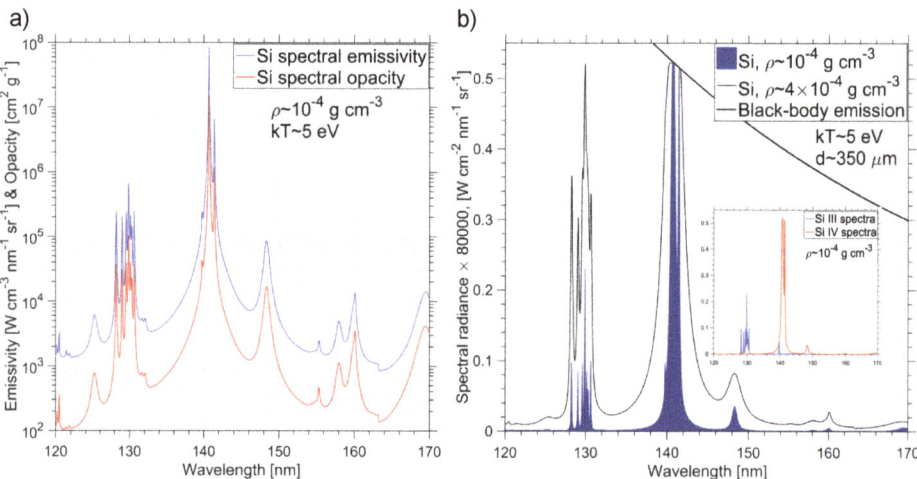

Figure 2. (**a**): Calculated spectral emissivity and opacity coefficients versus the wavelength at $\rho \approx 10^{-4}$ g cm^{-3} and kT $\approx$ 5 eV; (**b**): the calculated spectral radiance for an artificial homogeneous Si plasma at $\rho \approx 10^{-4}$ g cm^{-3} (blue shaded area) and $\approx 4 \times 10^{-4}$ g cm^{-3} (dark solid line), kT $\approx$ 5 eV, and d $\approx$ 350 µm. The black-body emission curve versus the wavelength at the same temperature is also shown. The spectral contributions of the main individual Si ions (i.e., Si III and Si IV) are also presented. Note that the ordinates of (**a**,**b**) are not in the same scale.

4. Results and Discussion

Under the LTE hypothesis, the radiation of thermal light sources is governed by the fundamental laws of thermodynamics. Their intensity and spectral distribution, which depend on temperature, can be determined with the Kirchhoff's law of absorption–emission and Planck's equation, respectively, [23]. For a truly black-body over the wavelength range from zero to infinity, the radiation power emitted by the surface is given by the Stefan–Boltzmann's law. When the temperature of a black-body radiator increases, the overall radiated energy increases and the peak of the radiation curve moves to shorter wavelengths according to the Wien's displacement law. In this framework, the peak of the radiation curve (i.e., λ_W [nm] T_{bb}[eV] $\approx$ 250, where λ_W and T_{bb} are the peak of black-body radiation curve and its temperature, respectively) varies in the wavelength range of $\approx$170–120 nm for a black-body temperature (i.e., the radiation temperature) of $\approx$1.5–2 eV, respectively. Typical radiation-hydrodynamic calculations for the laser irradiance relevant to the LPP EUV/XR source experiments (not shown here) show that a maximum of the local radiation temperature in the plasma core is much less than local electron temperature. Thus, to produce an efficient pulsed plasma FUV light source, it is expected that the electron temperature should be higher than T_{bb}. On the other hand, the measured plasma threshold fluences (F_{th}) for the various metal targets in the air at atmospheric pressure are reported to be in the region of $0.9 \leq F_{th} \leq 8.5$ J cm^{-2} for a Q-switched 1.0 µm, ns Nd:YAG solid-state laser [24]. For example, the measured F_{th} is $\approx$0.9, 3, and 8.5 J cm^{-2} for the zinc (Zn), molybdenum (Mo) and tungsten (W) metal targets, respectively. Therefore, the necessary plasma threshold laser irradiances for 10 ns, 60 ns, and 100 ns FWHM pulses are approximately in the range of $\approx$(0.9–9) $\times 10^8$, (0.2–2) $\times 10^8$, and (0.1–0.9) $\times 10^8$ W cm^{-2} for Zn, Mo and W metal targets, respectively. Note that the plasma threshold fluence is defined using the emission of a given spectral resonance lines of neutral element, e.g., the strong radiation originated from transitions among 3d^{10}4s4p-3d^{10}4s4d of Zn I in the wavelength region of 320–340 nm [22]. Our calculations show, using the FAC code, low-ionized charge states, e.g., Zn III–Zn IV radiate strongly over the wavelength region of 120–170 nm. Thus, a somewhat higher laser fluence (or irradiance) than F_{th} is needed to produce an efficient FUV plasma light source.

The spectral features of various gases, liquid metal droplets [20] (not shown here), and metal targets were generated by a 1.0 μm fiber laser with 60–100 ns FWHM and 2–20 kHz repetition rates at a low laser irradiance region of $\approx 10^6$ to 5×10^9 W cm^{-2}. Typical calibrated FUV spectral irradiances (in units of μW cm^{-2} nm^{-1}) of the Si (Z = 14), Zn (Z = 30), and tin (Sn, Z = 50) plasmas at a distance of 100 cm from the target over a wavelength region of $\approx$123 to 164 nm are shown in Figure 3. The laser irradiance is estimated using the measurement of the average laser power for each experiment by an OPHIR laser power meter (serial number 517845). We recorded the plasma FUV emission (e.g., using the Zn solid target) for the laser irradiance as low as $\approx 5 \times 10^6$ W cm^{-2} using 100 ns FWHM and 20 kHz pulses. A high repetition rate of 20 kHz enables improving the signal-to-noise ratio at this low laser irradiance, i.e., to detect a clear FUV spectral emission over the wavelength region of $\approx$123–165 nm. This laser irradiance gives a $F_{th} \approx 0.5$ J cm^{-2}. This value is equal to the calculated theoretical plasma threshold fluence for the Zn metal target, as can be seen in Ref. [24]. It is worth mentioning that the previous report [24] shows that there is approximately no significant difference in F_{th} using single-shot irradiation with each pulse hitting a fresh sample spot or accumulating ten pulse shots on the same target surface. Our experimental and atomic physics calculations [6,17,21] show that the Zn plasma radiates strong FUV spectral band with a CE as high as $\approx 3\%/2\pi$sr at a laser irradiance of $\approx 5 \times 10^9$ W cm^{-2} for 2 kHz, 60 ns pulse. The corresponding Zn spectrum is shown in Figure 3 (right ordinate: the spectrum is marked with a rectangle). The unresolved transitions arrays from $3d^9\ 4l$-$3d^9\ 4l'$ and $3d^8\ 4l$-$3d^8\ 4l'$ orbitals in Zn III and Zn IV ions produce an efficient Zn plasma FUV light source. Here, l and l' are the orbital quantum numbers (i.e., s, p, d, f, ...). An inspection of Figures 1, 2b and 3 reveals the main charge states responsible for the Si and Zn plasma FUV radiations are the Si III, Si IV and Zn III, Zn IV ions, respectively. Furthermore, our study shows that the Sn III, Sn IV, and Sn V ions are major contributors to the FUV emission in Sn plasma. Figure 3 shows the Si spectra is somewhat more powerful (with a CE $\approx 1\%/2\pi$sr) than the emission from Zn and Sn plasmas at the laser irradiance of $\approx 10^9$ W cm^{-2} for 60 ns pulse at 2 kHz operation. A reason may come from the fact that the spectral lines of Si plasma are strong resonance lines in Si III and Si IV ions that are radiatively coupled to the ground states, whereas for Zn III and Zn IV ions, the transitions are generated among the singly excited states. Additionally, the low-ionized Si III–Si IV charge states remain stable over a wider electron temperature region than Zn III–Zn IV and Sn III–Sn V ions. For example, the average ionic charge states of Si and Sn are $\approx$3.9 and $\approx$6.2 at the electron temperature of $\approx$10 eV, respectively. Thus, a plasma over-ionization effect is less severe for the Si than Zn and/or Sn plasmas. Comparison of the Si spectra in Figures 1 and 3 show the two strong spectral lines around 140 nm (i.e., transitions of $2p^6\ 3s$-$2p^6\ 3p$ in Si IV) are broadened and merged in the plasma created by the longer pulse of 60 ns width at a lower laser irradiance of $\approx 10^9$ W cm^{-2}. The reason may be understood based on the calculation using the CR solver for an artificial homogeneous plasma. Figure 2b shows the spectral lines of Si IV around 140 nm can become optically thick (i.e., no object at a given temperature can emit more than black-body emission limit) at a high density region or a long photon path length owing to a larger plasma size for the 60 ns than 10 ns pulse. Thus, in the case of a collision-dominated plasma or an optically thick medium [25], it is expected that these two resonance spectral lines broadened and merged together at a typical areal density of Si plasma $\approx \rho \times d \geq 10^{-5}$ g cm^{-2} and a temperature of 5 eV. Note that, in the CR calculation, we used the Voigt spectral line shape that includes the collisional (i.e., the impact pressure) and Doppler broadening mechanisms (Figure 2b) [23]. It is worth noting that the instrumental broadening is not taken into account in the calculation. There are a few discrepancies between the calculated and the measured Si spectral emission. Particularly, the calculated continuum emission is much less than the measured spectra. Figure 3 shows the Si spectral lines around 130 nm and at shorter wavelengths are stronger than the corresponding lines in Figure 1. The reason is due to the lower temperature of Si plasma in conditions relevant to Figure 3 compared to Figure 1 owing to the lower laser irradiance. Thus, the spectral radiations originated from the lower charge state of Si III are stronger than Si IV. Moreover, the calculations using the CR solver show (Figure 2b) the ratio of spectral lines around 130–140 nm increases by raising the plasma opacity, i.e., by increasing the plasma density or the photon path length.

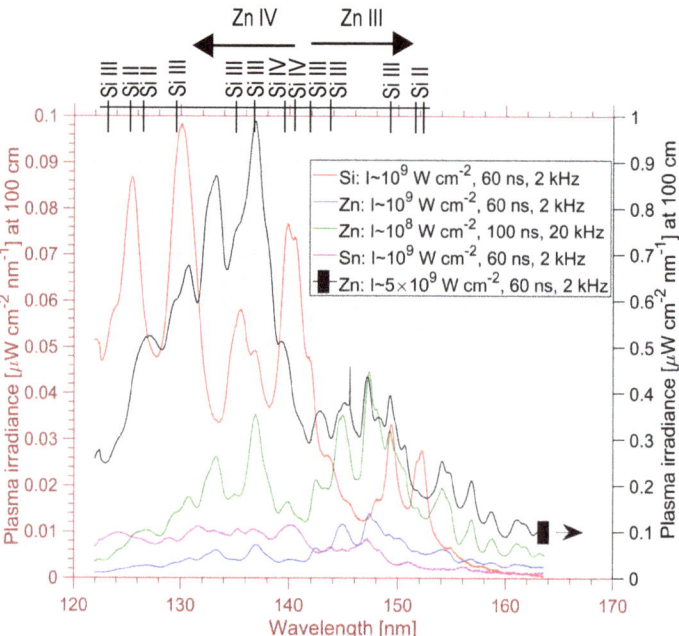

Figure 3. Measured FUV spectral irradiances of the Si, Zn and Sn plasmas at a distance of 100 cm from the target over the ≈123–164 nm wavelength region. Plasmas were generated by a 1.0 μm laser at two operation regimes: with pulse widths of 60 and 100 ns FWHM and the repetition rates of 2 and 20 kHz. Note that the right ordinate is used for one of the Zn spectra (marked with a filled rectangle) for better view. Here, the laser irradiances (pulse energies) for 2 and 20 kHz rep-rates are ≈10^9 W cm^{-2} (≈3 mJ), ≈5×10^9 W cm^{-2} (≈15 mJ), and ≈10^8 W cm^{-2} (20 kHz, 100 ns FWHM laser pulse energy ≈0.6 mJ), respectively. Positions of Si spectral lines are shown (on top) using the NIST atomic database [22].

The spectral features of several targets were also generated with 10 ns FWHM, 100 Hz laser at different laser irradiances in the range of $I \approx 10^{10}$ to 2.5×10^{11} Wcm^{-2}. Note that at this laser condition, the target rotated fast enough to provide a fresh sample in each laser shot. Figure 4a presents the calibrated spectral plasma irradiances (in units of μW cm^{-2} nm^{-1}) of the Si, Zn, Mo, Sn and tantalum (Ta, Z = 73) planar targets at a distance of 100 cm from the target over the wavelength range of ≈123–164 nm. Here, the laser irradiance was ≈2.5×10^{11} Wcm^{-2}. This irradiance is well beyond the plasma threshold fluence of all refractory metals. At this laser irradiance, all spectra were calculated after averaging ≈3000 pulses. As previously discussed, the main spectral features of the Si and Zn plasmas were mainly created from the low-ionized charge states of Si III–Si IV and Zn III–Zn IV ions, respectively. Inspection of Figures 3 and 4a reveals the main spectral lines of Si IV (around ≈140 nm) and Zn IV (≤140 nm) are brighter than Si III (around ≈130 nm) and Zn III (≥140 nm) in plasma generated by a 10 ns pulse than 60 ns due to the higher laser irradiance, consequently, a higher temperature. Additionally, as stated before, the low-ionized Sn III, Sn IV, and Sn V ions are main contributors in the measured Sn spectra (Figure 4a). Figure 4a shows that the Mo and Ta plasmas generate a weaker spectral FUV emission compared to the Zn and Sn ions. The reason may be due to plasma over-ionization, i.e., the Mo and Ta plasma radiations may be increased at the lower laser irradiance region. Figure 4a shows that all of the measured plasma spectral radiations have a continuum on which the emission lines are superimposed.

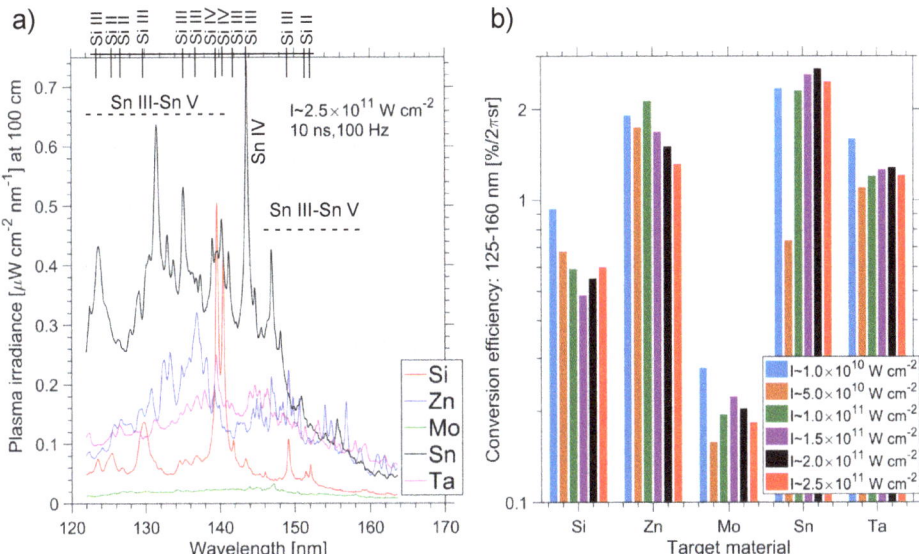

Figure 4. (**a**) Measured spectral irradiances of the Si, Zn, Mo, Sn and Ta plasmas at a distance of 100 cm from the target over the wavelength region of ≈123–164 nm. Here, a plasma generated by a 1.0 µm, 100 Hz, 10 ns pulse at the laser irradiance of ≈2.5 × 10^{11} W cm^{-2} (pulse energy ≈ 230 mJ). The observed Si spectral lines are shown (on top) using the NIST database [22]; (**b**) measured radiation conversion efficiency (in units of % into 2πsr) over the wavelength spectral band of 125–160 nm for various laser irradiances (pulse energies) of ≈10^{10} (≈10 mJ), 5 × 10^{10} (≈44 mJ), 1.0 × 10^{11} (≈90 mJ), 1.5 × 10^{11} (≈140 mJ), 2 × 10^{11} (≈190 mJ) and 2.5 × 10^{11} Wcm^{-2} (≈230 mJ).

Figure 4b presents the measured radiation conversion efficiencies (in units of % into 2πsr) over the wavelength region of 125–160 nm versus the peak laser irradiances in the range of ≈10^{10} to 2.5 × 10^{11} W cm^{-2}. For these experimental conditions, maximum radiation conversion efficiencies in the range of 1–3%/2πsr were measured. All conditions that are known were kept constant during the experiments. However, note that at the low laser irradiance in contrast to the high region, around 60,000 pulses were accumulated to obtain each spectrum. All of the emission signals were corrected by the subtraction of the noise (dark) signal of the detector, which were separately measured for the same corresponding exposure time. Figure 4b shows the Si, Mo and Ta plasmas generate higher conversion efficiencies at the lowest laser irradiance of ≈10^{10} Wcm^{-2}. We expect that low-ionized charge states of the heavy elements with the open d-sub-shell, for example, Mo (with the neutral ground configuration $4d^5 5s$), Ta (with the neutral ground configuration $5d^3 6s^2$) and tungsten (with the neutral ground configuration $5d^4 6s^2$ [26]) generate a strong continuum-like FUV spectra at the lower laser irradiance than ≈10^{10} Wcm^{-2}. In particular, it is predicted through preliminary calculations that an optically thick Ta (or the tungsten) plasma radiates a strong broad quasi-flat FUV emission at a temperature region less than 5 eV. Indeed, more experiments needed to investigate the best target condition by considering the debris issue. Previous experiments demonstrated that a low-debris LPP plasma source is possible by using, e.g., gas [8] or droplet targets. For example, George et al. [4] demonstrated that the realization of a high CE low-debris LPP Sn EUV source is possible by reducing the mass of tin target, which is accomplished by using tin-doped droplet targets. These features are now under investigation, especially the debris issue in high repetition-rates experiments at a low laser fluence region.

Due to the lack of experimental information on the evolution of plasma parameters, a picture of the plasma dynamics may be obtained using the radiation-hydrodynamics model. Here, a radiation-hydrodynamics code, FLASH is used to investigate the plasma temperature and density at a given peak laser irradiance of $\approx 10^{10}$ Wcm^{-2}. Figure 5a–c present typical 2D spatial distributions of the electron temperature, the plasma density, and electron density near the peak laser irradiance, respectively. Here, this code is employed to study the plasma dynamics for the case of a planar solid Si target (with the initial density of ≈ 2.33 g cm^{-3}) irradiated by a 1.06 µm, 10 ns FWHM Gaussian-temporal-spatial-shaped laser pulse with a peak irradiance of $\approx 10^{10}$ Wcm^{-2}. In the simulation model, a single laser beam illuminates a planar target in the radius-Z (R-Z) cylindrical geometry. The laser is focused on the Z axis and enters the domain at a 90-degree angle, i.e., laser beam is normal to the target. It is assumed that the Si target is in a low-density air environment related to the pressure of 1.3×10^{-4} Pa at the vacuum chamber. The laser spot size diameter is assumed to be ≈ 120 µm ($1/e^2$ width ≈ 200 µm). The FLASH code predicts a maximum of electron temperature ≈ 20 eV for the plasma core at the peak laser irradiance. This plasma temperature is high enough to produce an average ionic charge state higher than ≈ 4, especially for elements with a high atomic number such as Mo or Ta. Our calculations (not shown here) predict that at such a high temperature, the plasma should also strongly emit at the wavelengths shorter than 120 nm. The calculation also shows at the maximum laser irradiance, this dense high-temperature plasma close to the target radiates intense continuum emission. Figure 5a also presents a dashed-lines contour to emphasize plasma regions with the electron temperatures in the range of 0.5–8 eV. Our study reveals that the dense low-temperature plasma, especially close to the target (as can be seen in Figure 5b for the region of $\rho \geq 10^{-4}$ g cm^{-3}), strongly radiates in the FUV region. The reason may be understood based on a comparison between the calculated Si spectral radiance (Figure 2b) and measured signal (Figure 4a). Due to the lack of experimental information, an effective plasma size may be estimated by the simulation as ≈ 300 µm. Indeed, more experiments and the radiation-hydrodynamic calculations coupled to the CR solver are required to investigate the conversion efficiency versus the laser spot diameter, pulse width and emission angle (angle-resolved spectra) in the laser plasma FUV light source. These features are now under investigation.

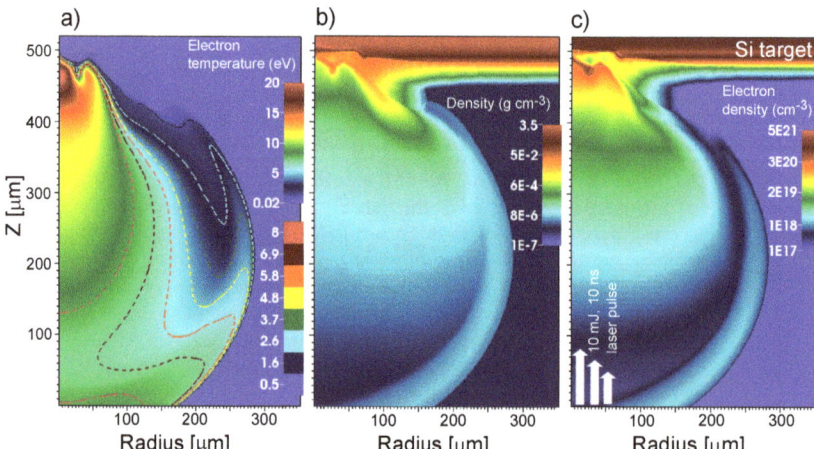

Figure 5. (a) The spatial distributions of the plasma electron temperature (in units of eV); (b) the plasma density (in units of g cm^{-3}); and (c) the plasma electron density (in units of cm^{-3}) for a 10 ns LPP near the peak irradiance of $\approx 10^{10}$ Wcm^{-2} over the Radius-Z space calculated using a 2D Eulerian FLASH code. The laser beam propagates along the Z direction as shown in (c). Here, a dashed-lines contour in Figure 5a shows the locations with the electron temperatures in the range of ≈ 0.5–8 eV.

5. Conclusions

We discussed in detail the analysis of short-wavelength data obtained from a laser plasma light source, characterized with an aberration-corrected McPherson Seya–Namioka type monochromator sensitive to the vacuum-ultraviolet spectral range. Absolute spectral irradiance calibration of laser plasmas for a wavelength FUV band from $\approx$123 to 164 nm was performed using a standard Deuterium lamp. Plasmas were created from fast rotating solid targets (Si, Zn, Mo, Sn and Ta) by two 1.0 µm lasers, separately; a Q-switched Nd:YAG solid-state laser producing 10 ns FWHM pulses at 100 Hz repetition rates and a fiber laser operating with pulse widths (60–100 ns FWHM) and repetition rates (2–20 kHz). Plasma FUV emission is detected for the laser irradiance as low as $\approx 5 \times 10^6$ W cm^{-2} using 100 ns FWHM and 20 kHz pulses. It was demonstrated that high-density laser plasmas created by nanosecond laser pulses radiate strongly over the FUV wavelength region. Calculations using a developed collisional-radiative solver and radiation-hydrodynamic code reveal that the FUV spectral radiation mainly consists of a strong continuum emission due to a dense plasma core close to the target, which was superimposed by a vast spectral lines of low-ionized charge states. We measured a maximum conversion efficiency of $\approx$(1–3)%/2πsr of the laser light to the FUV spectral band from a few selected targets by both lasers, i.e., 10 and 60 ns FWHM pulses. Particularly, the calculation and experimental results show emission from specific wavelength regions can be enhanced by proper optimization of target and laser parameters. These results are valuable for the lithography and metrology tools in the semiconductor industry as well as to design a high-power incoherent point-like FUV light sources driven by Q-switched mJ infrared laser pulses.

Author Contributions: Project administration, M.R.; supervision and analyzing measurements, M.M., M.R.; software-computational modeling, M.M.; writing—review and editing, M.M., M.R. All authors have read and agreed to the published version of the manuscript.

Funding: This work was supported in part by the State of Florida.

Data Availability Statement: All the data generated and analyzed that support the findings of this study are available from the corresponding author upon request.

Acknowledgments: The authors gratefully acknowledge the University of Chicago for making the FLASH code available.

Conflicts of Interest: The authors declare that they have no known competing financial interests or personal relationships that could have appeared to influence the work reported in this paper.

References

1. ISO21348 Definitions of Solar Irradiance Spectral Categories. Archived from Space Weather (spacewx.com). 2013. Available online: https://web.archive.org/web/20131029233428/http://www.spacewx.com/pdf/SET_21348_2004.pdf (accessed on 27 July 2021).
2. Rice, B. Extreme Ultraviolet (EUV) Lithography. In *Nanolithography: The Art of Fabricating Nanoelectronic and Nanophotonic Devices and Systems*; Feldman, M., Ed.; Woodhead Publishing: Cambridge, UK, 2014; pp. 1–80.
3. Fomenkov, I. EUV Source for High Volume Manufacturing: Performance at 250 W and Key Technologies for Power Scaling. EUV Source Workshop, Dublin, Ireland. 2017. Available online: https://www.euvlitho.com/2017/S1.pdf (accessed on 27 July 2021).
4. George, S.A.; Silfvast, W.T.; Takenoshita, K.; Bernath, R.T.; Koay, C.-S.; Shimkaveg, G.; Richardson, M.C. Comparative Extreme Ultraviolet Emission Measurements for Lithium and Tin Laser Plasmas. *Opt. Lett.* **2007**, *8*, 997–999. [CrossRef] [PubMed]
5. O'Sullivan, G. The Origin of Line-Free XUV Continuum Emission From Laser-Produced Plasmas of The Elements $62 \leq Z \leq 74$. *J. Phys. B At. Mol. Phys.* **1983**, *16*, 3291–3304. [CrossRef]
6. Szilagyi, J.; Parchamy, H.; Masnavi, M.; Richardson, M. Spectral Irradiance of Singly and Doubly Ionized Zinc in Low-Intensity Laser-Plasma Ultraviolet Light Sources. *J. Appl. Phys.* **2017**, *121*, 033303–033309. [CrossRef]
7. Di Palma, T.M.; Borghese, A. Characterization of a UV-VUV Light Source Based on a Gas-Target ns-Laser-Produced Plasma. *Nucl. Instr. Meth. B* **2007**, *254*, 193–199. [CrossRef]
8. Arikkatt, A.J.; Wachulak, P.; Fiedorowicz, H.; Bartnik, A.; Czwartos, J. Wideband Spectral Emission Measurements from Laser-Produced Plasma EUV/SXR Source Based on a Double Gas Puff Target. *Metrol. Meas. Syst.* **2020**, *27*, 701–719.
9. Xu, Q.; Deng, X.; Tian, H.; Zhao, Y.; Wang, Q. Influence of Pre-Ionized Plasma on the Dynamics of a Tin Laser-Triggered Discharge-Plasma. *Appl. Sci.* **2019**, *9*, 4981. [CrossRef]

10. Bezel, I.; Derstine, M.; Gross, K.; Shchemelinin, A.; Szilagyi, J.; Shortt, D. High Power Laser-Sustained Plasma Light Sources for KLA-Tencor Broadband Wafer Inspection Tools. EUV Source Workshop, Dublin, Ireland. 2017. Available online: https://www.euvlitho.com/2017/S63.pdf (accessed on 27 July 2021).
11. Beckers, J.; Van De Ven, T.; Van Der Horst, R.; Astakhov, D.; Banine, V. EUV-Induced Plasma: A Peculiar Phenomenon of a Modern Lithographic Technology. *Appl. Sci.* **2019**, *9*, 2827. [CrossRef]
12. Sinha, H.; Ren, H.; Nichols, M.T.; Lauer, J.L.; Tomoyasu, M.; Russell, N.M.; Jiang, G.; Antonelli, G.A.; Fuller, N.C.; Engelmann, S.U.; et al. The Effects of Vacuum Ultraviolet Radiation on Low-k Dielectric Films. *J. Appl. Phys.* **2012**, *112*, 111101–111121. [CrossRef]
13. Takahashi, A.; Okada, T.; Hiyama, T.; Maeda, M.; Uchino, K.; Nohdomi, R.; Mizoguchi, H. Ar_2 Excimer Emission From a Laser-Heated Plasma in a High-Pressure Argon Gas. *Appl. Phys. Lett.* **2000**, *77*, 4115–4117. [CrossRef]
14. Kogelschatz, U.; Esrom, H.; Zhang, J.-Y.; Boyd, I.W. High-Intensity Sources of Incoherent UV and VUV Excimer Radiation for Low-Temperature Materials Processing. *Appl. Surf. Sci.* **2000**, *168*, 29–36. [CrossRef]
15. Gu, F.M. The Flexible Atomic Code. *Can. J. Phys.* **2008**, *86*, 675–696. [CrossRef]
16. Masnavi, M.; Nakajima, M.; Hotta, E.; Horioka, K. Estimation of the Lyman-α Line Intensity in a Lithium-Based Discharge-Produced Plasma Source. *J. Appl. Phys.* **2008**, *103*, 013303–013311. [CrossRef]
17. Masnavi, M.; Szilagyi, J.; Parchamy, H.; Richardson, M. Laser-Plasma Source Parameters for Kr, Gd, and Tb Ions at 6.6 nm. *Appl. Phys. Lett.* **2013**, *102*, 164102–164105. [CrossRef]
18. Parchamy, H.; Szilagyi, J.; Masnavi, M.; Richardson, M. Ultraviolet Out-of-Band Radiation Studies in Laser Tin Plasma Sources. *J. Appl. Phys.* **2017**, *122*, 173303–173310. [CrossRef]
19. Fu, W.; Liang, E.P.; Fatenejad, M.; Lamb, D.Q.; Grosskopf, M.; Park, H.-S.; Remington, B.; Spitkovsky, A. Increase of the Density, Temperature and Velocity of Plasma Jets Driven by a Ring of High Energy Laser Beams. *High Energy Density Phys.* **2013**, *9*, 336–340. [CrossRef]
20. Richardson, M.C.; Koay, C.-S.; Takenoshita, K.; Keyser, C. High Conversion Efficiency Mass-Limited Sn-Based Laser Plasma Source for EUV Lithography. *J. Vac. Sci. Technol. B* **2004**, *22*, 785–790. [CrossRef]
21. Parchamy, H.; Szilagyi, J.; Masnavi, M.; Richardson, M. Quantitative Analysis of Vacuum-Ultraviolet Radiation From Nanosecond Laser-Zinc Interaction. *Opt. Laser. Technol.* **2018**, *103*, 1–7. [CrossRef]
22. Atomic Spectra Database. Available online: https://physics.nist.gov/PhysRefData/ASD/levels_form.html (accessed on 27 July 2021).
23. Masnavi, M.; Nakajima, M.; Hotta, E.; Horioka, K.; Niimi, G.; Sasaki, A. Estimation of Optimum Density and Temperature for Maximum Efficiency of Tin Ions in Z Discharge Extreme Ultraviolet Sources. *J. Appl. Phys.* **2007**, *101*, 033306–033317. [CrossRef]
24. Cabalin, L.M.; Laserna, J.J. Experimental Determination of Laser Induced Breakdown Thresholds of Metals Under Nanosecond Q-Switched Laser Operation. *Spectrochim. Acta Part B* **1998**, *53*, 723–730. [CrossRef]
25. Fujimoto, T. *Plasma Spectroscopy*; Clarendon Press; Oxford University Press: New York, NY, USA, 2004; pp 236–256.
26. Abdallah, J., Jr.; Colgan, J.; Clark, R.E.H.; Fontes, C.J.; Zhang, H.L. A Collisional-Radiative Study of Low Temperature Tungsten Plasma. *J. Phys. B At. Mol. Phys.* **2011**, *44*, 075701–075707. [CrossRef]

Article

Dosimetric Optimization of a Laser-Driven Irradiation Facility Using the G4-ELIMED Application

Sergio Mingo Barba [1,2,*], Francesco Schillaci [3], Roberto Catalano [4,5], Giada Petringa [3,4], Daniele Margarone [3,6] and Giuseppe Antonio Pablo Cirrone [4,5]

1. School of Engineering, Zurich University of Applied Sciences, 8400 Winterthur, Switzerland
2. Chemistry Department, University of Fribourg, 1700 Fribourg, Switzerland
3. ELI–Beamlines Center, Institute of Physics, Czech Academy of Sciences, 252 41 Dolní Břežany, Czech Republic; francesco.schillaci@eli-beams.eu (F.S.); giada.petringa@lns.infn.it (G.P.); D.Margarone@qub.ac.uk (D.M.)
4. Laboratori Nazionali del SUD, Istituto Nazionale di Fisica Nucleare (LNS-INFN), 95125 Catania, Italy; catalano@lns.infn.it (R.C.); pablo.cirrone@infn.it (G.A.P.C.)
5. Physics and Astronomy Department "E Majorana", University of Catania, 95125 Catania, Italy
6. Centre for Plasma Physics, School of Mathematics and Physics, Queen's University of Belfast, Belfast BT7 1NN, UK
* Correspondence: ming@zhaw.ch

Abstract: ELIMED has been developed and installed at ELI beamlines as a part of the ELIMAIA beamline to transport, monitor, and use laser-driven ion beams suitable for multidisciplinary applications, including biomedical ones. This paper aims to investigate the feasibility to perform radiobiological experiments using laser-accelerated proton beams with intermediate energies (up to 30 MeV). To reach this goal, we simulate a proton source based on experimental data like the ones expected to be available in the first phase of ELIMED commissioning by using the G4-ELIMED application (an application based on the Geant4 toolkit that simulates the full ELIMED beamline). This allows the study of transmission efficiency and the final characteristics of the proton beam at the sample irradiation point. The Energy Selector System is used as an active energy modulator to obtain the desired beam features in a relatively short irradiation time (around 6 min). Furthermore, we demonstrate the capability of the beamline to filter out other ion contaminants, typically co-accelerated in a laser-plasma environment. These results can be considered as a detailed feasibility study for the use of ELIMED for various user applications such as radiobiological experiments with ultrahigh dose rate proton beams.

Keywords: Monte Carlo simulations; Geant4; laser-accelerated ion beams

1. Introduction

High power laser-plasma interaction is a new and innovative approach to produce and accelerate particle beams [1]. The interaction of ultrahigh laser intensities (>10^{19} W/cm^2) with a thin (~µm) solid target results in the generation of extremely high magnetic and electric fields that produce a plasma and relativistic electrons (known as "hot electrons") propagating into the vacuum and creating a quasi-static sheath electric field at the target-vacuum interface. Such a field ionizes the target rear side and accelerates the ions outwards. The characteristics of the laser-accelerated ion beam will depend on the used laser and target parameters.

A laser-plasma ion accelerator can be considered as a "multi-color" source where different kinds of ionizing radiations (protons/ions, gamma/X-rays, electrons, and neutrons) can be produced simultaneously. Additionally, such accelerators are expected to generate ultra-high dose rate beams, which are orders of magnitude higher than those currently being proposed for the "FLASH" radiotherapy approach [2,3]. Moreover, a laser-based approach could potentially reduce the overall size and cost of an accelerator installation.

In this framework, the ELIMAIA (ELI Multidisciplinary Applications of laser-Ion Acceleration) beamline [4] at the ELI Beamlines (Extreme Light Infrastructure) Centre aims to provide ion beams accelerated by high repetition-rate petawatt-class lasers suitable for multidisciplinary user applications. The two major subsystems of ELIMAIA are the Ion Accelerator and ELIMED (ELI Beamlines MEDical and multidisciplinary applications) sections [5,6]. ELIMED, in turn, consists of three main sub-sections: (i) the ion collection and focusing part, (ii) the ion energy selection, and (iii) the in-air transport section. The collection and focusing section aims to collimate the laser-accelerated ion beam and reduce its peculiar large divergence. This part is made of a set of five Permanent-Magnet Quadrupoles (PMQs). As described in [7], the PMQs have different lengths (one is 160 mm long, two are 120 mm, and the other two 80 mm) and a field gradient of around 100 T/m over a 36 mm magnetic bore. The PMQs are used to properly inject the accelerated particles downstream into the Energy Selection System (ESS). Hence, the full section from the target to the first collimator of the chicane is arranged in a way that the matching condition between collection and selection sections are respected. This means that the drift between quadrupoles is chosen to keep the emittance and Twiss Parameters within the required values of the chicane (Table 1). Also, the transport matrix conditions to have a waist on the horizontal axis and a parallel beam on the vertical axis are respected (it means M12 = 0 and M44 = 0). The ESS is a chicane made of four laminated resistive dipoles [8]. The technology used for the laminated yokes of the magnets (98% of packing factor) allows fast changes (1 Hz) in the magnetic field intensity based on the required ion species, ion energy, and energy bandwidth. This allows to change the selected ion energy between different shots, i.e., the ESS can be used as an active energy modulator. This is a unique feature of the ELIMED beamline not available at other laser-based accelerator facilities. Downstream of the ESS, a set of electromagnets (two electromagnetic quadrupoles and two steerers) are available to allow a final shaping of the particle beam and to correct for systematic misalignments prior to its final delivery onto the user sample in the in-air dosimetry end-station, which is separated from the in-vacuum section by a thin kapton window. A detailed description of the ELIMAIA beamline, along with the ELIMED transport magnetic elements can be found here [4,6,9].

Table 1. ESS acceptance parameters. The parameters are defined in [8] and summarized here.

	$X\theta_x$	$Y\theta_y$	XY
α	0.8401	0.3556	0.0002
β (mm/π·mrad)	2.7094	2.4484	0.9112
Emit. Norm (rms) π mm·mrad	2.9506	3.9324	24.15 mm^2
X_{max}	Y_{max}	$\theta_{x, max}$	$\theta_{y, max}$
14.97 mm	14.99 mm	8.632 mrad	7.162 mrad

The ion and proton beams transported along ELIMED are characterized and monitored online in terms of energy, fluence, and spatial profile through a set of in-line detectors [10]. Diamond and silicon carbide detectors are extensively used in a Time-Of-Flight (TOF) configuration [11,12] to rapidly retrieve the beam energy spectra at different positions along the beamline. Furthermore, accurate shot-to-shot measurements of the dose released at the end of the beamline (where the user samples are placed) can be performed. ELIMED's absolute dosimetry systems are independent of the ultra-high dose rate (up to 10^9 Gy/s) and allow to perform online absolute dose determination with an accuracy better than 5%, thus satisfying the internationally established clinical requirements [13–15]. The ELIMED dosimetry system is based on three main devices: (i) a Secondary Electron Monitoring (SEM), (ii) a Multi-Gap Ionization Chamber (MGIC), and (iii) a Faraday Cup (FC) for absolute dosimetry. Passive detectors, such as CR39 and radiochromic films (RCF), are also used to benchmark active ion diagnostic and dosimetry devices. The entire ELIMED beamline (considering the initial ion source as an input) can be fully simulated using the developed ELIMED application of the Geant4 Monte Carlo toolkit [16–18].

In this study, the capability of the G4-ELIMED application was exploited to optimize the transmission efficiency along the beamline and the dosimetric characteristics of the final beam. The beamline configuration was optimized to obtain a final beam suitable for pilot radiobiology experiments by using laser-generated proton beams centered around 20 MeV. A Spread-Out Bragg Peak (SOBP) was generated using the ESS as an active energy modulator, which was the main aim of this study and at the same time producing a depth-dose profile similar to the ones required to carry out radiobiological experiments. Additionally, the removal of unwanted ion species accelerated in the laser-generated plasma, such as carbon ions, was studied to assure the capability of the beamline to filter out ion beam contaminants that can be detrimental for accurate dosimetric studies.

2. Materials and Methods

2.1. The G4-ELIMED Application

A dedicated Monte Carlo application has been developed to simulate the full ELIMED beamline and, in particular, to assess the dosimetric features of the ion beam on the user sample [16]. The Geant4 (GEometry ANd Tracking) toolkit [19–21], version 10.03, was selected as the most appropriate code for the ELIMED transport and dosimetry beamline simulation for its robustness, versatility, and reliability of the implemented physical processes.

The G4-ELIMED application realistically reproduces each element of the beamline, both in terms of geometry and magnetic features; it includes the detectors for the beam diagnostics and dosimetry (e.g., the SEM detector and the Faraday cup) and allows to retrieve complementary key information, such as secondary radiation emission along the beam transport section, ion dose distributions at the irradiated sample, and many others.

Since the ELIMED beamline was designed and realized to work in a wide range of applications (e.g., radiation chemistry like pulsed radiolysis of water [22,23], nuclear physics for generation of isotopes for Positron Emission Tomography (PET) [24,25], cultural heritage using proton activation analysis (PAA) techniques [26], and material science through radiation stress-tests, including electronics for space application [27,28]), the beamline setup can be easily modified, thus the simulation tools should support the exploitation of such beamline modularity. The user-friendly interface of the code allows its simple use also by non-expert users.

In this work, all the simulations were carried out with 10^5 initial particles and a maximum simulation step of 50 µm. These values were chosen to obtain high-quality results while maintaining a reasonable computational time.

2.2. Source Implementation

Since experimental data from the ELIMAIA-ELIMED source are not available yet, a realistic experimental source term (based on data from the J-KAREN-P PW-class laser facility in Japan [29]) was implemented in the simulation. The energy and angular distributions were based on the data from Dover et al. [30], where they used a laser beam with an irradiance of 5×10^{21} W·cm^{-2} and a stainless steel target with a thickness of 5 µm placed at 45^0 with respect to the laser direction. On the other hand, the spatial distribution was assumed to be Gaussian with a standard deviation equal to 10 µm. All the distributions are presented in Figure 1.

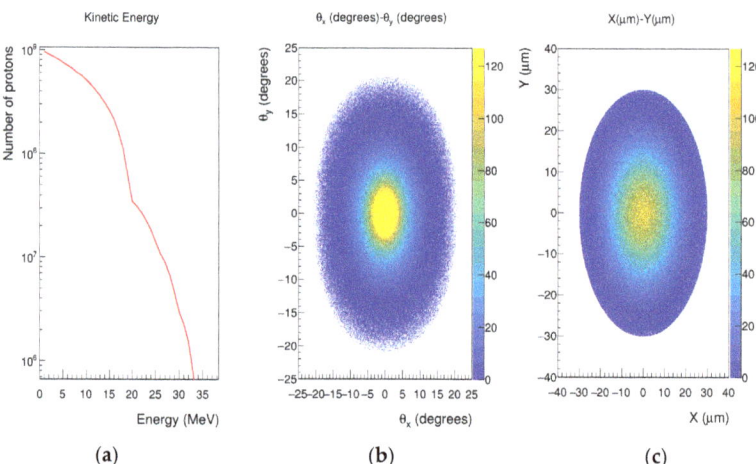

Figure 1. Distributions of the implemented source: (**a**) Initial kinetic energy distribution following the data presented in Dover et al. [30]; (**b**) Initial angular distribution. Protons at different energies have a maximum half-angle between 2.4 (highest energy) and 21 (lowest energy) degrees according to the data presented in Dover et al. [30]; (**c**) Initial position of the protons in the XY plane.

2.3. Depth-Dose Profile Generation

Clinical irradiations with ion beams are usually carried out using a Spread-Out Bragg Peak (or SOBP), i.e., a flat depth dose distribution is needed to uniformly irradiate a solid tumor.

The SOBP is the result of many beams of different energies and intensities added up with an appropriate weighting function. Usually, the energy change is done by some passive energy modulation system (e.g., a wheel modulator [31] or a ridge filter [32]) coupled with additional range shifters. These components are not required along the ELIMED beamline because the initial energy spectrum of laser-accelerated beams is intrinsically poly-energetic and the ESS can be used as an active energy modulator.

The only problem with such an approach is that the configuration of the focusing system needs to be changed to properly inject protons at different kinetic energies into the ESS. This will increase the time required to perform a certain experiment. For this reason, only the configurations to focus four different energies (18, 20, 22, and 25 MeV) were considered in this work. These changes have been calculated keeping the same sequence of magnets and limiting the displacement as much as possible in order to reduce the time necessary for repositioning the magnets. In such a way the transmission efficiency is not optimal, but the full irradiation time is limited to about 6 min. On the other hand, four setups calculated to maximize the transmission efficiency would require changing the sequence of the magnets, which means several hours because this operation cannot be performed under vacuum and involves the manipulation of heavy objects (the weight of the smaller quadrupole is about 70 kg).

In the simulated configurations, the first and the fourth PMQs have a length equal to 120 mm and positive polarity, while the second and the third PMQs have a length of 80 mm and negative polarity. The initial positions of the PMQs to transport the different energies are summarized in Table 2 and the relative distances between elements (D1, D2, D3, and D4) are clarified in Figure 2 where the generic scheme of the setup is presented.

Table 2. Initial positions of the four PMQs for the configurations used to focus different energy beams. The distances are calculated with respect to the position of the source.

Energy (MeV)	D1 (mm)	D2 (mm)	D3 (mm)	D4 (mm)
18	56.8	218.4	772.0	901.1
20	60.2	228.3	798.2	924.0
22	59.4	253.1	836.2	956.2
25	61.5	281.7	885.5	1005.5

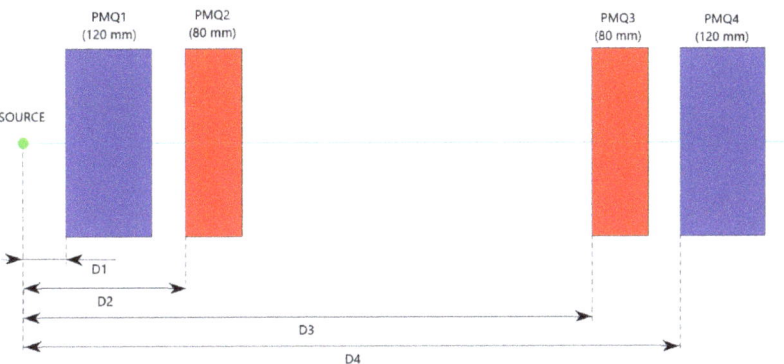

Figure 2. Layout of the collection and focusing section configuration. Values of the initial relative positions of the quadrupoles (D1, D2, D3, and D4) per each energy configuration are given in Table 2.

As mentioned above, the ESS can be used as an active energy modulator. This is realized by changing the magnetic field, i.e., the current intensity, of the dipoles to select different energies at different shots. Herein, the magnetic field values used in the energy selector are 0.243 T, 0.257 T, 0.269 T, and 0.287 T which are the necessary parameters to obtain protons with energies of 18 MeV, 20 MeV, 22 MeV, and 25 MeV, respectively, streaming on the reference trajectory. On the other hand, both the energy spread and the transmission efficiency depend on the aperture of the slit placed in the center of the ESS to select ions at different kinetic energies. Thus, a slit aperture equal to 30 mm was used to increase the transmission of protons, except in the 25 MeV case where a 20 mm slit aperture was used to reduce the energy spread and, hence, the distal fall-off of the SOBP.

2.4. In-Air Configuration of the Beamline

The detectors used for the online beam diagnostic and dosimetry were included in the simulations to consider the effect that they may introduce into the beam transport section. A brass scattering foil with a radius of 3 cm and a tantalum in-air collimator with 1.75 and 25 cm of inner and outer radius respectively were added to improve the characteristics of the final proton beam. To produce a proper SOBP, the thickness of the scattering foil (used to improve the lateral profiles) was varied between 200 and 320 µm. Furthermore, the in-air section length was decreased from 200 to 33 cm to reduce the scattering with the air and the loss of protons, which were important because of the low proton kinetic energies. A schematic layout of the in-air part configuration is presented in Figure 3.

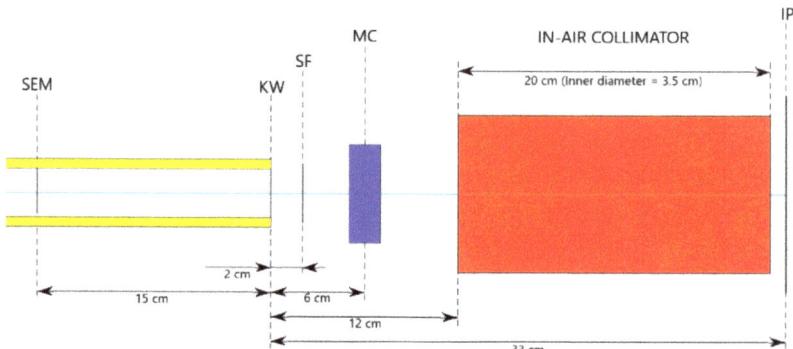

Figure 3. Layout of the in-air part of the beamline. The relative distances of the Secondary Electron Monitor (SEM), the Scattering Foil (SF), the Monitor Chamber (MC), the In-air Collimator, and the Irradiation Point (IP) are referred with respect to the Kapton Window (KW).

3. Results

Medical applications demand a high control of the beam characteristics. In this section, several clinically accepted parameters connected to the beam quality [33] were studied at the irradiation point to verify the capability of using the beamline to perform radiobiological experiments. The capability of the beamline to filter out unwanted carbon ions was additionally studied and discussed.

3.1. Lateral Profiles

The lateral profiles represent the relative dose distributions measured along the transversal axes with respect to the proton beam direction (in our case, the X and Y axes). To irradiate cells, flat distributions with very sharp lateral penumbras are desirable to ensure a homogeneous irradiation over all the cells. In this study, to reduce the impact of the noise produced by a lack of statistics in the quality parameters, the lateral profiles were normalized to the average value of the signal. The obtained lateral profiles are shown in Figure 4 and the corresponding beam quality parameters are summarized in Table 3.

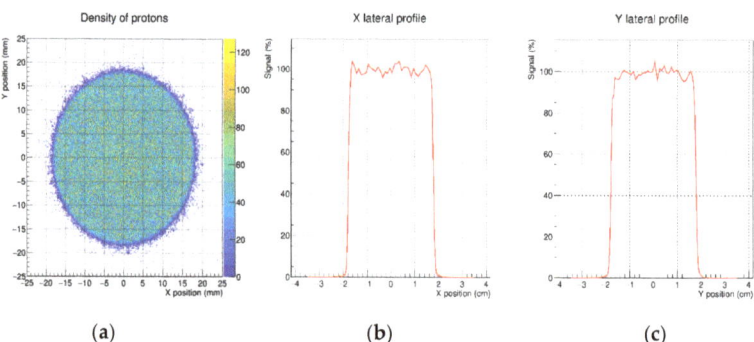

Figure 4. Distributions related with the lateral profiles at the irradiation point: (**a**) Density of protons in the XY plane produced by the combination of different energy beams; (**b**) Normalized lateral dose profiles on the X-axis obtained by the combination of different energy beams at the irradiation point; (**c**) Normalized lateral dose profiles on the Y-axis obtained by the combination of different energy beams at the irradiation point.

Table 3. Beam quality parameter tolerances and obtained results of the final lateral dose profiles. The calculation of quality parameters is defined in detail in [34,35].

Parameter	Tolerance	X Profile	Y Profile
FWHM	As close as possible to the beam diameter	3.57 cm	3.56 cm
Left penumbra	≤1.5 mm	0.85 mm	0.91 mm
Right penumbra	≤1.5 mm	0.82 mm	0.96 mm
Ratio 90%/50%	>0.9	0.96	0.95
Flatness	≤3%	4.1%	4.7%
Symmetry	97–103%	101.2%	100.1%

As observed in Table 3, the only parameter which was not falling within the required tolerances was the flatness. But, as it is observed in Figure 4, the profiles had a certain noise which was probably generated by a lack of statistics in the simulated proton histories.

3.2. Depth-Dose Profile

The depth-dose profile represents the dose deposited along the beam direction (in our case, the Z-axis). Herein, as previously mentioned, we tried to reproduce a SOBP with the combination of four different beam energies. The values of the depth-dose profile quality parameters are presented in Table 4 and the contribution of each energy together with their final combination are shown in Figure 5.

Table 4. Beam quality parameter tolerances and obtained results of the final depth-dose profile. The calculation of quality parameters is defined in detail in [31]. Here, the distal fall-off was defined as the 80–20% Penumbra.

Parameter	Tolerance	Result
M_{95}	≥1 mm	1.96 mm
Distal fall-off	<1.5 mm	0.94 mm
Flatness	<5%	3.6%

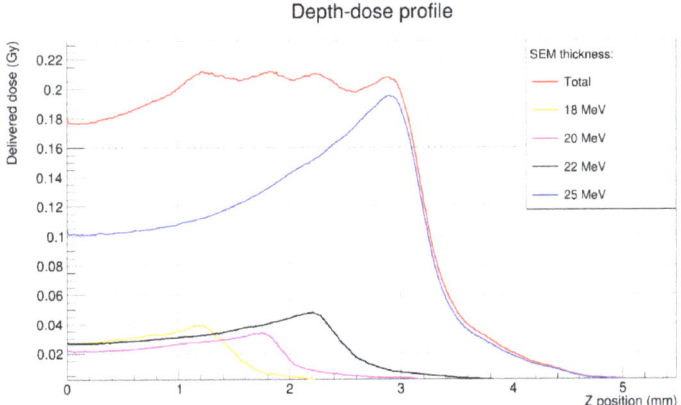

Figure 5. Depth-dose profile obtained at the irradiation point with the contribution of the four selected energies: 18 (yellow line), 20 (magenta line), 22 (black line), and 25 (blue line) MeV; while the red line corresponds to the combination of all them.

In this case, all the beam quality parameters were within the tolerances recommended of the international dosimetry code of practice [33], therefore this depth-dose distribution would be acceptable for clinically relevant radiobiology irradiation.

3.3. Transmission Efficiency

Another important aspect to be discussed is the capability of the beamline to efficiently transport protons around a given energy. The transmission efficiency was defined as the percentage of transmitted protons within ±10% of the selected kinetic energy (e.g., in the 20 MeV case, we would consider protons with kinetic energy between 18 and 22 MeV). The transmission efficiencies at diverse positions along the beamline are compiled in Table 5.

Table 5. Transmission efficiency values for different energy configurations and at different points along the ELIMED beamline.

Energy (MeV)	After PMQs (%)	After ESS (%)	After Kapton Window (%)	Final (%)
18	39	2.93	2.67	0.37
20	42.7	6.38	5.77	0.91
22	37.1	6.56	6.2	0.81
25	34.4	6.31	5.98	0.75

Despite the relatively low transmission efficiency for the given source term [30], it is important to stress that the low transmission values reported in Table 5 are still acceptable thanks to the relatively large proton number at the source. Ultimately, considering the available laser repetition rate, we focus our study on the time required to perform a sample irradiation experiment, i.e., the time needed to deliver the required dose at the irradiation point.

In radiobiology experiments, doses of the order of 1–2 Gy are typically required. Hence, the number of shots necessary to reach a 2 Gy dose level was calculated considering 10^{10} initial protons in the full energy spectrum (i.e., between 0 and 33 MeV) and the transmission efficiency of every single energy. A total number of 2812 shots were obtained. Considering that the L3 HAPLS laser system at ELI Beamlines [36] can deliver PW-class laser pulses at 10 Hz, approximately 280 s will be needed to reach the required dose on the user sample. However, this does not consider the time required to change the position of the PMQs, which was calculated considering a speed of 1 mm/s, thus returning about 110 s. Ultimately, the whole irradiation time is estimated to be approximately 6 min for the given source term.

3.4. Transmission of Unwanted Ion Species

In all the simulations presented above, only protons were considered. However, depending on the specific target used to produce the proton beam, some heavier, high-energy ions may be generated. The presence of such unwanted ion species could be detrimental for the sample irradiation if they are not properly filtered out by means of the beamline elements, thus affecting the results of the experiment. Therefore, the heavy-ion transmission effects must be studied prior to the proton beam irradiation. The transmissions of carbon ions with different charge states (from C^{1+} to C^{6+}) were considered at this stage. Such simulations were performed using a Carbon ion source similar to the proton one, but with a maximum cut-off energy calculated using the following empirical formula:

$$E_{cut-off}^{n+} = E_{cut-off}^{p} \cdot n/2, \tag{1}$$

where $E_{cut-off}^{n+}$ and $E_{cut-off}^{p}$ = 33 MeV are the maximum cut-off energies for carbon ions with a charge state equal to n and for protons, respectively.

The simulations were carried out only up to the exit of the ESS where the C^{1+}, C^{2+}, and C^{3+} beams were filtered out, while the C^{4+}, C^{5+}, and C^{6+} beams presented a transmission over the total initial number of carbon ions of 10^{-2}%, 3×10^{-2}% and 5×10^{-2}%, respectively. The simulations could be extended to the whole beamline but, as it is shown in Figure 6, the maximum kinetic energy after the ESS was around 70 MeV for C^{5+} ions, and the maximum range in the air for these ions is around 21 cm (according to ICRU range tables [37]). So, these ions would never be able to reach the irradiation point. Therefore, we can conclude that carbon ions in the given energy range are filtered out in the ELIMED beamline.

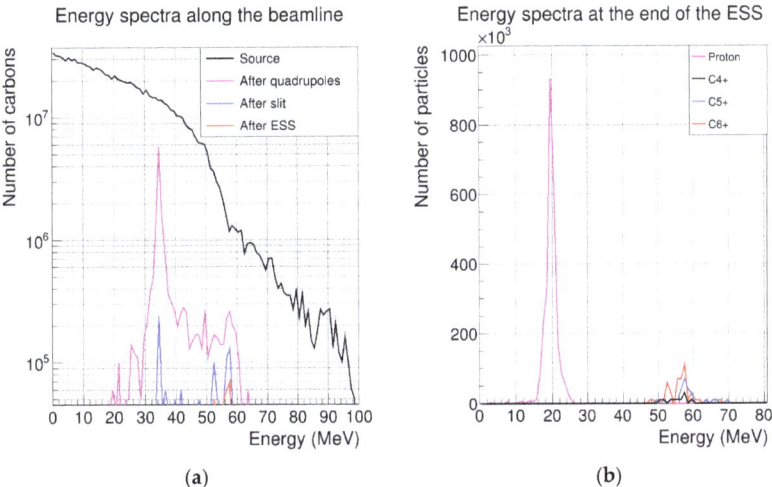

Figure 6. Energy spectra of carbon ions along ELIMED beamline: (**a**) Absolute energy spectra of C^{6+} ions at different points along the ELIMED beamline; (**b**) Absolute energy spectra of protons (magenta line), C^{4+} (black line), C^{5+} (blue line) and C^{6+} (red line) ions after the ESS. The spectra of C^{1+}, C^{2+}, and C^{3+} beams are not included because they are fully filtered before the end of the ESS.

4. Discussion

The presented simulations used a realistic (experimental) high-power laser-accelerated proton source term as input for modeling its selection and transport. A relatively low kinetic energy window (centered at 20 MeV) was considered of interest for the pilot, in-vitro radiobiology experiments at the ELIMAIA-ELIMED beamline. The use of the Energy Selection System (ESS) as an active energy modulator was proven to be feasible, but it showed the drawback related to the need to re-positioning the four PMQs to transport protons with different kinetic energies. However, these changes in the configuration of the collecting system (PMQs) are not expected to drastically increase the overall irradiation time (approximately 2 additional minutes), thus it would enable radiobiological irradiations in a reasonable amount of time (around 6 min). Moreover, it is expected that at higher energies (around 60 MeV, i.e., already laying in the clinical window) a single configuration of the beam focusing system would allow a more efficient transport and injection into the ESS, both for low and high proton energies based on the presence of given resonances [38], thus potentially shortening the overall sample irradiation time required to create a clinical SOBP. Finally, it is noteworthy that the experimental source term (laser-driven proton source) can be improved in terms of total proton flux, thus enhancing the final dose delivered onto the user sample.

The numerical results presented are promising in terms of final particle beam properties and demonstrate to fulfill the quality requirements for clinical applications. Furthermore, it was shown that unwanted plasma ion species, such as carbon ions, are properly filtered out in the ELIMED beamline. Thus, once the experimental characterization of the proton source at ELIMAIA will be carried out, the ELIMED beamline can be fine-tuned based on the actual initial proton beam spectral and spatial features at the source, and ultimately be optimized for pilot radiobiological tests with ultrahigh dose-rate, ultrashort laser-accelerated beams.

Author Contributions: The paper's initial idea was proposed by D.M., G.A.P.C., G.P. and F.S. The conceptualization is by D.M., G.A.P.C., G.P., F.S. and S.M.B.; the software work and analysis were performed by S.M.B.; Supervision by R.C. and G.P. The original draft preparation was by S.M.B., G.A.P.C. and F.S. and the review and editing were performed by S.M.B., D.M., G.A.P.C. and F.S. All authors have read and agreed to the published version of the manuscript.

Funding: This research was funded by INFN in the framework of the Interdisciplinary Committee and by the MC-INFN and ELIMED projects; it was also funded by the Ministry of Education, Youth, and Sports of the Czech Republic through the project "Advanced Research Using High-Intensity Laser-Produced Photons and Particles" (CZ.02.1.010.00.016_0190000789).

Data Availability Statement: Data are available from the corresponding authors upon reasonable request.

Conflicts of Interest: The authors declare no conflict of interest.

References

1. Macchi, A.; Borghesi, M.; Passoni, M. Ion acceleration by superintense laser-plasma interaction. *Rev. Mod. Phys.* **2013**, *85*, 751–793. [CrossRef]
2. Favaudon, V.; Caplier, L.; Monceau, V.; Pouzoulet, F.; Sayarath, M.; Fouillade, C.; Poupon, M.F.; Brito, I.; Hupé, P.; Bourhis, J.; et al. Ultrahigh dose-rate FLASH irradiation increases the differential response between normal and tumor tissue in mice. *Sci. Transl. Med.* **2014**, *6*, 245ra93. [CrossRef]
3. Vozenin, M.C.; Hendry, J.H.; Limoli, C.L. Biological Benefits of Ultra-high Dose Rate FLASH Radiotherapy: Sleeping Beauty Awoken. *Clin. Oncol.* **2019**, *31*, 407–415. [CrossRef]
4. Margarone, D.; Cirrone, G.; Cuttone, G.; Amico, A.; Andò, L.; Borghesi, M.; Bulanov, S.; Bulanov, S.; Chatain, D.; Fajstavr, A.; et al. ELIMAIA: A Laser-Driven Ion Accelerator for Multidisciplinary Applications. *Quantum Beam Sci.* **2018**, *2*, 8. [CrossRef]
5. Cirrone, G.A.P.; Romano, F.; Scuderi, V.; Amato, A.; Candiano, G.; Cuttone, G.; Giove, D.; Korn, G.; Krasa, J.; Leanza, R.; et al. Transport and dosimetric solutions for the ELIMED laser-driven beam line. *Nucl. Instruments Methods Phys. Res. Sect. A Accel. Spectrometers Detect. Assoc. Equip.* **2015**, *796*, 99–103. [CrossRef]
6. Cirrone, G.A.P.; Petringa, G.; Catalano, R.; Schillaci, F.; Allegra, L.; Amato, A.; Avolio, R.; Costa, M.; Cuttone, G.; Fajstavr, A.; et al. ELIMED-ELIMAIA: The First Open User Irradiation Beamline for Laser-Plasma-Accelerated Ion Beams. *Front. Phys.* **2020**, *8*, 564907. [CrossRef]
7. Schillaci, F.; Cirrone, G.A.P.; Cuttone, G.; Maggiore, M.; Andó, L.; Amato, A.; Costa, M.; Gallo, G.; Korn, G.; Larosa, G.; et al. Design of the ELIMAIA ion collection system. *J. Instrum.* **2015**, *10*, T12001. [CrossRef]
8. Schillaci, F.; Maggiore, M.; Andó, L.; Cirrone, G.A.P.; Cuttone, G.; Romano, F.; Scuderi, V.; Allegra, L.; Amato, A.; Gallo, G.; et al. Design of a large acceptance, high efficiency energy selection system for the ELIMAIA beam-line. *J. Instrum.* **2016**, *11*, P08022. [CrossRef]
9. Petringa, G.; Cirrone, G.A.P.; Catalano, R.; Cuttone, G.; Miluzzo, G.; Schillaci, F.; Tudisco, S.S.; Margarone, D. Status of the ELIMED-ELIMAIA beamline and innovative development of dosimetric devices for laser-driven ion beams. In *Proceedings of the Applying Laser-Driven Particle Acceleration II, Medical and Nonmedical Uses of Distinctive Energetic Particle and Photon Sources: SPIE Optics + Optoelectronics Industry Event*; Bolton, P.R., Ed.; SPIE: Bellingham, WA, USA, 2021; Volume 11790, p. 11.
10. Scuderi, V.; Amato, A.; Amico, A.; Borghesi, M.; Cirrone, G.; Cuttone, G.; Fajstavr, A.; Giuffrida, L.; Grepl, F.; Korn, G.; et al. Diagnostics and Dosimetry Solutions for Multidisciplinary Applications at the ELIMAIA Beamline. *Appl. Sci.* **2018**, *8*, 1415. [CrossRef]
11. Margarone, D.; Krsa, J.; Giuffrida, L.; Picciotto, A.; Torrisi, L.; Nowak, T.; Musumeci, P.; Velyhan, A.; Prokpek, J.; Lska, L.; et al. Full characterization of laser-accelerated ion beams using Faraday cup, silicon carbide, and single-crystal diamond detectors. *J. Appl. Phys.* **2011**, *109*, 103302. [CrossRef]
12. Scuderi, V.; Milluzzo, G.; Doria, D.; Alejo, A.; Amico, A.G.; Booth, N.; Cuttone, G.; Green, J.S.; Kar, S.; Korn, G.; et al. TOF diagnosis of laser accelerated, high-energy protons. *Nucl. Instruments Methods Phys. Res. Sect. A Accel. Spectrometers Detect. Assoc. Equip.* **2020**, *978*, 164369. [CrossRef]
13. Brahme, A.; Chavaudra, J.; McCullogh, E.; Nüsllin, F.; Rawlinson, J.E.; Svensson, G.; Svensson, H. Accuracy requirements and quality assurance of external beam therapy with photons and electrons. *Acta Oncol.* **1988**, *27* (Suppl. 1).
14. Goitein, M. Calculation of the uncertainty in the dose delivered during radiation therapy. *Med. Phys.* **1985**, *12*, 608–612. [CrossRef]
15. Mijnheer, B.J.; Battermann, J.J.; Wambersie, A. What degree of accuracy is required and can be achieved in photon and neutron therapy? *Radiother. Oncol.* **1987**, *8*, 237–252. [CrossRef]
16. Pipek, J.; Romano, F.; Milluzzo, G.; Cirrone, G.A.P.; Cuttone, G.; Amico, A.G.; Margarone, D.; Larosa, G.; Leanza, R.; Petringa, G.; et al. Monte Carlo simulation of the ELIMED beamline using Geant4. *J. Instrum.* **2017**, *12*, C03027. [CrossRef]
17. Milluzzo, G.; Pipek, J.; Amico, A.G.; Cirrone, G.A.P.; Cuttone, G.; Korn, G.; Larosa, G.; Leanza, R.; Margarone, D.; Petringa, G.; et al. Transversal dose distribution optimization for laser-accelerated proton beam medical applications by means of Geant4. *Phys. Medica* **2018**, *54*, 166–172. [CrossRef] [PubMed]

18. Milluzzo, G.; Pipek, J.; Amico, A.G.; Cirrone, G.A.P.; Cuttone, G.; Korn, G.; Larosa, G.; Leanza, R.; Margarone, D.; Petringa, G.; et al. Geant4 simulation of the ELIMED transport and dosimetry beam line for high-energy laser-driven ion beam multidisciplinary applications. *Nucl. Instruments Methods Phys. Res. Sect. A Accel. Spectrometers Detect. Assoc. Equip.* **2018**, *909*, 298–302. [CrossRef]
19. Agostinelli, S.; Allison, J.; Amako, K.; Apostolakis, J.; Araujo, H.; Arce, P.; Asai, M.; Axen, D.; Banerjee, S.; Barrand, G.; et al. GEANT4—A simulation toolkit. *Nucl. Instruments Methods Phys. Res. Sect. A Accel. Spectrometers Detect. Assoc. Equip.* **2003**, *506*, 250–303. [CrossRef]
20. Allison, J.; Amako, K.; Apostolakis, J.; Araujo, H.; Dubois, P.A.; Asai, M.; Barrand, G.; Capra, R.; Chauvie, S.; Chytracek, R.; et al. Geant4 developments and applications. *IEEE Trans. Nucl. Sci.* **2006**, *53*, 270–278. [CrossRef]
21. Allison, J.; Amako, K.; Apostolakis, J.; Arce, P.; Asai, M.; Aso, T.; Bagli, E.; Bagulya, A.; Banerjee, S.; Barrand, G.; et al. Recent developments in GEANT4. *Nucl. Instruments Methods Phys. Res. Sect. A Accel. Spectrometers Detect. Assoc. Equip.* **2016**, *835*, 186–225. [CrossRef]
22. Raschke, S.; Spickermann, S.; Toncian, T.; Swantusch, M.; Boeker, J.; Giesen, U.; Iliakis, G.; Willi, O.; Boege, F. Ultra-short laser-accelerated proton pulses have similar DNA-damaging effectiveness but produce less immediate nitroxidative stress than conventional proton beams. *Sci. Rep.* **2016**, *6*, 1–9. [CrossRef] [PubMed]
23. Dromey, B.; Coughlan, M.; Senje, L.; Taylor, M.; Kuschel, S.; Villagomez-Bernabe, B.; Stefanuik, R.; Nersisyan, G.; Stella, L.; Kohanoff, J.; et al. Picosecond metrology of laser-driven proton bursts. *Nat. Commun.* **2016**, *7*, 1–6. [CrossRef] [PubMed]
24. Amato, E.; Italiano, A.; Margarone, D.; Pagano, B.; Baldari, S.; Korn, G. Future laser-accelerated proton beams at ELI-Beamlines as potential source of positron emitters for PET. *J. Instrum.* **2016**, *11*, C04007. [CrossRef]
25. Italiano, A.; Amato, E.; Margarone, D.; Psikal, J.; Korn, G.; Nazionale, I.; Catania, S. Laser-accelerated Proton Beams from a Solid Hydrogen Target as a Future Source of Radionuclides for Positron Emission Tomography. *J. Sci. Eng. Res.* **2017**, *4*, 173–176.
26. Mirani, F.; Maffini, A.; Casamichiela, F.; Pazzaglia, A.; Formenti, A.; Dellasega, D.; Russo, V.; Vavassori, D.; Bortot, D.; Huault, M.; et al. Integrated quantitative PIXE analysis and EDX spectroscopy using a laser-driven particle source. *Sci. Adv.* **2021**, *7*, eabc8660. [CrossRef] [PubMed]
27. Asavei, T.; Tomut, M.; Bobeica, M.; Aogaki, S.; Cernaianu, M.O.; Ganciu, M. Materials in extreme environments dor energy, accelerators and space applications at ELI-NP facilities like the Facility for Antiproton and Ion Research (FAIR), the High Luminosity Large Hadron Collider (HL-LHC), the Facility for Rare Isotope Beams. *Rom. Rep. Phys.* **2016**, *68*, 275–347.
28. Barberio, M.; Sciscià, M.; Vallières, S.; Cardelli, F.; Chen, S.N.; Famulari, G.; Gangolf, T.; Revet, G.; Schiavi, A.; Senzacqua, M.; et al. Laser-accelerated particle beams for stress testing of materials. *Nat. Commun.* **2018**, *9*, 1–7. [CrossRef]
29. Kiriyama, H.; Mori, M.; Pirozhkov, A.S.; Ogura, K.; Sagisaka, A.; Kon, A.; Esirkepov, T.Z.; Hayashi, Y.; Kotaki, H.; Kanasaki, M.; et al. High-contrast, high-intensity petawatt-class laser and applications. *IEEE J. Sel. Top. Quantum Electron.* **2015**, *21*, 232–249. [CrossRef]
30. Dover, N.P.; Nishiuchi, M.; Sakaki, H.; Kondo, K.; Alkhimova, M.A.; Faenov, A.Y.; Hata, M.; Iwata, N.; Kiriyama, H.; Koga, J.K.; et al. Effect of Small Focus on Electron Heating and Proton Acceleration in Ultrarelativistic Laser-Solid Interactions. *Phys. Rev. Lett.* **2020**, *124*, 084802. [CrossRef]
31. Jia, S.B.; Romano, F.; Cirrone, G.A.P.; Cuttone, G.; Hadizadeh, M.H.; Mowlavi, A.A.; Raffaele, L. Designing a range modulator wheel to spread-out the Bragg peak for a passive proton therapy facility. *Nucl. Instruments Methods Phys. Res. Sect. A Accel. Spectrometers Detect. Assoc. Equip.* **2015**, *806*, 101–108. [CrossRef]
32. Kostjuchenko, V.; Nichiporov, D.; Luckjashin, V. A compact ridge filter for spread out Bragg peak production in pulsed proton clinical beams. *Med. Phys.* **2001**, *28*, 1427–1430. [CrossRef] [PubMed]
33. Musolino, S.V. Absorbed Dose Determination in External Beam Radiotherapy: An International Code of Practice for Dosimetry Based on Standards of Absorbed Dose to Water; Technical Reports Series No. 398. *Health Phys.* **2001**, *81*, 592–593. [CrossRef]
34. Catalano, R.; Petringa, G.; Cuttone, G.; Bonanno, V.P.; Chiappara, D.; Musumeci, M.S.; Puglia, S.M.R.; Stella, G.; Scifoni, E.; Tommasino, F.; et al. Transversal dose profile reconstruction for clinical proton beams: A detectors inter-comparison. *Phys. Medica* **2020**, *70*, 133–138. [CrossRef] [PubMed]
35. Cirrone, G.A.P.; Coco, S.; Cuttone, G.; De Martinis, C.; Giove, D.; Lojacono, P.A.; Mauri, M.; Messina, R. A fast monitoring system for radiotherapeutic proton beams based on scintillating screens and a CCD camera. *IEEE Trans. Nucl. Sci.* **2004**, *51*, 1402–1406. [CrossRef]
36. Sistrunk, E.; Spinka, T.; Bayramian, A.; Betts, S.; Bopp, R.; Buck, S.; Charron, K.; Cupal, J.; Deri, R.; Drouin, M.; et al. All diode-pumped, high-repetition-rate advanced petawatt laser system (HAPLS). In *Proceedings of the 2017 Conference on Lasers and Electro-Optics, CLEO 2017—Proceedings*; Institute of Electrical and Electronics Engineers Inc.: Piscataway, NJ, USA, 2017; Volume 2017, pp. 1–2.
37. ICRU. Key data for ionizing-radiation dosimetry: Measurements standards and applications (ICRU Report 90). *J. Int. Comm. Radiat. Units Meas.* **2016**, *14*. NP. Available online: http://fulir.irb.hr/3302/ (accessed on 10 September 2021).
38. Wiedemann, H. *Particle Accelerator Physics, Graduate Texts in Physics*; Springer International Publishing: Cham, Switzerland, 2015; ISBN 978-3-319-18316-9.

Article

In-Target Proton–Boron Nuclear Fusion Using a PW-Class Laser

Daniele Margarone [1,2,*], Julien Bonvalet [3], Lorenzo Giuffrida [2], Alessio Morace [4], Vasiliki Kantarelou [2], Marco Tosca [2,5], Didier Raffestin [3], Philippe Nicolai [3], Antonino Picciotto [6], Yuki Abe [4], Yasunobu Arikawa [4], Shinsuke Fujioka [4], Yuji Fukuda [7], Yasuhiro Kuramitsu [8], Hideaki Habara [8] and Dimitri Batani [3,9]

1. Centre for Plasma Physics, School of Mathematics and Physics, Queen's University of Belfast, Belfast BT7 1NN, UK
2. ELI–Beamlines Center, Institute of Physics, Czech Academy of Sciences, Za Radnicí 835, 252 41 Dolní Břežany, Czech Republic; Lorenzo.Giuffrida@eli-beams.eu (L.G.); Vasiliki.Kantarelou@eli-beams.eu (V.K.); Marco.Tosca@eli-beams.eu (M.T.)
3. CELIA (Centre Lasers Intenses et Applications), CNRS, CEA, Université de Bordeaux, UMR 5107, F-33405 Talence, France; julien.bonvalet@u-bordeaux.fr (J.B.); didier.raffestin@u-bordeaux.fr (D.R.); philippe.nicolai@u-bordeaux.fr (P.N.); dimitri.batani@u-bordeaux.fr (D.B.)
4. Institute of Laser Engineering, Osaka University, 2-6 Yamada-oka, Suita 565-0871, Japan; morace@ile.osaka-u.ac.jp (A.M.); abe.yuki@eei.eng.osaka-u.ac.jp (Y.A.); arikawa-y@ile.osaka-u.ac.jp (Y.A.); sfujioka@ile.osaka-u.ac.jp (S.F.)
5. Department of Macromolecular Physics, Faculty of Mathematics and Physics, Charles University, V Holešovičkách 2, 180 00 Prague, Czech Republic
6. MNF—The Micro Nano Characterization and Fabrication Facility, Bruno Kessler Foundation, Via Sommarive 18, 38122 Trento, Italy; picciotto@fbk.eu
7. Kansai Photon Science Institute (KPSI), National Institutes for Quantum and Science and Technology (QST), 8-1-7 Umemidai, Kizugawa-shi 619-0215, Japan; fukuda.yuji@qst.go.jp
8. Graduate School of Engineering, Osaka University, 2-1 Yamada-oka, Suita 565-0871, Japan; kuramitsu@eei.eng.osaka-u.ac.jp (Y.K.); habara@eei.eng.osaka-u.ac.jp (H.H.)
9. HB11 Energy Holdings pty. Ltd., 11 Windora Avenue, Sydney, NSW 2096, Australia
* Correspondence: d.margarone@qub.ac.uk

Abstract: Nuclear reactions between protons and boron-11 nuclei (p–B fusion) that were used to yield energetic α-particles were initiated in a plasma that was generated by the interaction between a PW-class laser operating at relativistic intensities (~3 × 10^{19} W/cm^2) and a 0.2-mm thick boron nitride (BN) target. A high p–B fusion reaction rate and hence, a large α-particle flux was generated and measured, thanks to a proton stream accelerated at the target's front surface. This was the first proof of principle experiment to demonstrate the efficient generation of α-particles (~10^{10}/sr) through p–B fusion reactions using a PW-class laser in the "in-target" geometry.

Keywords: proton–boron fusion; laser–plasma acceleration; α-particle beam

1. Introduction

The conventional route of nuclear fusion for power generation is based on the reaction between deuterium and tritium nuclei, which yields one α-particle and one neutron. Formidable technological challenges, however, stem from the production and handling of tritium, as well as from the radiation damage and radioactivity induced by the high-energy neutrons in the reactor materials. In this respect, the nuclear reaction between a proton and a boron-11 nucleus (p–B fusion) to yield three energetic α-particles is very attractive, as it only involves abundant and stable isotopes in the reactants and there is no neutron in the reaction products. Previous studies have reported a main resonance of such nuclear reactions occurring for incoming proton beam energies at 675 keV [1], which shows a corresponding cross-section of about 1.2 barn. The α-particles generated from p–B fusion present a broad energy spectrum that peaks around 4 MeV [1]; however, cutoff energies up to 10 MeV have been demonstrated experimentally [2–6]. In the last 15 years, p–B fusion has been effectively induced by means of high-power lasers, which has

reported an impressive progression in the reaction yield [2,4,7,8], thus has become a point of interest for the energy sector where it is being considered as an alternative approach to conventional inertial confinement fusion schemes [9–11] and also potentially for medicine where intense α-particle beams can be used for radioisotope production [12]. However, an extensive systematic investigation of laser-based p–B fusion of the deep understanding of the underpinning physics is still missing [13]. An overview of the recent experimental progression in p–B fusion in terms of α-particle flux (or flux per input laser energy) is shown in Figure 1, both for the "in-target" [2–4,7,14] and "pitcher–catcher" geometries [5,6,8,15]. In this work, we show the first experimental results of efficient α-particle production from p–B fusion using a PW-class laser in the "in-target" (i.e., direct irradiation) configuration. The results that were achieved during the same campaign in the "pitcher–catcher" geometry have been published elsewhere [5,6].

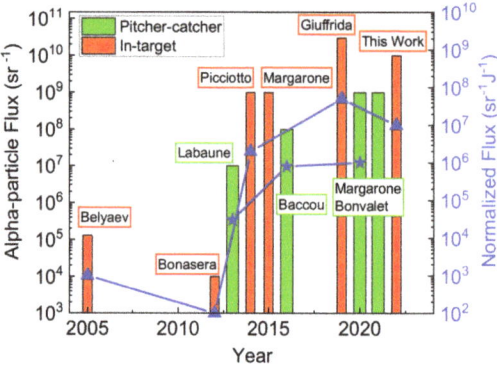

Figure 1. The experimental progress in p–B fusion, measured in terms of α-particle production in the "in-target" [2–4,7,14] and "pitcher–catcher" [5,6,8,15] geometries. The left-hand scale indicates the absolute α-particle flux (particles/sr), while the right-hand scale is normalized to the laser energy delivered on target (particles/sr/J).

2. Materials and Methods

The relatively short-pulse (2.2 ps) and high-energy (~1.4 kJ) PW-class laser system LFEX [16], which was operated at relativistic intensities (~3 × 10^{19} W/cm^2) at the Institute of Laser Engineering of the Osaka University (Japan), was focused onto the front surface (normal incidence) of a boron nitride (BN) target with a thickness of 0.2 mm. The concentration of hydrogen in the sample was a few %, which came from the chemical synthesis of the material during the manufacturing process.

As schematically shown in Figure 2, a Thomson parabola (TP) spectrometer was placed in the forward direction along the target normal to monitor the proton/ion plasma emission from the target's rear surface, which was based on an acceleration mechanism commonly known as "target normal sheath acceleration" (TNSA) [17]. Protons that were accelerated via TNSA at the target's rear side did not contribute to the generation of α-particles from p–B fusion; however, the determination of their cutoff energy was important to confirm that that particular laser shot was representative of an optimal laser–plasma coupling (a high laser intensity on the target's front surface allows the generation of electrons with high temperature, also known as "hot electrons", hence efficient TNSA at the target's rear side and protons with high cutoff energies). Plasma ions were deflected by parallel electric and magnetic fields based on their charge-to-mass ratio and were ultimately recorded on an imaging plate [18]. The presence of protons with cutoff energies of ~25 MeV confirmed that relativistic electrons were efficiently produced at the target's front side, thanks to the relatively high intensity and long pulse width of the incoming laser beam. The main α-particle diagnostic was a CR39 nuclear track detector that was shielded with Al filters of different thicknesses (10 µm and 30 µm), which was aimed at the target's front side and placed at a distance of 144 cm from the target and at an angle of ~80° from the target normal. Such a large detection angle was deliberately chosen so that the CR39 sample would be out of the main blow-off plasma emission cone, thus excluding the presence of energetic heavy ions (B and N) emitted backwards and impinging on the detector. The calibration of the CR39 detectors with various Al filters is reported elsewhere, along with the etching procedure that was used in this work [6]. We note that tracks that were ascribable to the low-energy blow-off plasma protons (very small pits in the CR39 sample) were unambiguously distinguishable from those ascribable to α-particles from p–B fusion events (larger pits) when the etching time was kept short enough (≤1 h), and that high-energy protons were not visible on the CR39 since they would have generated tracks with diameters below the resolution of the optical microscope that was used to map the sample after particle irradiation (<1 µm).

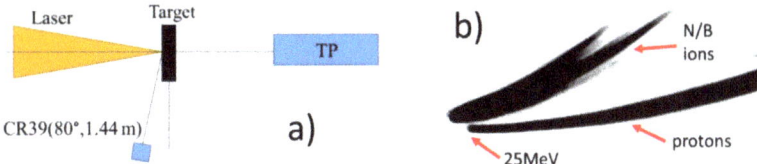

Figure 2. (a) The experimental setup; (b) the Thomson parabola (TP) snapshot showing the presence of protons and heavier ions being accelerated forwards from the target's rear surface (TNSA acceleration mechanism), i.e., not contributing to the generation of α-particles via p–B fusion.

A set of start-to-end numerical simulations was carried out with the aim of providing a qualitative interpretation of the experimental results. Additionally, 2D hydrodynamic simulations were performed using the CHIC code [19] with the aim of modeling the interaction of the relatively long (~2 ns) laser pedestal with the solid target. Then, 2D particle-in-cell (PIC) simulations were run using the SMILEI code [20] with the goal of modeling the acceleration of the protons at the target's front surface toward the target bulk (i.e., the protons moving forwards), thus highlighting the ongoing mechanism known as hole-boring radiation pressure acceleration (HB-RPA) [21,22]. The collision between the forward accelerated protons and the BN target bulk (assumed to be "cold" for simplicity) was modeled in 3D using the Monte Carlo FLUKA code [23,24] with the aim of estimating the relative flux and energy distribution of the α-particles that were generated by p–B fusion events and propagated backward. Although the PIC simulation was performed in 2D due to computational constraints, this was a reasonable approximation since the HB-RPA that occurred at the target's front surface was weakly affected by the number of dimensions in the numerical simulation in terms of proton energies. In fact, the maximum proton energy was directly linked to the radiation pressure of the laser pulse at the center of the focal spot where the intensity was maximized (e.g., the proton energy calculated by 3D PIC simulations can be even larger than that in 2D PIC simulations) [25].

3. Results

The energy spectrum of the α-particles that were emitted backward from the target's front surface is shown in Figure 3a. This energy distribution was recalculated from the signal recorded by the CR39 detectors that were covered by 10-µm and 30-µm Al filters (Figure 3b,c, respectively). The measured α-particle flux in the energy range of 5-10 MeV and at the detection angle of 80° (with respect to the target normal) was 1.2×10^{10}/sr ± 17%. This estimation was carried out by integrating the curve shown in Figure 3a and using a reasonable extrapolation (the red dashed line in Figure 3a) of the spectrum between 7 and 8 MeV (this was not measured due to the limitations of our calibration [6]). Particles with energy <5 MeV could not be detected since they were stopped in the 10-µm Al filter, and particles with energy potentially >10 MeV (diameter < 4 µm) were not counted since they were outside the CR39 calibration.

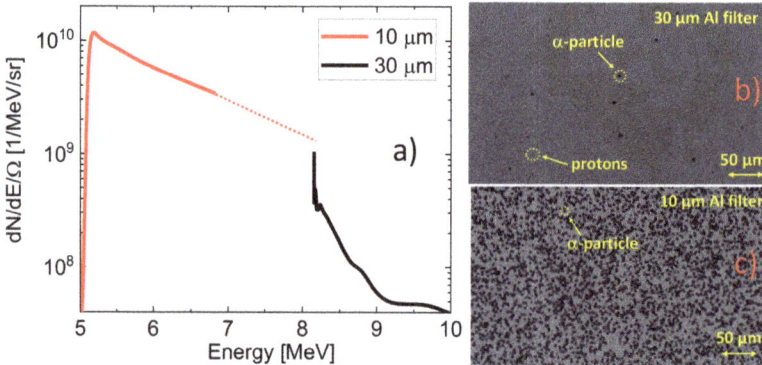

Figure 3. (**a**) The experimental spectrum of the α-particles that were emitted in the backward direction from the target's front surface; (**b**) the corresponding CR39 raw image in the case of the 30-μm Al filter and (**c**) the 10-μm Al filter.

The presence of a relatively large pre-plasma region that longitudinally extended for a length of ~100 μm in front of the target was estimated by the 2D hydrodynamic simulations. This information was implemented in the geometry that was used for the 2D PIC run, as shown in the proton density map of Figure 4a (the red dashed rectangle). The interface between the pre-plasma and the solid density region (around 175 μm in Figure 4a) along with the relatively long laser pulse feature (~2 ps) allowed the onset of an effective HB-RPA process at the target's front surface [21,22], which ultimately led to the efficient acceleration of the protons that were propagating forward into the target bulk. This can be clearly seen in Figure 4b, which reports the proton phase space plot ($p_x > 0$). The energy distribution of the protons that were propagating forward, which was obtained from the 2D PIC simulation, is shown in Figure 4c (the black line). Protons with an energy of 0.5–19 MeV were accelerated toward the BN target interior, thus generating p–B fusion events inside the target. We noted that, according to the simulation outputs, the highest proton flux lay in the range of 0.5–1 MeV, which was an optimal condition for an efficient p–B fusion process (the high cross-section of the nuclear reaction). Furthermore, the flux of protons with energies > 8 MeV was relatively low, hence their contribution in terms of p–B fusion yield was negligible (also due to the low cross-section of the nuclear reaction at such energies). Therefore, the low-energy part of the proton spectrum was responsible for the high-flux α-particle streams that were propagating backward, as predicted by the 3D Monte Carlo simulation output shown in Figure 4d. The corresponding α-particle energy distribution that was calculated by the Monte Carlo simulation for an angle corresponding to the position of the CR39 detector (80°) is reported in Figure 4c (the red line). The energy cutoff of the α-particle stream that was calculated numerically was ~14 MeV, but this could not be verified experimentally due to the limitations in the available α-particle calibration.

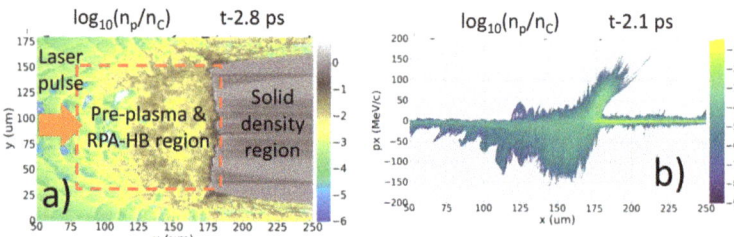

Figure 4. *Cont.*

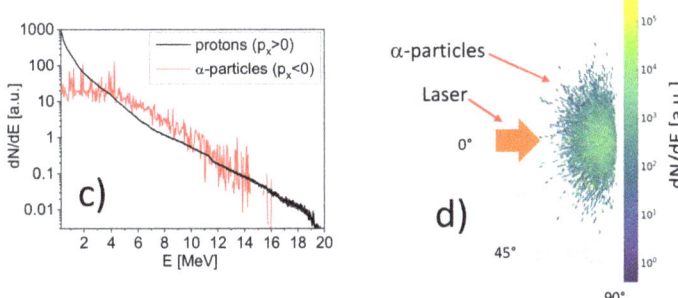

Figure 4. (**a**) The proton density map that was calculated by 2D PIC simulations at t = 2.8 ps (i.e., 1.2 ps after the highest intensity peak entered the highest density part of the target); (**b**) the proton phase space plot at t = 2.1 ps (the proton density is shown in units of plasma critical density); (**c**) the proton energy distribution ($p_x > 0$) and α-particle energy distribution at the target's front side from PIC and Monte Carlo simulations, respectively; and (**d**) the α-particle angular distribution from the same simulation run.

4. Discussion and Conclusions

The results presented in this work provide the first proof of principle experimental demonstration of efficient α-particle generation from p–B fusion using a PW-class laser and the "in-target" geometry. The measured α-particle flux was ~10^{10}/sr, thus one order of magnitude higher than previous results that were obtained with the same laser parameters but in the "pitcher–catcher" geometry [5,6]. This achievement is in line with the experimental progress in p–B fusion that has been reported in the last 15 years (see Figure 1) and confirms the advantage of triggering p–B fusion reactions using a direct irradiation scheme, at least in terms of α-particle flux [2–4]. A crude estimate of the total α-particle generation could be provided under the assumption of quasi-isotropic emission, which was based on the fact that the kinetic energy of the accelerated protons was relatively low (unlike the pitcher–catcher geometry that was reported in our previous p–B fusion experiment at LFEX [6]), hence there was no substantial momentum transfer from the protons to the α-particles. Therefore, under such a rough assumption, the total number of α-particles (including those particles absorbed inside the thick BN target) was ~1.4×10^{11}. However, despite the high α-particle flux that was experimentally measured, we noted that the overall conversion efficiency of the process (laser to α-particle energy) was still low (~0.005%). It is worth noting that the α-particle flux that was measured experimentally was a clear underestimation of the number of α-particles that were emitted backward due to the limited energy range (5–10 MeV) that was detectable by the diagnostics that were used. In fact, the numerically predicted α-particle energy range was much broader (1–14 MeV). Thus, considering the diagnostic limitations, we could expect a produced α-particle flux and conversion efficiency in line with the previous results that were reported in [4] with a kJ (TW-class) laser and in-target geometry (see Figure 1). Nevertheless, the start-to-end numerical simulation study that was performed (hydrodynamic, PIC, and Monte Carlo) allowed the qualitative support of the basic mechanism of multi-MeV proton acceleration at the target's front side and the subsequent generation of α-particles via p–B fusion that occurred inside the BN target.

These results are propaedeutic for the preparation of future experiments with PW-class lasers with the aim of generating high-flux α-particle streams in the laser–plasma environment that are tunable in energy, which is of potential interest for the study of ion stopping power in plasma, including the related implications in inertial confinement fusion schemes [26–29]. In fact, in contrast with TW-class kJ-laser pulses, the use of PW-class kJ-laser beams allows us to achieve high laser intensities on target (10^{19}–10^{20} W/cm^2) and thus, to explore acceleration regimes occurring at the target's front surface (e.g., HB-RPA) that could potentially be used to tune the energy of the protons that are responsible for p–B fusion reactions in the target bulk and, ultimately, to tune the average kinetic energy of the α-particles.

Author Contributions: The paper's initial idea was proposed by D.M., L.G. and D.B.; the conceptualization was realized by D.M., L.G., D.B., A.M. and P.N.; the experiment was carried out by A.M., Y.A. (Yuki Abe), D.M., L.G., V.K., D.R., J.B., P.N., Y.F., Y.K. and H.H.; the data analysis was performed by V.K., M.T. and D.R.; the numerical simulations were carried out by J.B. and P.N.; the original draft preparation was prepared by D.M. and the review and editing was performed by D.M., D.B., J.B., L.G., A.M., V.K., M.T., D.R., P.N., A.P., Y.A. (Yuki Abe), Y.A. (Yasunobu Arikawa), S.F., Y.F., Y.K. and H.H. All authors have read and agreed to the published version of the manuscript.

Funding: This research was funded by the Ministry of Education, Youth, and Sports of the Czech Republic through the project "Advanced Research Using High-Intensity Laser-Produced Photons and Particles" (CZ.02.1.010.00.016_0190000789), JSPS KAKENHI No. 19H00668, and the EUROfusion Consortium, which was funded by the European Union via the Euratom Research and Training Programme (Grant Agreement No 101052200—EUROfusion). However, the views and opinions expressed are those of the authors only and do not necessarily reflect those of the European Union or the European Commission. Neither the European Union nor the European Commission can be held responsible for them. The teams involved have operated within the framework of the Enabling Research Project: ENR-IFE.01.CEA "Advancing shock ignition for direct-drive inertial fusion". The authors warmly acknowledge the technical support of the laser team at the Institute of Laser Engineering of Osaka University. The inspiring and fascinating scientific discussions on proton–boron fusion and related applications that were undertaken within the international network organized by HB11 Energy Holdings Pty Ltd. are also acknowledged.

Institutional Review Board Statement: Not applicable.

Informed Consent Statement: Not applicable.

Data Availability Statement: Data are available from the corresponding authors upon reasonable request.

Conflicts of Interest: The authors declare no conflict of interest.

References

1. Stave, S.; Ahmed, M.W.; France, R.H.; Henshaw, S.S.; Müller, B.; Perdue, B.A.; Prior, R.M.; Spraker, M.C.; Weller, H.R. Understanding the B11(p,α)αα reaction at the 0.675 MeV resonance. *Phys. Lett. B* **2011**, *696*, 26. [CrossRef]
2. Picciotto, A.; Margarone, D.; Velyhan, A.; Bellutti, P.; Krasa, J.; Szydlowsky, A.; Bertuccio, G.; Shi, Y.; Mangione, A.; Prokupek, J.; et al. Boron-Proton Nuclear-Fusion Enhancement Induced in Boron-Doped Silicon Targets by Low-Contrast Pulsed Laser. *Phys. Rev. X* **2014**, *4*, 031030. [CrossRef]
3. Margarone, D.; Picciotto, A.; Velyhan, A.; Krasa, J.; Kucharik, M.; Mangione, A.; Szydlowsky, A.; Malinowska, A.; Bertuccio, G.; Shi, Y.; et al. Advanced scheme for high-yield laser driven nuclear reactions. *Plasma Phys. Contr. Fusion* **2015**, *57*, 014030. [CrossRef]
4. Giuffrida, L.; Belloni, F.; Margarone, D.; Petringa, G.; Milluzzo, G.; Scuderi, V.; Velyhan, A.; Rosinski, M.; Picciotto, A.; Kucharik, M.; et al. High-current stream of energetic α particles from laser-driven proton-boron fusion. *Phys. Rev. E* **2020**, *101*, 013204. [CrossRef] [PubMed]
5. Margarone, D.; Morace, A.; Bonvalet, J.; Abe, Y.; Kantarelou, V.; Raffestin, D.; Giuffrida, L.; Nicolai, P.; Tosca, M.; Picciotto, A.; et al. Generation of α-Particle Beams with a Multi-kJ, Peta-Watt Class Laser System. *Front. Phys.* **2020**, *8*, 343. [CrossRef]
6. Bonvalet, J.; Nicolai, P.; Raffestin, D.; D'humieres, E.; Batani, D.; Tikhonchuk, V.; Kantarelou, V.; Giuffrida, L.; Tosca, M.; Korn, G.; et al. Energetic α-particle sources produced through proton-boron reactions by high-energy high-intensity laser beams. *Phys. Rev. E* **2021**, *103*, 053202. [CrossRef] [PubMed]
7. Belyaev, V.S.; Matafonov, A.P.; Vinogradov, V.I.; Krainov, V.P.; Lisitsa, V.S.; Roussetski, A.S.; Ignatyev, G.N.; Andrianov, V.P. Observation of neutronless fusion reactions in picosecond laser plasmas. *Phys. Rev. E* **2015**, *72*, 026406. [CrossRef]
8. Labaune, C.; Baccou, C.; Depierreux, S.; Goyon, C.; Loisel, G.; Yahia, V.; Rafelski, J. Fusion reactions initiated by laser-accelerated particle beams in a laser-produced plasma. *Nat. Commun.* **2013**, *4*, 2506. [CrossRef]
9. Hora, H.; Korn, G.; Giuffrida, L.; Margarone, D.; Picciotto, A.; Krasa, J.; Jungwirth, K.; Ullschmied, J.; Lalousis, P.; Eliezer, S.; et al. Fusion energy using avalanche increased boron reactions for block-ignition by ultrahigh power picosecond laser pulses. *Laser Part. Beams* **2015**, *33*, 607–619. [CrossRef]
10. ENERGY TOKEN. Available online: https://hb11.energy.com (accessed on 21 December 2021).
11. MarvelFusion. Available online: https://marvelfusion.com (accessed on 21 December 2021).

12. Qaim, S.M.; Spahn, I.; Scholten, B.; Neumaier, B. Uses of alpha particles, especially in nuclear reaction studies and medical radionuclide production. *Radiochim. Acta* **2016**, *104*, 601. [CrossRef]
13. Belloni, F. On a fusion chain reaction via suprathermal ions in high-density H–11B plasma. *Plasma Phys. Contr. Fusion* **2021**, *63*, 055020. [CrossRef]
14. Bonasera, A.; Caruso, A.; Strangio, C.; Aglione, M.; Anzalone, A.; Kimura, S.; Leanza, D.; Spitaleri, A.; Immè, S.; Morelli, D.; et al. Measuring the astrophysical S-factor in plasmas. In Proceedings of the 4th International Conference on Fission and Properties of Neutron Rich Nuclei, Sanibel Island, FL, USA, 11–17 November 2007; Hamilton, J.H., Ed.; World Scientific: Fort Lauderdale, FL, USA, 2013; pp. 503–507.
15. Baccou, C.; Depierreux, S.; Yahia, V.; Neuville, C.; Goyon, C.; de Angelis, R.; Consoli, F.; Ducret, J.E.; Boutoux, G.; Rafelski, J.; et al. New scheme to produce aneutronic fusion reactions by laser-accelerated ions. *Laser Part. Beams* **2015**, *33*, 117. [CrossRef]
16. Morace, A.; Iwata, N.; Sentoku, Y.; Mima, K.; Arikawa, Y.; Yogo, A.; Tosaki, S.; Vaisseau, X.; Abe, Y.; Kojima, S.; et al. Enhancing laser beam performance by interfering intense laser beamlets. *Nat. Commun.* **2019**, *10*, 2995. [CrossRef] [PubMed]
17. Macchi, A.; Borghesi, M.; Passoni, M. Ion acceleration by superintense laser-plasma interaction. *Rev. Mod. Phys.* **2013**, *85*, 751. [CrossRef]
18. Rabhi, N.; Batani, D.; Boutoux, G.; Ducret, J.-E.; Jakubowska, K.; Lantuejoul-Thfoin, I.; Nauraye, C.; Patriarca, A.; Sa'd, A.; Semsoum, A.; et al. Calibration of imaging plate detectors to mono-energetic protons in the range 1–200 MeV. *Rev. Sci. Instrum.* **2017**, *88*, 113301. [CrossRef] [PubMed]
19. Breil, J.; Galera, S.; Maire, P.H. Multi-material ALE computation in inertial confinement fusion code CHIC. *Comput. Fluids* **2011**, *46*, 161. [CrossRef]
20. Derouillat, J.; Beck, A.; Pérez, F.; Vinci, T.; Chiaramello, M.; Grassi, A.; Fle, M.; Bouchard, G.; Plotnikov, I.; Aunai, N.; et al. SMILEI: A collaborative, open-source, multi-purpose particle-in-cell code for plasma simulation. *Comput. Phys. Commun.* **2018**, *222*, 351. [CrossRef]
21. Robinson, A.P.L.; Gibbon, P.; Zepf, M.; Kar3, S.; Evans, R.G.; Bellei, C. Relativistically correct hole-boring and ion acceleration by circularly polarized laser pulses. *Plasma Phys. Contr. Fusion* **2009**, *51*, 024004. [CrossRef]
22. Wilks, S.C.; Kruer, W.L.; Tabak, M.; Langdon, A.B. Absorption of ultra-intense laser pulses. *PRL* **1992**, *69*, 1383. [CrossRef]
23. Bohlen, T.T.; Cerutti, F.; Chin, M.P.W.; Fasso, A.; Ferrari, A.; Ortega, P.G.; Mairani, A.; Sala, P.R.; Smirnov, G.; Vlachoudis, V. The FLUKA Code: Developments and Challenges for High Energy and Medical Applications. *Nucl. Data Sheets* **2014**, *120*, 211–214. [CrossRef]
24. Ferrari, A.; Sala, P.R.; Fasso, A.; Ranft, J. *FLUKA: A Multi-Particle Transport Code*; CERN-2005-10 (2005), INFN/TC_05/11, SLAC-R-773; CERN: Geneva, Switzerland, 2005.
25. Tamburini, M.; Liseykina, T.V.; Pegoraro, F.; Macchi, A. Radiation-pressure-dominant acceleration: Polarization and radiation reaction effects and energy increase in three-dimensional simulations. *Phys. Rev. E* **2012**, *85*, 016407. [CrossRef] [PubMed]
26. Chen, S.N.; Atzeni, S.; Gangolf, T.; Gauthier, M.; Higginson, D.P.; Hua, R.; Kim, J.; Mangia, F.; McGuffey, C.; Marquès, J.-R.; et al. Experimental evidence for the enhanced and reduced stopping regimes for protons propagating through hot plasmas. *Sci. Rep.* **2018**, *8*, 14586. [CrossRef] [PubMed]
27. Zylstra, A.B.; Frenje, J.A.; Grabowski, P.E.; Li, C.K.; Collins, G.W.; Fitzsimmons, P.; Glenzer, S.; Graziani, F.; Hansen, S.B.; Hu, S.X.; et al. Measurement of Charged-Particle Stopping in Warm Dense Plasma. *Phys. Rev. Lett.* **2015**, *114*, 215002. [CrossRef] [PubMed]
28. Cayzac, W.; Frank, A.; Ortner, A.; Bagnoud, V.; Basko, M.M.; Bedacht, S.; Bläser, C.; Blažević, A.; Busold, S.; Deppert, O.; et al. Experimental discrimination of ion stopping models near the Bragg peak in highly ionized matter. *Nat. Comm.* **2017**, *8*, 15693. [CrossRef]
29. Temporal, M.; Canaud, B.; Cayzac, W.; Ramis, R.; Singleton, R.L. Effects of alpha stopping power modelling on the ignition threshold in a directly-driven inertial confinement fusion capsule. *Eur. Phys. J. D* **2017**, *71*, 132. [CrossRef]

MDPI
St. Alban-Anlage 66
4052 Basel
Switzerland
Tel. +41 61 683 77 34
Fax +41 61 302 89 18
www.mdpi.com

Applied Sciences Editorial Office
E-mail: applsci@mdpi.com
www.mdpi.com/journal/applsci

www.ingramcontent.com/pod-product-compliance
Lightning Source LLC
LaVergne TN
LVHW070554100526
838202LV00012B/459